CATCH AND GLEE CULTURE
IN EIGHTEENTH-CENTURY ENGLAND

CATCH AND GLEE CULTURE IN EIGHTEENTH-CENTURY ENGLAND

BRIAN ROBINS

THE BOYDELL PRESS

© Brian Robins 2006

All Rights Reserved. Except as permitted under current legislation no part of this work may be photocopied, stored in a retrieval system, published, performed in public, adapted, broadcast, transmitted, recorded or reproduced in any form or by any means, without the prior permission of the copyright owner

The right of Brian Robins to be identified as the author of this work has been asserted in accordance with sections 77 and 78 of the Copyright, Designs and Patents Act 1988

First published 2006
The Boydell Press, Woodbridge

ISBN 1 84383 212 7

The Boydell Press is an imprint of Boydell & Brewer Ltd
PO Box 9, Woodbridge, Suffolk IP12 3DF, UK
and of Boydell & Brewer Inc.
668 Mt Hope Avenue, Rochester, NY 14620, USA
website: www.boydellandbrewer.com

A catalogue record of this publication is available
from the British Library

This publication is printed on acid-free paper

Printed in Great Britain by
Biddles Ltd, King's Lynn, Norfolk

Contents

List of Tables		vi
Preface		vii
1.	A Thoroughly English Music: The Seventeenth-Century Background and Early Clubs	1
2.	Club Life in Eighteenth-Century London – The Academy of Vocal Music and The Madrigal Society	16
3.	The Catch Club	32
4.	The Expansion of London Catch Club Culture	72
5.	Provincial Catch and Glee Clubs	88
6.	The Catch and Glee in Other Performance Contexts	103
7.	The Glee: Aesthetics, Form and Poetry	135
8.	Epilogue: Later Reception of the Eighteenth-Century Catch and Glee	150
Appendix A	Members of the Catch Club	155
Appendix B	Prize Medals Awarded by The Catch Club	160
Appendix C	Select List of Eighteenth Century Catch & Glee Publications	162
Bibliography		165
Index		169

Tables

Table 1: Proportion of 'Old' Music Included in the Catch Club
Books & the Warren Collection — 38

Table 2: Proportion of Works by Foreign Composers in the
Catch Club Books & the Warren Collection — 53

Table 3: Income of the Catch Club 1763–1775 — 62

Table 4: Proportion of Glees, Catches & Canons Included in
the Catch Club Books and the Warren Collection — 64

Table 5: Composer Representation in the Catch Club Books
& the Warren Collection — 69

Table 6: Composer Representation in the Books of the Canterbury
Catch Club — 94

Table 7: Programme of the Opening Concert of the Vocal Concerts
Given at Willis's Rooms on 11 February 1792 — 121

Table 8: Dramatic Works by William Shield Incorporating Glees & Catches — 132

Table 9: Principal Topics of Glees Included in the Warren Collection — 141

Preface

This book owes its genesis to a streak of perverseness in the make-up of its author. In the course of a youthful enthusiasm for music and music history during which I soaked up as much of both as was possible, one particular question came to dominate my thoughts. Could the picture of English music of the eighteenth century truly be as bleak as so many writers painted it? Was it really possible that my fellow countrymen had produced nothing more than the near-worthless, slavish imitations of Handel I consistently read about? Patriotic hackles aroused, the desire to investigate further and, if possible, challenge what frequently appeared to be received opinion became irresistible. It did not take too long to draw the conclusion that while Handel had indeed cast a giant shadow over the music of his adopted countrymen, the music of the best English composers, men like Arne and Boyce, in fact achieved a level of individuality, a hazily-defined 'Englishness', that could be clearly differentiated from that of the colossus.

Somewhat later curiosity became more sharply focussed. In particular, it came to revolve around the question of the symphony, the new genre that spread like wildfire through continental Europe in the 1760s and 1770s. But not among English composers, so it seemed. Why was this so? After all, English audiences had been perfectly happy to turn up to concerts to hear the symphonies of émigrés such as J. C. Bach and Abel. Then, amidst a significant list of names of English composers whose interest in the symphony had been largely marginal, came the discovery of John Marsh. Here at last was an English composer who had devoted himself with some assiduity to the symphony, in fact more than forty of them, making Marsh the most prolific of all English symphonists. But there was more to Marsh than just symphonies, the majority of which are in any event now lost. Throughout his life Marsh had also painstakingly chronicled the musical and everyday events he witnessed. His writings are preserved in a huge set of manuscript journals, now housed in the Huntington Library in San Marino, California, that I subsequently set out to edit and eventually publish. Among the dozens of social and musical topics covered by Marsh's writings was his involvement with the catch clubs he encountered (and established) in the cities in which he lived and worked. Here it seemed was a uniquely English musical and social phenomenon in need of further investigation. Preliminary research soon established that it was indeed a topic that had to date received scant attention from scholars, a notable exception being the work done by the American Emanuel Leo Rubin, whose 1968 doctoral thesis on the glee subsequently came to form an axis around which some at least of the substance of the present book revolved. I am happy to acknowledge my considerable debt to Rubin's pioneering work.

Notwithstanding that debt, my approach differs from that of Rubin in that this is not a book *about* the glee (or catch, for that matter), much needed though such a survey might be. Rather is it concerned with the culture that encouraged the development of the two genres in the clubs formed for their performance and subsequently witnessed their dissemination into an enthusiastic wider world. Those seeking substantive critical analysis of an enormous repertoire must therefore await the scholar with the time, energy and resources to undertake what will be a Herculean task.

No artistic movement or development emerges from a vacuum. Following an introduction and description of the two forms, the opening chapter is therefore devoted to a survey of their seventeenth-century forbears, particularly relevant in the case of the catch. It concludes by noting the emergence of music clubs during the latter part of the century, a topic taken up in the following chapter, the first part of which draws on a wide variety of sources to examine the increasing importance of club life within the social fabric of early eighteenth-century Britain. Several music societies and organisations are then placed within this context, most relevantly the Madrigal Society, whose extensive records housed in the British Library (generally referred to as BL in footnotes) provide valuable insights into its structure, membership, repertoire and *modus operandi*.

The heart of the book will be found in Chapter 3, which deals with the Catch Club. Once again we are fortunate that the British Library holds extensive records relating to what was at one and the same time the first and infinitely the most important club to be formed for the performance and encouragement of the repertoire. This hugely important source was not available to Rubin, who believed it to have been lost during World War II, although Viscount Gladstone had previously drawn on it for his slim volume on the Catch Club. My own detailed examination of the Catch Club's Minutes and other records has allowed for many new observations and conclusions to be drawn concerning its membership and repertoire.

The following three chapters move, as it were, concentrically outwards. The first plots the expansion of catch club culture in London, a development directly inspired by the Catch Club itself. Once again original club records have been employed and drawn upon where they are extant. These and the personal observations of contemporary observers have been used to show the degree to which these clubs and societies either emulated or differed from the Catch Club in their social make-up, constitution, repertoire and aims. Chapter 5 moves out to provincial England for an overview of how the culture of the catch club spread to many towns and cities throughout the country. While as comprehensive as is possible at present, few detailed records of such clubs have to date emerged, so this is a part of the book that depends to a considerable extent on anecdotal contemporary observation. The chapter is a revised and expanded version of an essay that originally appeared in *Concert Life in Eighteenth-Century Britain*. I am grateful to Ashgate Publishing Limited for their permission to re-use much of the material. The succeeding chapter moves us away from the confines of club culture into the wider world of domestic music making, the concert hall (and pleasure gardens), and the opera house, a phenomenon accounted for by the extraordinary popularity attained by the glee. Paradoxically, the conclusion is drawn that such wide dissemination at least in part accounts for the decline in quality of the genre by the end of the century.

The penultimate chapter is in two distinct parts, the first of which is concerned with an attempt to place the glee within the context of the prevailing musical aesthetics of the day. That leads to a brief discussion of the variety of formal construction employed by the glee composers, and the poetry on which they drew. Finally, an epilogue examines the later reception of the eighteenth-century glee and catch repertoire, noting especially the importance of the nationalistic undertones with which the glee had gradually but surely become imbued.

One of the ambitions of the book is that it might in its modest way serve to encourage deeper analysis of the music itself and, even more importantly, inspire one or more of today's many excellent small vocal ensembles to revive the best examples of a large and richly diversified repertoire. With this in mind, Appendix C is a select list of eighteenth-century catch and glee publications that might serve as an aid.

No book with academic pretensions is written without assistance and help. On the question of finance, I must express my profound gratitude to both the Leverhulme Trust for the award of a two-year Fellowship, and the British Academy for the award of an Exchange Fellowship that enabled me to use the unrivalled resources of the Huntington Library in San Marino, California for two months. The staff of a number of institutions deserve thanks for their help and courtesy, among them those of the British Library, the Huntington Library, the Guildhall Library, Westminster Library, the library of Canterbury Cathedral and the library of the Guildford School of Music. City and county archivists throughout England replied promptly and helpfully, if largely negatively, regarding my requests for information on provincial catch clubs.

I am also indebted to the following individuals for the help and support they have given: Mark Argent, Michael Bellesiles, Donald Bewley, Barra Boydell, Donald Burrows, Annette Farquharson, Wendy Harrisson, Robert D. Hume, Harry Johnstone, Simon McVeigh, Andrew Pink, Mary Robertson, the late Stanley Sadie, Roz Southey, Ian Spink and William Weber. My very special thanks go to Pierre Dubois, Peter Holman and Philip Olleson, all of whom have at one time or another read either individual chapters or, in the case of Philip Olleson, the entire book. I am deeply grateful to them for the comments, opinions and helpful criticism that have made it a better book than it would otherwise have been. Following time-honoured tradition, it goes without saying that any remaining errors are entirely my responsibility. I would also like to thank the staff of Boydell & Brewer Ltd for the unfailing support they have provided in the course of publication, with Editorial Director Caroline Palmer deserving special mention for her good humoured and always valuable help.

Finally, I must pay tribute to my long-standing partner, Anne Young, who has not only once again given me unstinting moral support through the many trials and tribulations involved in producing a book, but also undertook the proof reading, prepared the index, and gave me invaluable assistance with the formatting. My debt to her is incalculable.

Chapter 1

A Thoroughly English Music:
The Seventeenth-Century Background and Early Clubs

'None give so harsh a report of Englishmen than the English themselves' - Henry Lawes.[1]

Music composed by Englishmen during the eighteenth century has in general had a poor press, not least from their fellow countrymen. The stance is both deeply rooted and of long duration. Writing in the early 1770s on a broad range of topics concerning 'the present state of England', the observations of an anonymous writer may be taken as representing a widely held opinion: 'All Europe except France is supplied by Italian musicians', he claimed, before continuing, 'And among the rest England enters so fully into that stile that we have no musick but Italian; Handell struck out in a manner of his own. Since the death of that great man, we have been a mere colony from Italy; all the great singers that have figured in our theatres have been Italians, except a few good voices, prostituted to the bawling of ballads to entertain the mob.'[2]

It is hardly surprising that many cultivated foreign visitors were only too ready to echo such sentiments. In 1765 a member of the French Royal Academy undertaking a tour of England noted: 'In the present age Handel, a German by birth, brought about the same revolution in England, which Lully the Italian had effected in France in the last century. Since that era the English flatter themselves that they have a national music: but it is no more than a dialect of the Germans, as the latter itself is a dialect of the Italian.'[3]

Thus emerged the concept of a *Land ohne Musik*, an image formulated in the nineteenth century and lazily adopted by the twentieth. While more recently writers such as Simon McVeigh and William Weber have exploded the absurd myth of the 'land without music' in general terms,[4] few beyond the confines of a small dedicated group of scholars and musicians have been prepared to accept the merits or advance the cause of native-born composers. As comparatively recently as 1967, a student of the history of British music would have learned from one of its senior practitioners of the 'painful insularity' of English eighteenth-century musicians, whose 'blind adoration of Handelian methods in almost every branch of the art laid a dead weight on English music which crushed out of ninety-nine of every hundred composers any vital originality that they might otherwise have displayed'.[5]

---

[1] Quoted in William Chappell, *Popular Music of the Olden Time*, 2 vols (London, 1859).
[2] *Letters Concerning the Present State of England Particularly respecting the Politics, Arts, Manners and Literature of the Times* (London, 1772), Letter XXV 'The Present State of Musick', p. 274.
[3] M. Grosley, *A Tour of London; or New Observations on England and its Inhabitants*, translated from the French by Thomas Nugent, 2 vols (London, 1772), vol. 2, p. 112.
[4] Simon McVeigh, *Concert Life in London from Mozart to Haydn* (Cambridge, 1993); William Weber, *The Rise of Musical Classics in Eighteenth-Century England* (Oxford, 1992).
[5] Percy M. Young, *A History of British Music* (London, 1967), pp. 404 & 271.

Notwithstanding such damaging assessments, English music had in fact developed indigenous forms that owe little or nothing to the influence of Handel or the Italians. Two of the most important, the catch and the glee,[6] form the basis of this study, which rather than attempting a systematic musical survey of the two forms is concerned specifically with their seminal place within the musical and social fabric of the period.[7] Neither, particularly the catch, can truly be considered an invention of the eighteenth century, but it was certainly during the second half of that century that they attained the highest point of their development and popularity.

Both the catch and the glee can essentially be defined as unaccompanied part songs composed for anything from between three and six solo parts, until the last decades of the eighteenth century normally intended for performance exclusively by male voices. The catch is the simpler in musical construction, being dependent upon the entry of successive voices a line of verse apart. As the seventeenth-century composer Christopher Simpson observed: 'The contrivance thereof is not intricate; for if you [...] place one part at the end of another, so that they aptly make one continued tune, you have finished a catch.'[8] Once the end is reached the singer goes back to the start and begins again. In theory a catch could therefore continue indefinitely, but in practice it had of course to be concluded. This could be achieved by one singer at a time dropping out until the last to enter is left alone to draw the performance to a close, or by means of settling on a pre-arranged chord to end it. The catch is thus a type of canon resembling a round (often no differentiation was made between the two terms), but can be distinguished from the latter by the interruption of the line at various points to allow the words of another part or parts to be clearly heard. An anonymous mid eighteenth-century writer provided this admirable description: 'A catch is that species of composition, in which the words and music are so contrived, that the sense of one line *catches* on, or plays into that of another; and, by so doing, conveys a meaning and humour, which did not occur in the cursory reading.'[9] The skill in the setting is consequently not so much musical as in organising it in such a fashion that the words of the different parts will at times be juxtaposed to allow new meanings to be heard explicitly or, more subtly, inferred. For this reason the great majority of catches were composed to convivial, humorous, bawdy, or even grossly indecent words, a characteristic that would ultimately come to distinguish the form from its generally more refined cousin, the glee. As will later be seen, the rise of 'polite' society in the last decades of the century would place the more unruly catch at a distinct disadvantage. Overwhelmingly suited to convivial male gatherings in inns and clubs, the catch was markedly less acceptable in the wider

---

[6] But see Ian Spink, 'Introduction' to *The Works of Henry Purcell*, vol. 22a (London, 2000), p. x. Spink suggests that a collection such as Caldara's *Divertimenti musicali per campagna, canoni all unisono* contains works that are analogous to the catch, thus forming part of a pan-European form of convivial middle-class music making that may also be considered to include the *chansons à boire* popular in 17th-century France.

[7] For the most comprehensive survey of the glee to date see Emanuel Leo Rubin, 'The English Glee from William Hayes to William Horsley', Ph.D. Diss. U. of Pittsburgh (1968). No equivalent work exists on the catch.

[8] Christopher Simpson, *Compendium, or Introduction to Practicall Musick* (1656).

[9] Preface to 'The Words of the favourite Catches and Glees, performed at the Ranelagh House, on the Twelfth of May'. The Music by Thomas Arne (London, 1767). It is likely that Arne was the author of this preface.

musical circles that enthusiastically embraced the glee in the concert hall and the home.

While the seventeenth century produced a small body of works termed 'glees', and there are other extended part-songs and even madrigals that bore a close enough relationship to the eighteenth-century form to be included as glees in the books of catch clubs and publications,[10] the genre may safely be considered, fundamentally, to belong to the second half of the eighteenth century. During its early years one finds the lack of a clear identity, up to the end of the 1760s many glees being ambiguously termed catches or glees, according to the source, while some early 'glees' are little more than catches in disguise. Both the word itself and its etymology have caused confusion. Contrary to what its name might imply and more recent association with American glee clubs, the Georgian glee dealt in large part with serious or semi-serious topics. While it is certainly true that humorous examples exist, at the height of its attainment and popular influence the glee tapped above all into the vein of male sociability and the fashionable exploitation of the 'sentimental'.

Some authorities have suggested that the word 'glee' derives from the Anglo-Saxon *gliw* or *gléo*,[11] literally entertainment and specifically the kind of entertainment provided by minstrels. Others are of the opinion that the true derivation is from *gligg* or *gligge*, which simply means 'music'. W. A. Barrett, one of the first musical educationalists to make a serious study of the form, suggested in the course of a series of lectures given in 1877 that the word *gligg* originally meant 'combination' in the sense that it might be applied to the diverse activities of minstrels – music, dancing, tumbling, joking etc, thus neatly effecting a union between the two possible derivations.[12] The sense of combination or association has pertinent connotations for the later social significance of both the glee and the catch. Barrett also discovered a link with minstrelsy in *Promptorium Parvulorum*, a Latin and English dictionary compiled around 1440, in which the word *gle* is significantly defined as 'armonia', or 'minstrelsy'. Various other theories have been advanced, but whatever the truth the name had certainly changed meaning by the seventeenth century, rendering arcane searches for further etymological explanations otiose. The glee most probably gained its first footings from the eighteenth-century revival of interest in 'ancient' music (and particularly the English madrigal) so penetratingly charted by William Weber.[13] That was certainly the view of John Wall Callcott, one of the most prolific glee composers, who was unequivocal in his view that 'the Madrigal is the original source of Glee'.[14] Undoubtedly the majority of glees share with the madrigal the important characteristic of realising the text with due regard for its expressive qualities. Indeed, many glee composers appear to have chosen their texts with a deliberate eye to their inherent expressive and occasionally dramatic possibilities rather than their literary standard, which was at times poor. Conversely, other composers seem to have

---

[10] See below p. 37–8.
[11] *Gléo* is the choice of the *New Oxford Dictionary*, which defines the word as 'entertainment, music, fun', adding that it is of Germanic origin.
[12] William Alexander Barrett, 'English Glee and Madrigal Writers' – Two lectures read at the London Institution on 18 January and 15 February 1877 (London, ?1877).
[13] Weber, *Musical Classics*.
[14] John Wall Callcott, 'Essays on Musical Subjects': Essay III – 'On the Catch Club', 31 August 1801, BL. Add. MS 27646. fol. 148.

almost self-consciously set older, more 'madrigalian' texts by canonic poets of high literary standing, as the names of Shakespeare, Tasso, Ben Jonson, and Dryden among many other distinguished authors readily attest.[15] During the 1780s it even became fashionable among some composers to use the term 'madrigal' to describe pieces that are in every essential glees, while it is notable that later in the nineteenth century some composers employed the rubric to distinguish works in which they sought to return to the 'pure' unaccompanied glee of the previous century.

Notwithstanding such cross-relationships, the association between the madrigal and the glee should not be overestimated. The structure of the former invariably involved a greater degree of contrapuntal complexity than is normally found in glees, whose looser musical form and introduction of solo passages were also often dictated by the text, and could range from short, simple through-composed works to lengthy multi-sectional compositions responding to the fluctuating sentiments of the words. Such pieces employ a wide diversity of tempo, dynamics, texture, and even at times key. Although glee composers may have modelled the principle of their newly created genre on that of the madrigal, their aim (with a few deliberate and self-conscious exceptions) was not the revival of an archaic form, but the creation of a living, contemporary style. The measure of their achievement was summed up admirably by Barrett, who in the course of his concluding comments told his audience: 'Glee music forms a splendid literature in itself. It is thoroughly English in style, manly, straightforward and vigorous, with a tenderness and pathos, which like the veins in marble take away nothing of its solidity, but add greatly to its beauty.'[16] Barrett's 'splendid literature' is a huge and largely untapped source. The American scholar Emanuel Rubin identified and listed incipits for over 2500 glees composed between roughly 1760 and 1810, the true figure being almost certainly substantially higher, while the number of catches written during the same period is likely to be at least as large.[17]

To discover the genesis of this enormous repertoire, it is necessary to turn the clock back more than two centuries before its heyday. The relationship between the round and the catch has already been noted and *Sumer is icumen in*, the most famous of all rounds, originally dates from the thirteenth century. A few other relevant early secular part songs such as the round *Ah! Robin, gentil Robin* have also survived, but it is not until 1580 that a significant catch repertoire emerges. Collected in a manuscript known as the Lant Roll, now housed in the Rowe Music Library in Cambridge, is an anthology of 57 pieces made in 1580 by Thomas Lant, a herald of the College of Arms. The introduction is explicit in making clear that during the Elizabethan period no distinction was made between catches and rounds, announcing that its reader will find 'Here wthn this rowle divers fine catches, otherwise called Rowndes of 3, 4, and 5 parts in one'.[18]

There can be little doubt that by the time Lant made his compilation the singing of catches was a well-established pastime, almost exclusively conducted within a

---

[15] See Chapter 7 for a more detailed discussion of texts.
[16] Barrett, Lectures, p. 42.
[17] Rubin, 'The English Glee'.
[18] MS 1, Rowe Music Library, King's College, Cambridge. For more on the Lant Roll see Jill Vlasto, 'An Elizabethan Anthology of Rounds', *Musical Quarterly* 40 (1954), p. 222.

convivial context. In 1573 a morality play called *New Customs* includes a dialogue between the allegorical characters Avarice and Cruelty that makes a clear allusion to the singing of catches:

> Avarice: But, sirs, because we have tarried so long,
> If you be good fellows let us depart with a song.
> Cruelty: I am well pleased, and therefore, let every man
> *Follow after in order* as well as he can.[19]

Shakespeare's plays also include a number of oft-quoted references to catches. The stage instructions for Act 2, Scene 3 of *Twelfth Night* (c. 1601) explicitly calls for the catch 'Hold thy peace' to be sung by Sir Toby Belch, Sir Andrew Aguecheek, and the clown Feste, who, significantly, have just eaten and imbibed.[20] Disturbed from sleep by their 'performance', Malvolio exclaims:

> My masters, are you mad? [...] Have you no wit, manners, nor honesty, but to gabble like tinkers at this time of night? Do ye make an ale-house of my lady's [Olivia's] house, that ye squeak out your cozier's catches without any mitigation or remorse of voice?[21]

The steward's words are revealing, for they establish the social class of those expected to be found singing catches. Malvolio obviously considers it undignified for knights to sing them (particularly late at night!), catches being associated in his mind with tinkers and coziers (tailors), a view substantiated in other dramatic works of the period, where there are references to catches being sung by a smith and a saddler,[22] and by soldiers,[23] while in Ben Jonson's *Silent Woman* (1609–10) a character complains of having caught a cold 'sitting up late and singing catches with cloth workers'. Significantly, Malvolio also makes clear in the speech quoted above that he associates the singing of catches with alehouses, identified by Peter Clark as the smallest and rudest of the three types of victualing house (the others being the inn and the tavern) found in England until late in the seventeenth century.[24] Clark also draws attention to the importance of the alehouse as a communal meeting place for the class we have recognised as being associated with catch singing. Such establishments provided a focal point in both town and country for various forms of entertainment and games, and were also the haunt of itinerant minstrels and later, ballad singers. The repertoire was traditional, with bawdy topics and drinking songs providing the bulk of material.[25] There is no reason to suppose that the singing of

---

[19] Quoted in Edward Francis Rimbault, *The Rounds, Catches and Canons of England*, (London, c. 1860). The italics are mine. Rimbault's preface is a valuable source of such relevant quotations, but he published his collection of texts in bowdlerised form, the words having been adapted 'to modern use' by the Rev. J. P. Metcalfe, a reflection of the embarrassment of many editors faced with risqué original texts. Not unlike today's film censors, Rimbault and his collaborator found it necessary 'to wade through seas of filth to extract a few drops of sweet perfume', p. xxxiii.
[20] 'Hold thy peace' is included in Ravenscroft's *Pammelia*, discussed below.
[21] Peter Alexander (ed.), *The Complete Works of Shakespeare* (London, 1951).
[22] In Ben Jonson's *New Inn* (London, 1626).
[23] In Beaumont and Fletcher's *Faithful Friends* (London, c 1608).
[24] Peter Clark, *The English Alehouse 1200–1830* (Harlow, 1983), p. 5.
[25] Clark, *The English Alehouse*, p. 155.

rounds and catches was any less prevalent, since it was necessary to learn only a few tunes that were probably transmitted orally and fitted with new words, while performance requirements were sufficiently modest for artisans of the kind mentioned above to master.

The ability of those of little musical competence to sing catches was a topic taken up by Thomas Ravenscroft in the preface to his *Pammelia*, the first published collection of catches and a volume that contains many of the same items as the Lant Roll, some slightly differently texted or musically more complex versions.[26] Doubtless with an eye geared to business, Ravenscroft informs his reader that catches are 'so generally affected [...] because they are so consonant to all ordinaryie musicall capacity, being such indeed, as such whose loue of Musicke exceeds their skill, cannot but commend'. The author continues by extolling the broader merits of the catch, finding in it 'Good Art in all, for the more musicall, good mirth and melodie for the more Iouiall, sweet harmonie, mixed with much varietie, and both with great facilitie.' 'The onely intent', concludes Ravenscroft, 'is to giue generall content, composed by Art to make thee disposed to mirth.' The universal usage of catch tunes is again emphasised by the Melvill Manuscript.[27] A collection made by David Melvill of Aberdeen in 1604, it includes 90 catches, of which 75, now decked out with Scottish words, also appeared in one or other of Ravenscroft's publications.

Neither the musical nor the social significance of *Pammelia* or that of Ravenscroft's companion anthologies, *Deuteromelia* (1609) and *Melismata* (1611) have to date been subjected to detailed study.[28] All the works contained are anonymous and all three collections encompass a wide variety of items ranging from Latin texts to street cries and tavern songs. A similar lacuna exists where subsequent kindred publications are concerned. Extant records and commentaries are notable for the absence of references to catch publications until the middle of the century, when two concurrent and probably not unconnected events significantly advance the story of the catch and the glee. The first was the arrival on the scene of John Playford (1623–86), who in 1648 set up as a bookseller and publisher in London's Inner Temple. Two years later Playford, who had received musical training as a choirboy, issued *The English Dancing Master*, the publication that brought him lasting fame and a work that ran into numerous editions.[29] The following year his presses produced *A Musicall Banquet*, a compilation divided into three parts, of which the third is devoted to a 'New and Choyce' selection of 'Catches or Rounds for three or foure voices'. A dozen catches and rounds were included in the *Banquet*, including the canon *Non nobis Domine*, once widely attributed to William Byrd, and a piece that would achieve

---

[26] Thomas Ravenscroft, *Pammelia. Mvsicks Miscellanie* (London, 1609).
[27] The manuscript is housed in the Library of Congress, Washington, MS M1490.M535A5. In 1916 the collection was transcribed as *The Melvill Book of Roundels* by Granville Bantock and H. Orsmond Anderton for private publication by the Roxburgh Club (rep. New York, 1972).
[28] Modern facsimile editions of all three of Ravenscroft's publications have been published by Da Capo Press (New York, 1971) and the American Folklore Society (Philadelphia, 1961), the latter with an introduction by M. A. Shaaber.
[29] Wilfred Mellers fails to recognise the importance of either Ravenscroft or Playford in 'Music: Paradise and Paradox in the Seventeenth Century'. Included in *Seventeenth-Century Britain*, ed. Boris Ford; The Cambridge Cultural History series (Cambridge, 1989), pp. 181–6.

canonic status as a post-dinner grace in the world of the eighteenth-century catch club.

In 1652 Playford followed the *Banquet* with what was destined to become one of the seminal works of the seventeenth-century catch literature. *Catch that Catch Can, or a Choice Collection of Catches, Rounds, & Canons for 3 or 4 Voyces* was a selection compiled by John Hilton (1599–1657) including over a hundred catches or rounds in addition to sacred canons. Unlike Playford, Hilton was a professional musician who in 1628 had become organist of St Margaret's, Westminster, and his collection includes works of his own in addition to those of Henry and William Lawes, William Child, Richard Dering, John Jenkins and others. Addressing the dedication of his Preface to 'My much Honoured Friend, Mr. Robert Coleman, a true Lover of Musick', Hilton punningly presumes to offer his dedicatee '*Endeavours*, not snacht up at random, nor catcht at with an uncivill and rude hand, but gathered with a reverend and carefull collection, to avoid offence and scandal. And if that *Generall Good* I ayme at therein shall acceed my wishes, (being the Mutuall *Society* of Friends in a modest *Recreation*) I have catch't the happinesse of my desires.' Notwithstanding Hilton's claims of reverence and avoidance of 'a rude hand' and 'offence and scandall', it is worth noting *Catch that Catch Can* includes its fair share of bawdy pieces. The second part of the Preface, directed more generally 'To all Lovers of Musick', includes a further convoluted series of puns (including the title, borrowed from Ravenscroft), but is of value for making clear the popularity of catch singing. Suggesting that his rounds 'may shift for themselves; so might,' he adds, 'the Catches themselves in these Times, when Catches and Catchers were never so much in request; all kind of Catches are abroad'. This, incidentally, seems to be the first occasion on which a distinction was made between rounds and catches.

Hilton's mention of 'these Times' brings us to the second of the mid-century events that had a crucial impact on the development of the catch. He was of course writing only a short while after the ultimate conclusion of the Civil Wars that had intermittently raged in England for nearly ten years. It seems entirely possible that Hilton's desire to avoid 'scandall' over his collection stemmed from a desire to stay out of possible trouble, and that his assertion that 'all kinds of Catches are abroad' may have had a double meaning. While Playford was an ardent Royalist who published political tracts during the Commonwealth,[30] the political leanings of Hilton are not known, but both must have been well aware that the publication of indecent catches could have provoked the Puritan government of the day, even if most of its ire was directed toward church music and the severest repression still lay in the future. Percy A. Scholes, the first writer to question the received notion that Puritanism was antagonistic toward nearly all music,[31] argues that since Playford and Hilton were also attached to churches with strongly 'puritanised' connections (Playford was Parish Clerk of the Temple Church, the lawyers' church, while Hilton was Clerk of St Margaret's, Westminster, the MPs' church) the authorities must have been fully aware of what they were up to and turned a blind eye. Scholes cites this as evidence of Puritan tolerance of music, which may or may not be the case, but it also

---

[30] I am grateful to Peter Holman for drawing my attention to this aspect of Playford's activities.
[31] Percy A. Scholes, *Music and Puritanism* (Vevey, Switzerland, 1934). Also *The Puritans and Music in England and New England* (Oxford, 1934; rep. 1969).

presumes that Playford and Hilton knew that they would be safe in publishing *Catch that Catch Can*, a more dubious proposition.[32]

Nevertheless, there can be little doubt that the wars and, to an even greater extent, the Puritan parliaments that Britain was shortly to experience, had crucial implications for convivial music making, and the development and extensive popularity of the catch already noted by Hilton in 1652. As the late seventeenth-century writer and lawyer Roger North observed, at the outset of the wars 'the whole of the masters of music in London were turned adrift, some went into the army [the most famous example being William Lawes, killed at the siege of Chester in 1645], others dispersed in the country and made music for the consolation of the Cavalier gentlemen'.[33] Those noted by North as having gone into the country 'gave great occasion to divers families to entertain the skill and practice of music, and to encourage the masters, to the great increase of composition'. Or to summarise in North's most frequently quoted words about the period, 'many chose rather to fidle at home, than to goe and be knockt on the head abroad'.[34] Others were less fortunate. While many unemployed church musicians found work as teachers, the closure of theatres left many musicians to lead an itinerant life that descended to little more than begging, a plight articulated by the author of *The Actor's Remonstrance or Complaint*, published in 1644:

> Our music that was held to be so delectable and precious that they scorned to come into a tavern for less than twenty shillings salary for two hours, now they wander with their instruments under their cloaks – I mean, such as have any – into all houses of good fellowship, saluting every room where there is company with, 'Will you have any music, gentlemen'.[35]

Music making during the period of the Civil Wars and Commonwealth was therefore largely divided between those who chose 'to fidle at home' (either their own or, in the instance of the best professional musicians, those of county landowners who could afford to employ them) and those professional musicians forced to ply their trade in taverns and alehouses. The latter development led to a major demographic change in the kind of person who might have been found providing entertainment in the victualing houses of Britain. While music was still sung by traditional habitués – tinkers, tailors, and soldiers – patrons could now also hear superior musicians in a repertoire that almost certainly included not only ballads but also catches. The incursion of such musicians into inns and taverns not only raised the standard of music making in the drinking house, but the increasing popularity of such activities ultimately brought rewards for both landlord and musician. Scholes even defines a new type of tavern that came into existence during this period, the 'Musick House'.[36] One such venue may have been the Black Horse in Aldersgate Street, London, where prior to 1654 one Edmund Chilmead ran a 'Musick

---

[32] Scholes, *Music and Puritanism*, p. 14.
[33] Quoted in Chappell, *Popular Music*, vol. 2, p. 479.
[34] John Wilson, ed., *Roger North on Music* (London, 1959), p. 294.
[35] Quoted in Henry Raynor, *A Social History of Music: From the Middle Ages to Beethoven* (London, 1972), p. 243.
[36] Scholes, *Music and Puritanism*, p. 26.

Meeting'. Further details of Chilmead's meetings are not known, although it has been suggested that they were the earliest public concerts in Britain.[37]

Much of the musical activity in taverns is likely to have involved instrumental music, but in 1657 an attempt by Cromwell's new (third) parliament to clamp down on such performances may unwittingly have provided further encouragement to vocal music. In June that year an ordinance was passed 'against vagrants and wandering idle dissolute persons' among whom were those 'commonly called fiddlers, or minstrels', who were warned that if at any time after 1 July they were 'taken fiddling, and making music, in any inn, alehouse or tavern, or shall be taken proffering themselves, or desiring, or intreating any person or persons to hear them play or make music in any of the places aforementioned' they were to be adjudged 'rogues, vagabonds and sturdy beggars, and proceeded against and punished accordingly'.[38] Chappell claims, without providing evidence, that while the ordinance obviously put at least some check on instrumental playing, the demand for entertainment at convivial drinking houses (a designation to which can now be added the coffee house) resulted in an upsurge in the singing of part-songs, catches and canons. In support of his contention, Chappell cites the anecdote in which Pepys mentions going to a coffee house by the Thames with Matthew Locke and 'Pursell' (possibly Henry's father) during the time General Monck was in London and still at least nominally a supporter of the Commonwealth (1659).[39] There an eight-part canon by Locke on the words *Domine, salvum fac Regem* (*God save the King*) was sung by the assembled company, a bold and potentially dangerous gesture at the time, suggests Chappell, somewhat weakening his own argument. While it may have been safer to go to one's favourite watering hole without the telltale shape of a violin or viol hidden beneath a cloak, the ordinance specifically forbade music making of any kind, including singing. To have been 'taken' singing (particularly a genre as dubious as the catch) would not have involved the perpetrator in a lesser penalty than if he had been found playing the violin or viol. Chappell, who followed the anti-Puritan line adopted by music historians from Hawkins and Burney onward, must be treated with as much caution as Scholes, whose admirable attempt to redress the balance is marred by the polemical fervour of a crusader.[40]

Some of the earliest recorded evidence of music clubs comes not from the inn or tavern, but the Oxford colleges that were the haunt of the indefatigable diarist and observer Anthony Wood (1632–95), whose writings provide rare and invaluable insight into the early club life of the university city.[41] By 1656 Wood was a member of a weekly music club run for profit and held at the house (situated opposite the site on which the Sheldonian Theatre would later be built) of William Ellis, who before the Civil Wars had been organist of St John's College. Of eight professional

---

[37] Ian Spink, 'The Old Jewry Musick-Society: A 17th-Century Catch-Club', *Musicology II: Journal of The Musicological Society of Australia* (1965–67), p. 35.
[38] Quoted in Chappell, *Popular Music*, p. 479.
[39] *The Shorter Pepys*, ed. Robert Latham (London, 1985), p. 20.
[40] As to a lesser extent is that of Antonia Fraser in her *Cromwell: Our Chief of Men* (London, 1973). Fraser extols Cromwell's well-known love of music while omitting less savoury aspects of his policy towards it. The repressive 1657 Act, for example, is not mentioned.
[41] Anthony Wood, *The Life and Times of Anthony à Wood*, ed. Andrew Clark, 3 vols. (Oxford, 1892; 1894).

musicians Wood cites as being regulars at Ellis's meetings, three, Curteys ('a lutinist lately ejected from some choire or cath.'), Edward Low, former organist of Christ Church, and the chorister William Flexney were organists or choristers who had lost their jobs as a direct result of the Puritan suppression of church music.[42]

As Wood makes clear, the principal occupation of Ellis's club was the performance of instrumental consort music, the membership including John Wilson (1595–1674), the song-writer and lutenist who had started his career with Shakespeare's company and is named by Wood as 'the best at lute in all England'.[43] In 1660 Wilson published *Cheerfull Ayres*, which included a number of his songs arranged in three parts and termed 'glees', although they have been described as descendents of Elizabethan part-songs.[44] No fewer than four of Ellis's professional club members are also identified by Wood as singers, to which list can be added the name of Wilson. It therefore seems reasonable to assume, particularly given Wilson's membership, that instrumental performances were leavened by songs and catches, which may also have involved some or all of the eight amateur members also named by Wood. Ellis's club is probably therefore one of the earliest organised music clubs at which catches were regularly performed. Nor was Ellis's the only Oxford music society recorded by Wood: he also noted less formal winter meetings in the Queens College chambers of Christopher Harrison and those of Charles Perot at Oriel, Dr Narcissus Marsh at Exeter College, and the theorbist Thomas Janes at Magdalen, in addition to a regular weekly Friday meeting of the 'scholastical musitians'. This flurry of musical activity, which according to Wood was supported by the professional musicians attached to the university, was significantly curtailed after the Restoration, when Ellis's society was badly affected by the restoration of posts to the professionals who had been the backbone of the society. His meetings 'began to decay, because they were held up only by scholars, who wanted directors and instructors &c. so that in a few yeares after, the meeting in that house was totally layd aside'.[45]

In the absence of further documentary evidence, it is difficult to know just how much direct impetus the Civil Wars and the Commonwealth period contributed to the undeniable increase in the popularity of catch singing. It was certainly sufficient for Playford to feel confident in bringing out further publications. In 1652, the same year that *Catch that Catch Can* appeared, Playford also produced his *Ayres and Dialogues*, which included a number of part-songs by John Wilson and is notable for being the first known publication to employ the rubric 'glee' for a vocal composition. Some, like those later included in Wilson's *Cheerfull Ayres* were arranged from solo songs. A further edition of *Catch that Catch Can*, including an additional thirty-one pieces, appeared in 1658.

By the dawn of the Restoration the catch had undergone a profound change of social status. The exile of skilled musicians into inns and taverns following the closure of theatres and the mix of displaced professional musicians and gentleman

---

[42] Wood, *Life and Times*, vol. 1, p. 204.
[43] Ibid.
[44] See Ian Spink, ed., *The Blackwell History of Music in Britain: The Seventeenth Century* (Oxford, 1992): David Greer, 'Vocal Music I: Up to 1660', p. 174.
[45] Wood, *Life and Times*, vol. 1, p. 275.

enthusiasts such as Anthony Wood in the music clubs of Oxford (and doubtless elsewhere) not only raised performance levels, but also introduced convivial music making to a new social class. The singing of catches was no longer the exclusive province of the bucolic tradesman of Shakespeare's day, but a form of entertainment participated in by gentleman amateurs such as Samuel Pepys, who on 21 July 1660, just two months after the Restoration, records dining at a club with the Chancery clerk John Spong, at which they had three voices to sing catches.[46]

Further evidence of both the expansion of club life and the newly acquired social status of the catch comes with John Playford's *Musical Companion* (1667). This was divided into two parts; the first included the catches previously issued in earlier editions of *Catch that Catch Can*, with the addition of 'some new Rounds and Catches', while the second part consisted of simple part songs for two, three, and four voices. The collection includes 108 new compositions that can be defined broadly as 'glees',[47] among them the song *Sweet Tyraness*, attributed to Purcell as one of his earliest works, but possibly composed by his father. The Preface written by Playford (Hilton had died in 1657) is dedicated 'To his endeared friends of the late Musick-Society and meeting in the Old-Jury, London'. Playford names these friends as Charles Pidgeon, Esq; Mr Thomas Tempest, Gent.; Mr Herbert Pelham, Gent.; Mr John Pelling, Citizen; Mr Benjamin Wallington, Citizen, Mr George Piggot, Citizen; and Mr John Rogers, Gent. The social mix of gentlemen and 'citizens' establishes a pattern that, as we will see, would become one of the defining features of the burgeoning club life of late seventeenth- and eighteenth-century Britain.

Several of those named by Playford are known through association with that enthusiastic amateur Pepys. John Pelling was an apothecary and friend of Pepys who frequently visited the latter to make music. It was Pelling who appears to have been responsible for introducing Pepys to Piggot, Wallington, Rogers and Tempest ('a gentleman, a young man [...] who sings very well endeed and understands anything in the world at first sight').[48] His first recorded encounter with Wallington and Piggot took place in September 1667, when although 'we sung several good things' Pepys was left dissatisfied, confessing himself to be 'more and more confirmed that singing with many voices is not singing, but a sort of Instrumentall music, the sense of the words being lost by not being heard, and especially as they set them with Fuges of words'.[49] Pepys, it seems, did not share the widespread enthusiasm for the singing of canons and catches. He was no happier some six months later, repeating his complaints about concerted vocal music when Pelling brought Wallington, Tempest and Rogers to him 'by appointment' for more music, an occasion on which the company sang until the onset of night and 'drank my good store of wine'.[50]

The most interesting of Pepys' musical companions to us is Benjamin Wallington. At the time of their first meeting, in 1667, Pepys describes him as a poor goldsmith that 'goes without gloves on his hands', 'being a very little fellow' who 'did sing a

---

[46] *The Shorter Pepys*, p. 65.
[47] Spink, 'Old Jewry', p. 37.
[48] *The Shorter Pepys*, p. 873.
[49] *The Shorter Pepys*, p. 829.
[50] *The Shorter Pepys*, p. 873.

most excellent bass'.[51] Ben Wallington's fortunes must have improved, since he was to become the leading light of what Roger North called the earliest public concerts, probably, as we have seen, erroneously.[52] These events started out as private meetings but turned public, pre-dating the famously advertised 'concerts' of John Banister, which commenced in December 1672. According to North, Wallington's meetings were held in a large room in an alehouse situated in a lane behind the southwest corner of St Paul's. This was identified by Barrett as the Goose and Gridiron, an inn still standing at the time he was writing (1886), the name being a local corruption of the emblems of the swan and lyre employed by the landlord by way of advertising his establishment's musical credentials.[53] Rather more recently, Ian Spink has inclined to the view that Wallington's concerts are synonymous with those mentioned by the eighteenth-century historian Sir John Hawkins as taking place in 1664 at the Mitre, which stood in much the same vicinity.[54] Moreover, Spink has suggested that the Mitre meetings, which had ceased by the start of 1665, moved to become the Old Jewry Musick-Society to which Playford dedicated the 1667 edition of *Catch as Catch Can*.[55] Roger North, who may have had personal experience of Wallington's meetings (he was in his late teens at the time), recognised the radical nature of the musical events that took place there:

> The means of bringing that [revolution in music] forward was the humour of following publick consorts, and it will not be out of the way to deduce them from the beginning. The first of those was in a lane behind Paul's [sic], where there was a chamber organ that one Phillips played upon, and some shopkeepers and foremen came weekly to sing in consort, and to hear, and injoy ale and tobacco; and after some time the audience grew strong, and one Ben. Wallington got the reputation of [a] notable base voice, who also set up for a composer in print, but of a very low sence; and their music was chiefly out of Playford's Catch Book. But this showed an inclination of the citisens to follow musick. And the same was confirmed by many little entertainements the masters voluntarily made for their scollars, for being known they were always crowded.[56]

Elsewhere North supplemented this account with a more personal, if hardly flattering, picture recording that 'with help of a dull organist and miserable-singers, folks heard music out of the Catch-book [Playford's], and drank ale together. One Ben. Wallington came to the conduct of this celebrious meeting, whose voice was literally base and his compositions altogether rustik and inartificiall. It will be wondered when in old prints his songs are seen, that such musick could please anyone.'[57]

Whatever the standard of performance at these music meetings (and one suspects a certain degree of snobbery may have been involved in North's description) this

---

[51] *The Shorter Pepys*, p. 829.
[52] See above, pp. 8-9.
[53] Barrett, Lectures, p. 154.
[54] Spink, 'Old Jewry', p. 35.
[55] Ibid.
[56] *Roger North on Music*, p. 351. One of Wallington's songs is included in the 1672 edition of *Catch that Catch Can*.
[57] *Roger North on Music*, p. 304.

account of what can justly be regarded as the first catch club is highly significant. It shows that the appeal of catch singing still crossed social boundaries. The club not only looked backward in carrying echoes of the bourgeois heritage of catch singing in the early part of the century, but forward in the sense that its organisation laid down parameters for many an eighteenth-century catch club: the location of meetings in a hostelry of some description, ensuring the necessary juxtaposition of music making and a convivial atmosphere where drinking played an essential part in the entertainment, and the willing support of the landlord. Those who attended comprised both performer and auditor, but entry was restricted to males only. Such features would become paradigms of club life in the following century.

By the final decades of the century public, private, and even domestic music meetings had become highly fashionable, the last featured in Edward Ravenscoft's 1672 comedy *The Citizen turned Gentleman*, in which the citizen is told that if he is to appear a person of consequence, it will be necessary for him to hold a music club at his home once a week.[58] One citizen who followed such advice without any pretension to becoming a gentleman was Thomas Britton, who in 1678 famously began a series of concerts in the attic of his London home, which according to Hawkins was situated 'on the south side of Aylesbury-street, which extends from Clerkenwell Green to St. John's-street'.[59] Britton, a modest but intellectually lively minded man, pursued the profession of small coal man. In spite of his humble background and the uncomfortable nature of his accommodation, he managed to establish a weekly subscription series open to the public, initially free of charge. Extraordinarily, by the turn of the eighteenth century Britton's concerts had become a part of London's social life, attracting not only an audience that could boast such members of the *beau monde* as the Duchess of Queensberry, but notable professional instrumentalists including the violinist John Banister, himself the founder of a public concert series, John Christopher Pepusch and, later, Handel. The repertoire performed at Britton's concerts appears to have been principally chamber music, all the performers named by Hawkins being instrumentalists. That vocal music was also included is shown by an entry in the diary of the antiquarian and topographer Ralph Thoresby, which records that in June 1712 he and his companions called at Britton's where they heard 'a noble concert of music, vocal and instrumental, the best in town, which for many years past he has had weekly for his own entertainment, and of the gentry &c'.[60] Further, if more circumstantial, evidence suggesting the performance of vocal music, can be found in the catalogue of Britton's music, produced when it came up for sale after his death in 1714. Among a number of vocal collections can be found '3 Different Catch Books by Mr. Purcell and the best masters'.[61]

---

[58] Ravenscoft, *The Citizen turned Gentleman* (London, 1672). Quoted in Rimbault, *Rounds and Catches*.
[59] Sir John Hawkins, *A General History of the Science and Practice of Music* (London 1776, rep. 2 vols, New York, 1963), vol. 2, p. 790. Hawkins notes that even by the time he was writing, Britton's house had long gone.
[60] Quoted in A. Löffler, *Thomas Britton, the "Musical Smallcoal-Man"*, http://www.ph-erfurt.de/~neumann/eese/artic99/.
[61] The full catalogue is listed in Hawkins, *General History*, vol. 2, pp. 792–3.

The continuing success of the catch repertoire inspired Playford to bring out yet another edition of *Catch that Catch Can* in 1685, the year before his death. Among the new additions on this occasion were twelve catches by Purcell, who contributed nearly sixty examples of the genre in all. If hardly significant within the overall context of his output, they do show that, like his contemporaries John Blow, with fourteen catches to his credit, and Michael Wise, Purcell was not averse to adding to a minor, popular genre. Ian Spink, the modern editor of his catches, draws attention to technical shortcomings that give the impression they were carelessly written, but also notes that the composer's famed ability to match words and music, so much a feature of the solo songs, is also clearly evident in the catches.[62] The earliest have been dated to the late 1670s, while the latest were composed in the 1690s. Their subject matters range from the celebration of drink and conviviality, through political texts that reveal Purcell as an enthusiastic patriot with Tory rather than Whig sympathies, to those whose nature is sufficiently bawdy to have caused as much embarrassment to some of his biographers and admirers as Mozart's scatological letters and canons have to his.

One man unlikely to have been too concerned about Purcell's bawdier catches was the Oxford divine, scholar, architect, and collector of music Henry Aldrich (1648–1710), who became a canon in 1681 and thereafter appears to have been in charge of both secular and sacred music at Christ Church. From some time before this date he held a music meeting in his rooms to which all members of the cathedral choir were invited, thus following the lead of Ellis and others during the Commonwealth period. Notwithstanding his apparently impeccable academic and ecclesiastical credentials, Aldrich was a convivial man whose meetings combined music with sociability, and who contributed two well-known catches, *On Tobacco* and *Christ Church Bells*, to the repertoire in addition to a catch including the lines 'for the liquor will make a man shite, and the landlady make him spue'. Notwithstanding such a 'free, open and facetious manner' (to quote one of Aldrich's contemporaries), he ran his meetings to strict rules of etiquette, and insisted on punctuality. Defaulters were barred from the following meeting and those arriving late were reduced to drinking small beer rather than the excellent punch or claret served by the hospitable Aldrich, portents of the draconian laws adopted by more formal clubs in the eighteenth century.[63]

It may safely be assumed that by the end of the century numerous other music clubs and societies had been established in Britain, among them the Hibernian Catch Club of Dublin, founded around 1680 by the vicars choral of St Patrick's and Christ Church Cathedrals, thus emphasising the close relationship between the church and catch and glee singing that would come to be one of the defining features of many later clubs, particularly in the English provinces. For nearly a century the Hibernian Catch Club remained an exclusive society restricted to the vicars choral, lay members only being finally admitted in 1770, the year to which records go back.[64] It still exists today.

---

[62] Spink, 'Introduction' to *Works*, vol. 22a, p. xi.
[63] 'Introduction' to *The Aldrich Book of Catches*, ed. B. W. Robinson and R. F. Hall (London, 1989).
[64] Brian Boydell, *A Dublin Musical Calendar* (Dublin, 1988), p. 267.

The popularity of music clubs at the turn of the eighteenth century is well illustrated by the preface to the second edition of *The Pleasant Musical Companion*, published in 1701 by Playford's son Henry, who had taken over his father's imprints. In his preface Playford states the aim of his publication, which was 'chiefly for the encouragement of the musical societies which will be speedily set up in all the chief cities and towns of England'. The preface, written in the third person, is sufficiently innovative to be worth quoting *in extenso*:

> He has prevailed with his acquaintance and others in this City, to enter into several Clubs Weekly, at Taverns, of convenient distance from each other, having at each house a particular master of music belonging to the Society established in it, who may instruct those (if desired) who shall be unskilled in bearing a part in the several catches contained in this book, as well as others, and shall perfect those who already have some insight in things of this nature, that they shall be capable of entertaining the societies they belong to abroad. In order to do this, he has provided several articles to be drawn, printed, and put in handsome frames, to be put up in each respective room the societies shall meet in, and be observed as so many standing rules, which each respective society is to go by: and he questions not, but the several Cities, Towns, Corporations &c., in which the kingdom of Great Britain and Ireland, as well as Foreign Plantations, will follow the example of the well-wishers to Vocal and Instrumental Music in the famous City, by establishing Weekly Meetings as may render his undertaking as generally received as useful. And if any body or bodies of gentlemen are willing to enter into or compose such Societies, they may send to him, where they may be furnished with the books or articles. This much he thought was necessary to premise, and giving the reader a light into the knowledge of his design; but he shall leave his book without further vindication than the great names of the persons who obliged the world with the words, and those who (if anything can add to such finished pieces) have given a mitre to 'em by their Musical Composures; as Dr. Blow and the late famous Mr Henry Purcell, whose Catches have deservedly gained an universal applause.

This is an astonishing announcement, as striking in its commercialism as Ravenscroft's *Pammelia* preface of nearly a hundred years earlier, but going far beyond the earlier compiler in introducing a new didactic element to the business of selling music and entrepreneurship. No longer content with the simple objective of his publication giving 'generall content', Henry Playford has not only been instrumental in setting up a number of clubs in London, but also lays down with breathtaking confidence a blueprint for a nationwide, indeed empire-wide, network of music clubs to which are attached professional musicians who will instruct amateur members in the art of part singing. In addition, Playford has also drawn up a set of rules to be universally adopted by his network of clubs. His scheme was a grandiose conception and like most such schemes there is no suggestion that it achieved widespread success. But Playford was also a man ahead of his time. While the English are too independently-minded a nation readily to submit to a set of universally applied rules, particularly for their leisure activities, a looser version of Playford's vision of a nationwide network of catch clubs would ultimately emerge.

Chapter 2

Club Life in Eighteenth-Century London
The Academy of Vocal Music and The Madrigal Society

During the final years of the seventeenth century and the early part of the eighteenth century, the establishment of clubs of all kinds proliferated, a development that runs in close parallel with the increasing social amenities provided by inns and taverns. As Peter Clark noted in his major study of club life,[1] the rise of public drinking places was a vital ingredient in the expansion of the number of clubs and societies in early modern Britain, such establishments undertaking radical improvements in the amenities they provided by enlarging and improving premises, which frequently included purpose-built assembly rooms and other areas in which clubs and societies could hold their meetings in private. Clark estimates that before 1800 no fewer than nine out of ten club and society meetings took place in public drinking houses, which were, in his words, 'one of the main theatres of male sociability'.[2] By holding meetings at venues where alcoholic refreshment was readily available, the most essential component of conviviality was thus automatically incorporated.

By the 1720s one observer could speak of London having an 'infinity of clubs and societies for the improvement of learning and keeping up good humour and mirth'.[3] Such clubs were the near-exclusive preserve of men, particularly those devoted to conviviality, where the presence of women was felt to be inhibiting to the heavy drinking that frequently took place. However, such clubs were generally prepared to admit a wide social and age spread, having frequently the ancillary purpose of becoming a meeting place at which business could be conducted and new trade contacts made.

While a considerable number of informal clubs were established in the period under discussion, a striking development during the early years of the eighteenth century was the increasingly formal structure of clubs, which developed from the *ad hoc* meetings that had predominated in coffee houses and taverns during the previous century into societies with clearly defined sets of rules. Henry Playford's Preface dating from 1701 and quoted at the end of the previous chapter makes clear that those seeking to set up their own clubs with his assistance would be provided with a rulebook. The advantages of establishing a structure for an evening's entertainment were obviously particular in the case of music clubs and societies, where some kind of organised pattern was essential if meetings were to proceed in an orderly and coordinated manner that would allow full rein to their objective, the playing and singing of music. The establishment of charters, sets of rules and greater bureaucracy also allowed not only for the imposition of discipline within the context of club

---

[1] Peter Clark, *British Clubs and Societies 1580–1800* (Oxford, 2000).
[2] Clark, *British Clubs*, p. 164.
[3] Quoted in Clark, *British Clubs*, p. 1.

meetings, but also ensured that clubs could screen carefully prospective membership.

Typically, clubs organised themselves on a hierarchical, but democratic basis. The principal functionary at club meetings was the president, who was generally elected from among the membership on a strictly rotational basis, and whose principal function was to keep order and ensure that the club's rules were being correctly observed. He was usually conducted to his seat, generally placed on a raised dais, amidst great ceremony that was often, even in non-musical societies, accompanied by music. In musical organisations where the club had a specific agenda, the president was also frequently responsible for the choice of the entertainment to be given during the course of the evening. The president of the evening was assisted in his functions by a vice-president, who also served on a rotational basis, while in larger societies one would also expect to find a standing committee responsible for the overall functioning of the organisation.

It is noteworthy that the presence of music and singing is a recurrent feature of club life, clubs not specifically devoted to music frequently having recourse to it during their meetings. Typical is an account dating from 1722 of a Mug-house Club, so-called because each member drank ale from a personal mug, in Long Acre:

> They have a grave old Gentleman, in his own gray Hairs, now within a few months of Ninety years old, who is their President, and sits in an arm'd chair some steps higher than the rest of the company to keep the whole Room in order. A Harp plays all the time at the lower end of the Room; and every now and then one or other of the Company rises and entertains the rest with a song, and (by the by) some are good Masters. Here is nothing drunk but Ale, and every Gentleman hath his separate Mug, which he chalks on the Table where he sits as it is brought in; and everyone retires when he pleases, as in a Coffee-house.
>
> The Room is always so diverted with Songs, and drinking from one Table to another, to one another's healths, that there is no room for Politick's, or anything that can sow'r conversation. One must be there by seven to get Room, and after ten the Company are for the most part gone. This is a Winter's Amusement, that is agreeable to a Stranger once or twice, and he is well diverted with the different Humours, when the mugs overflow.[4]

In this account we find much of the essence of early eighteenth-century club life: a formally structured society, the presence of a chairman to keep order over meetings, albeit in this instance a venerable member who had apparently earned the office in perpetuity; a convivial atmosphere involving the frequent drinking of toasts; and a ban on the discussion of politics and other potentially contentious subjects. The statutes of many clubs and societies specifically forbade the discussion of religion or politics, the latter tending to be the preserve of clubs set up with the specific objective of being political debating societies. The Long Acre Mug-club also preserved elements of the older, looser kind of meetings in coffee-house clubs,

---

[4] J. Timms, *Club Life of London: With anecdotes of Clubs, Coffee-Houses and Taverns of the Metropolis during the 17th, 18th and 19th Centuries*, 2 vols. (London, 1866), vol. 1, p. 45.

members being allowed to come and go as they pleased, and visitors also being freely admitted.

The increasingly organised structure of music clubs is illustrated by the set of laws formulated by the Musical Society that held its meetings at the Castle Tavern in Pater Noster Row, just to the north of St Paul's Cathedral. This society, which admitted both performers and male auditors as members, dates from the early 1720s. According to Hawkins, it had its roots in private music meetings held in the St Paul's Churchyard home of the violinmaker John Young. Young's son Talbot founded a weekly meeting with a group of friends including the young Maurice Greene (1696–1755), who during the first half of the century would become a dominant figure in the English musical establishment and was already (since 1718) organist of St Paul's and musical director of the annual charitable Festival of the Sons of the Clergy. 'The fame of this concert', Hawkins relates, 'spread far and wide, and in a few winters the resort of gentlemen performers was greater than the house could admit to.'[5] A small subscription was introduced and a move made to the Queen's Head Tavern in Pater Noster Row, from where a further move was made in 1724 to the Castle. The society continued to thrive under the direction of Talbot Young and in March 1731 introduced a wide-ranging set of new laws.[6] This new rulebook, introduced on 14 March, contains no fewer than thirty-four laws, the fourth of which details the extraordinarily complex constitution of the officers of the society. In addition to a president, who was to be drawn from among the performing members and served on a monthly rotation basis, and treasurer, no less than four managers and six stewards were to be elected annually at the general meeting, held on the second Wednesday of each September. Nomination for membership could be made only by an existing performing member, no doubt a reflection of the society's origination as a performers' meeting. The nomination of auditor members then went forward to a ballot of the full membership that required a simple majority for admission, but potential performer members were subjected to practical trial that required the support of a three-quarters majority to be successful. Once elected the new member paid a joining fee of four guineas and thereafter an annual fee of two guineas, high rates that suggest the society was patronised by the wealthier professions of the city. This supports Hawkins' statement that the membership consisted of 'many young persons of professions and trades that depended upon a numerous acquaintance', who were 'thus induced by motives of interest to become members of the Castle concert'.[7] Membership lists have not survived, but here is clear evidence that many professional men joined successful clubs such as the Castle concerts not only to enjoy the convivial company of men of their own social class, but also to make new contacts that might further their business interests.

The By-Laws of the Castle concerts reveal that meetings were held every Wednesday evening between Michaelmas (29 September) and Lady Day (25 March) starting at seven. Between eight and nine there was an interval of thirty minutes, during which 'a sufficient Refreshment of wine' was to be provided by the officiating

---

[5] Hawkins, *A General History*, vol. 2, pp. 807–8.
[6] *The By-Laws of the Musical Society at the Castle Tavern, in Pater-Noster-Row* (London, 1731).
[7] Hawkins, *A General History*, vol. 2, p. 808.

steward, who had personally to make up any deficiency for a house bill that exceeded the stipulated limit of four pounds per evening. Concert evenings were governed by strict regulations, with a raft of fines imposed upon those in breach of them. These included lateness (a fine of 1s), not being seated by the time the music began (1s) and moving around during a performance (1s). For noises such as speaking aloud, clapping, hissing or making 'other loud Noise' the penalty rose to 2s. 6d. More serious infringements, such as bringing unauthorised guests or general misbehaviour at concerts (determined by 'the Opinion of the Majority of Members present'), met with a forfeit of a guinea or even expulsion. Rules XXVII and XXVIII deal with the question of ladies. While they were not permitted to become members, their introduction to concerts by existing members on a rotational basis to sit exclusively in the gallery and box of the concert room was allowed. Strict segregation was practised during the concert, with the male members directed not to remain in the gallery on pain of a fine of 5s. Despite (or perhaps because of) such stringent regulations the Castle concerts, whose repertoire consisted of both vocal and instrumental music, continued until about 1775, after which nothing more is heard of them.[8]

Although in some ways atypical of early eighteenth-century clubs, the foundation of the Academy of Vocal Music in 1726 represents another major step in the development of music societies. The choice of the word 'academy' had considerable significance, since it suggested a professional body much along the lines of the literary *academie* that flourished in seventeenth-century Italy. This, as William Weber has noted, was precisely the purpose behind the formation of the Academy, whose principal initial objective was 'gathering together the city's leading musicians'.[9] Its main instigator appears to have been John Christopher Pepusch (1667–1752), the German-born composer, performer, teacher, and collector who arrived in London from Berlin some time after September 1697. Pepusch's industry and range of activities was remarkable. Rapidly establishing himself among London's leading musicians, he had been able to further his career as a result of his marriage to the former opera singer Margherita de l'Epine, a wealthy woman in her own right. His passionate enthusiasm for old music was reflected in a large collection of books and music that included the early seventeenth-century keyboard collection now known as the *Fitzwilliam Virginal Book*, and the keyboard works of John Bull. On his death in 1752, Pepusch bequeathed most of his library to the Academy, by then renamed the Academy of Ancient Music, an organisation to which he devoted much time and energy. His many pupils include a number who would subsequently become catch and glee composers, notably Benjamin Cooke (1734–93), George Berg (?1730s–75), and John Travers (?–?).

In addition to Pepusch the assembly of thirteen included a number of leading figures in London musical life. Maurice Greene, already encountered above as a founder member of the Castle Concerts, was at thirty the youngest of the group. In its early years, Greene's position at St Paul's enabled the Academy to draw on boys from the cathedral choir to sing at its meetings, a number being present at the first

---

[8] McVeigh, *Concert Life*, pp. 32 & 35.
[9] Weber, *Musical Classics*, p. 17.

meeting. Sampson Estwick (*c.* 1656–1739), Francis Hughes (1666 or 7–1744), John Freeman (1666–1736), and Charles King (1687–1748) also had connections with St Paul's. The composer of a small body of both sacred and secular works, Estwick was a minor canon and also sacrist and succentor, while the countertenor Hughes left a stage career to become a member of not only the choir of St Paul's, but also those of the Chapel Royal and Westminster Abbey. The tenor and composer Freeman also served at both the Chapel Royal and Westminster Abbey in addition to St Paul's, while King was a noted composer of services who succeeded Jeremiah Clarke as Master of the Choristers at St Paul's. He is also one of the few composers during this period that can be positively identified with catch writing, his O *Absalom, my son* (1730) remaining sufficiently well known to enter the books of the Catch Club in 1763.[10] The bass and composer Bernard Gates became a Gentleman of the Chapel Royal.

The initial composition of the Academy was therefore drawn substantially from the church, the only positively identifiable exception in addition to Pepusch being John Ernest Galliard (*c.* 1687–1747), an immigrant German composer and oboist of French extraction. Galliard arrived in London around 1706, subsequently pursuing a career as a theatre composer and becoming the last composer to have an English opera, *Calypso and Telemachus* (1712) staged at the Queen's Theatre before it became totally dominated by Handel and the Italians.

The inaugural meeting of the Academy of Vocal Music was held on Friday 7 January 1726 at the Crown Tavern, situated close to St Clement's in the Strand. According to Estwick, it was formed as 'A Musick Meeting […] chiefly for [the performance of] Grave ancient vocal Musick'.[11] Among the works performed were two motets by Marenzio, a psalm by Morley and madrigals by Alessandro Stradella and Agostino Steffani, respectively late seventeenth- and early eighteenth-century examples of the *stile antico*, and so at least in spirit, 'Grave ancient vocal Musick'. The society was therefore from the outset dedicated to the revival of an Anglo-Italian repertoire of polyphonic music.[12]

The first meeting of the Academy also found the time to agree a set of rules and orders,[13] the third of which stresses the connections with the church in stating 'That any Gentleman of his Majesties Chappel Royal, or of the Cathedral [St Paul's] may be admitted of this Academy if they desire itt, and no other person but such as profess Musick, and shall be approved of by the Majority'. Another order stipulated that 'The doors be shut, and none admitted (for the present) but the members of the Academy'. The intent of this is somewhat ambiguous, since it is not clear if it applied specifically to the opening evening or more generally for the future. The former seems more likely, since the penultimate resolution carried by the meeting states 'That there be 18 Tickets given for the Gallery every night. Two to each Member as

---

[10] O *Absalom* was also included by Edmund Warren in the first of the collections he made for the Catch Club. See p. 33. For discussion of the Catch Club see Chapter 3.
[11] Quoted in Weber, *Musical Classics*, p. 58.
[12] For further discussion of the aims and repertoire of the Academy of Vocal Music see Weber, *Musical Classics*, pp. 56ff.
[13] 'Original papers relative to the first establishment of the "Academy of Vocal Music", which afterwards became the "King's Concerts of Ancient Music", 1725–30.' BL Add. MS 11732, fols. 1–2.

they Stand in the list [which presumably rotated] to be deliver'd after the performance of the night ensuing'. From the outset the Academy was thus prepared to admit visitors, although the strict regulation and control of ticketing ensured that it was not at this stage the public concert-giving organisation it would later become. Among other resolutions the Academy confirmed its day and place of meeting to be fortnightly on Fridays at the 'Crown Tavern against St Clement's Church in ye Strand', the meetings to commence at seven and end at nine. An opening quarterly subscription of half a guinea seems also to have been agreed, although it was not collected until the second meeting on 21 January, those attending the opening meeting paying a nominal fee of 2s. 6d to cover the expenses of the evening, which amounted to 18s and included 5s for the use of the room, fire and candles; 10s. 6d for wine and bread; and 2s to transport the boys from St Paul's by coach. Then comes a curious order that appears to contradict the admittance of singers of the Chapel Royal and St Paul's: 'Resolv'd – That composers (by general consent) may be admitted, tho' not vocal performers'. Quite where this placed a member like Francis Hughes, who is not known to have been a composer, is unclear. Unlike the majority of clubs and societies who worked on the principle of a rotating president, the Academy decided to elect a board of a maximum of seven managers to direct the musical proceedings by turn, the honour of doing so for the inaugural meeting falling to Galliard. These managers were also entrusted 'to make such Laws for ye governance of the Academy as they shall think fitt'. Finally, the Academy laid down rules for future membership, determining that election should be by ballot with at least two thirds of the membership necessary to form a quorum.

The invitation to singers of the Chapel Royal and St Paul's to attend was obviously intended to ensure a high quality of performance, and anticipates the Catch Club's incorporation of 'privileged' or professional members.[14] At the meeting of 1 March the Academy gained the accession of three further prominent immigrant members of London musical society: the composers Giovanni Bononcini (1670–1747) and Francesco Geminiani (1687–1762), and Nicola Haym (1678–1729), today best remembered as an opera impresario and librettist, but also a composer in his own right. Other prominent early members from the professional musical world included the composers William Croft (1678–1727), and the great castrato Francesco Bernardi (d. 1759), universally known as Senesino. In contradiction of its early rule, the Academy also began to elect prominent members of society, among them the clergyman Sir John Dolben (in 1726), a member of an old family with long-standing credentials as supporters of such music events as the Sons of the Clergy Festival,[15] while in 1728 the Lords Plymouth and Percival were elected, evidence that the Academy had moved beyond its original professional status to embrace aristocratic musical amateurs and other notable figures such as the painter William Hogarth, who became a member in 1729. In 1727 the Academy had pulled off another coup when it persuaded Agostino Steffani (1654–1728), Bishop of Spiga and a noted opera composer, to be life president, although he never visited Britain. By 1730 the Academy had become highly successful, boasting a list of eighty-three subscribers

---

[14] The Catch Club's incorporation of professional members is discussed below. See below p. 38ff.
[15] Weber, *Musical Classics*, p. 48.

each paying half a guinea. Notwithstanding such success, the Academy of Vocal Music had in common with many clubs and societies become affected by professional jealousy and disputes, the most serious of which brought about its reorganisation. The occasion was the well-known case of plagiarism brought against Bononcini, who had claimed authorship of a madrigal that was subsequently ruled to be the work of the Venetian Antonio Lotti. The ensuing row brought to the forefront the factionalism in the Academy, particularly the bitter rivalry that existed between Greene and Gates. The result was the departure of not only Bononcini, but also Greene, who naturally took with him the boys of St Paul's.[16] In the wake of this upheaval, the Academy resolved to change both its name and constitution.

On 26 May 1731 the Academy of Vocal Music formally became the Academy of Ancient Music, with the explanation that 'By ye Compositions of the Ancients is meant of such as lived before ye end of the Sixteenth Century'.[17] With the loss of the boys, Pepusch was put in charge of an educational programme that would allow the Academy to produce its own trebles, a development recounted by Sir John Hawkins when he came to write an account of the history of the Academy:

> The loss which the Academy sustained by the succession [sic] of some members, the death of others, and above all by the want of boys, laid them under great difficulties, and drove them to the necessity of trying what could be done without the assistance of treble voices; but the experience of one season drove them to the alternative of an encreased expence, or annihilation. In this predicament they resolved upon an expedient that should not only make good the loss they had sustained, but convey a benefit to posterity. In short, they determined upon such an establishment, and such a subscription, as would render the Academy at once a society for the entertainment of its members, and a seminary for the instruction of youth in the principles of music, and the laws of harmony. Invitations to parents, and offers of such an education for their children, as would fit them for trades and businesses, as the profession of music, were given by advertisements in the public papers: these brought in a great number of children, and such of them as were likely to be made capable of performing the *Soprano* part in vocal compositions, were retained; Dr. *Pepusch* generously undertook the care of their instruction for a stipend, the largest the Academy could afford, tho' greatly disproportionate to his merit, and succeeded so well in his endeavours to improve them, that some of the most eminent professors of the science owe their skill and reputation to his masterly method of tuition.[18]

The addition of a didactic programme to the activities of the Academy of Ancient Music reflects a thread that runs through musical activity in England throughout the eighteenth century. We will shortly encounter another example. Although not typical of early eighteenth-century clubs in that conviviality apparently played little part in the proceedings of what was essentially a serious professional body, the early days of the Academy of Vocal Music have been covered in some detail here because, like the

---

[16] The full story has been recounted frequently. See, for example, Weber, *Musical Classics*, p. 60. The secession of Greene was followed in 1734 by that of Gates and the boys of the Chapel Royal.
[17] 'Original papers', fol. 16.
[18] [John Hawkins] *An account of the Institution and Progress of the Academy of Ancient Music by A Member* (London, 1770).

Castle Concerts, its foundation represented a significant development in the organisation of music life in eighteenth-century England. Moreover, from its inception the Academy had chosen to propagate as a living entity music of a specialised nature, music of the old polyphonic style that had hitherto been the academic province of a very few enthusiasts. In that sense, it is a development that would prove significant to the forthcoming generation of catch and glee composers.

Among the members of the Academy of Vocal Music was one 'Mr Immins', who became a member in 1728. He is more accurately identified as John Immyns, the founder of a society that would have rather greater significance for the catch and glee than the Castle Concerts or the Academy of Vocal Music. According to Hawkins,[19] Immyns was an attorney by profession, apparently an unsuccessful one who had met with 'misfortunes' that resulted in him doing copying work for the Academy and acting as amanuensis to Pepusch. He was said to be the possessor of a strong, if not very flexible countertenor voice that served well in the performance of madrigals, of which he became so enamoured that in 1741 he decided to form his own club called the Madrigal Society. In contrast to the Academy of Vocal (Ancient) Music, the membership of the Madrigal Society was not initially professional, but on the contrary distinctly plebeian in character. Acquaintances used to singing psalmody were recruited by Immyns, who with the help of solmisation trained this disparate group of 'mechanics, weavers from Spitalfields and others from various trades and occupations' (Hawkins[20]) to sing both English and Italian madrigals. Among this group was Samuel Jeacock, a baker 'at the corner of Berkeley Street, in Red Lion Street, Clerkenwell', who is also noted by Hawkins as having attended private music meetings at the house of William Caslon, a letter-founder whose evenings concluded with wine, an 'excellent ale' of Caslon's own brewing and 'a song or two of Purcell's sung to the harpsichord, or a few catches'.[21] The first meeting place of the Madrigal Society was at the Twelve Bells, an alehouse situated in Bride Lane, Fleet Street. A subscription of 5s. 6d per quarter was charged to the members, the fee covering the cost of music books and paper in addition to providing porter and tobacco. Hawkins claimed that the Society had in its early days a membership of some twenty-five, and in 1749–50 it was reported to have had twenty-one members.[22] However attendance records show that it was rare for the full membership to gather for meetings, with those for 1774 and 1775 suggesting that numbers attending individual meetings were on average ten.[23] The funds of the society were never large, the account books showing that until 1775 it operated on a balance of no more than £10.[24] Thereafter the figure increased to a sum around £40 by 1775. During its earliest years, the Madrigal Society appears to have been run on a fairly loose constitutional basis, but by 1744 a system of rotating the presidency was in operation and in July 1745 a set of rules was agreed upon 'for the better management of this

---

[19] Hawkins, *A General History*, vol. 2, p. 886. Hawkins gives a detailed account of the history of the Madrigal Society, of which he was a member during the 1750s.
[20] Hawkins, *A General History*, vol. 2, p. 887.
[21] Hawkins, *A General History*, vol. 2, p. 807.
[22] Thomas Oliphant, *An Account of the Madrigal Society* (London, 1835), p. 8.
[23] Madrigal Society Records, BL, MadSoc.F1.
[24] Madrigal Society Records, BL, MadSoc.F5.

Society'.[25] Membership was to be restricted to twenty-one members (sixteen is crossed out), while those attending were required to subscribe for a period of a minimum of twelve meetings. The president was to be responsible for selecting scores taken in turn to ensure that all the society's music would be given performance, an idea that would later be adopted by the Catch Club.[26] Rule 4 has particular interest for the present study:

> In Order for the preservation of the Reputation of this Society as to keeping good hours it is agreed that all music and vocal performances shall cease at half an hour after ten a clock unless some of the Members shall be chearfully incited to sing Catches in which case it shall be a rule to End all performances by Eleven.[27]

As with a number of musical clubs, the Madrigal Society was from its early days therefore perfectly happy to relax at the end of the serious business of the evening by singing catches. This is not however to imply that the society was prepared to compromise on its principal *raison d'être*. Eating (and doubtless drinking) evidently started to impinge on the evening's music making. In November 1746 a new order was added to the rulebook expressly forbidding the eating of supper between the hours of half past eight and ten, those sufficiently overcome by pangs of hunger to breach the rule during these hours being liable to a fine of 6d.[28] When a revised set of rules was issued in 1757, this edict was expanded, the society calling to attention the fact that the music it had been formed to serve was 'a more refined and intellectual Pleasure' than filling the stomach.[29] Article 9 of the 1757 rulebook provides details of the scheme of meetings, which were divided into two halves ('Acts') during the course of which four madrigals ('if time will permit') were sung. An interval of 'about half an hour' divided the two parts, the evening being under the auspices of a president, who served for two successive nights. It was his task to lay out the music books needed for the evening's entertainment, and also to hold the key to the library and the society's books. The Madrigal Society thus took up a more aesthetic and temperate stance than was the case with many clubs and societies. Its one concession to true conviviality during the period up to 1760 was the occasional trip out of town. Such an outing on the Thames took place on Whit Monday in 1751, when a party of members breakfasted at Wandsworth, and took wine and dinner at Richmond. The expenses, which included £4 9s for dinner and £2 1 6d for the hire of a barge, were covered by an extra contribution.[30]

In its later years the substantial number of contemporary catch and glee publications in the library of the Madrigal Society suggests that the singing of both catches and glees was extended into the main part of the evening's entertainment, doubtless with a commensurate increase of conviviality. Among the first purchased

---

[25] Madrigal Society Records, BL, MadSoc.F1.
[26] See below p. 63 for a discussion of the Catch Club's adoption of a similar scheme.
[27] In the 1757 revision of the rules 'Eleven' was changed to 'at Pleasure'. Madrigal Society Records, BL, MadSoc.F2.
[28] Madrigal Society Records, BL, MadSoc.F1.
[29] Madrigal Society Records, BL, MadSoc.F2.
[30] Oliphant, 'Account' p. 10.

(in 1765) were 'four books of catches' by William Hayes (1708–77), presumably including his two seminal books of *Catches, Glees and Canons* published respectively in 1757 and 1764, while in 1766 the society started on a collection of the annual anthologies produced for the Catch Club under the auspices of its secretary, Edmund Warren, paying the compiler himself, a member of the Madrigal Society from 1762, two guineas for the second and third of his publications.[31] The account books show that further issues were obtained as they appeared. Subsequently the library was augmented by the purchase of catches and glees by Luffman Atterbury, Charles Dibdin, Thomas Arne, Samuel Webbe the elder and Benjamin Cooke, among others. Unlike the Academy of Ancient Music, the Madrigal Society did not therefore restrict itself entirely to a repertoire of old music, but rather from the mid-1760s played an important role in the performance and dissemination of a contemporary catch and glee repertoire.

The close links between the Madrigal Society and the emergent catch and glee are emphasised by the long list of composers and others associated with the repertoire that became members or were noted as frequent visitors. They include a number who held joint membership with the Catch Club, among them George Berg (a member of the Madrigal Society from 1758 and the Catch Club from 1764), Jonathan Battishill (c. 1760 and 1767 respectively), Luffman Atterbury (1765 and 1779), Thomas Arne (1765 and 1763), Benjamin Cooke (1769 and 1767), and R. J. S. Stevens (1798 and 1783). Arne's association with the society also produced the earliest recorded instance of glees being accompanied by a keyboard instrument, Stevens, who had been engaged as a treble, noting that in 1773 Arne accompanied 'some Glees, but his method of playing the Harpsichord, and his figure at the instrument being remarkable and rather ridiculous, could not help tickle the fancy of us boys'.[32] While never members, the names of both Samuel Webbes, father and son, frequently appear on the guest list during the 1790s. Other significant names include those of the scholar, prominent anti-slave campaigner, and collector of (among other music) catches and glees Granville Sharp (1735–1813),[33] who joined in 1768, and another keen collector, the antiquarian Thomas Bever (1725–97), who became a member in 1769 and would in 1787 become a founder member of the Glee Club.

While neither strictly a club nor a musical organisation, the establishment in 1754 of the tortuously named Society for the Encouragement of Arts, Manufactures, and Commerce is worth noting for the implications its activities would have for one of the important innovations of the Catch Club. Founded with the avowed aim of 'exciting a Spirit of Emulation, to encourage and reward Ingenuity and Industry',[34] the society instituted annual premiums for the best works submitted within six designated categories, of which one was devoted to the 'Polite and Liberal Arts'. The society, whose elected officers included a president, eight vice-presidents, a treasurer,

---

[31] For discussion of Warren's Catch Club anthologies see below p. 33.
[32] Mark Argent, ed., *Recollections of R. J. S. Stevens* (London, 1992), p. 10. As will be seen in Chapter 6, Arne was also a pioneer when it came to the orchestral accompaniment of glees.
[33] Sharpe's name appears in the subscription lists of a number of published collections of catches and glees, as does that of his brother William.
[34] *Rules and Orders of the Society, Established in London for the Encouragement of Arts, Manufactures, and Commerce* (London, 1758).

a registrar, and a secretary, met to do its business eight times a year during the winter months. A strong moral purpose can be detected in the set of 'Rules and Orders' drawn up in 1758, which suggest that 'The readiest Way perhaps of reforming Habits of Vice, is to remove those of idleness, itself the greatest political Vice', providing further evidence of the didactic or moral philosophy propounded by many societies. Members of the society were invited to propose worthwhile projects, which were then entered in a memorandum book kept 'for the Inspection of the Society' and duly considered by the committee elected to examine each category. Every effort was made to ensure impartiality, the rules stipulating the maintenance of anonymity for all entrants. Professional expertise from outside the ranks of the Society was called upon if necessary to evaluate entries, but a final decision rested with the relevant committee, which then put selected entries to confirmation by ballot of the membership. As will be seen in the succeeding chapter such rules conform closely to the regulations later established by the Catch Club for the award of premiums. There we will find the same preliminary examination by a group of 'privileged members', the same secrecy surrounding the identity of entrants, who were allowed to make only a distinguishing mark on their work and required to submit their names within a sealed envelope that was opened after judging was completed. As with the Society for Arts, final decisions were made by the membership, in the instance of the Catch Club by all members, who were subject to a fine for non-attendance on the day of judging.

A further reason for looking at the Society of Arts in relation to the Catch Club is the small, but significant congruent membership of the two societies. Although the Catch Club was by far the smaller and more select of the two, the older organisation boasted a large number of aristocratic and upper-class supporters, well over 200 out of a total membership listing in excess of 2500 issued in 1765.[35] Among them we find a number of prominent members of the Catch Club, including the Earl of Sandwich, the Duke of Queensbury, the Duke of Bedford, and the Earl of Exeter. While the Society offered no prizes for composition (although it did provide backing for the English manufacture of gut strings, a commodity largely imported from Italy at the time), its membership included a number of musicians. Notable from the viewpoint of our present interest are the names of Thomas Arne, one of the first honorary (or professional) members of the Catch Club, and Luffman Atterbury, winner of five Catch Club medals, who may have joined the Society of Arts as a carpenter, his trade by training. In a later membership list dating from 1770, Atterbury is no longer listed, but Arne's name is still there and has been joined by those of two more composers who feature prominently in the early days of the Catch Club, George Berg and Benjamin Cooke.[36]

The significant patriotic implications of the concept and aims of the Society of Arts have been discussed elsewhere,[37] but how far they extended to overt nationalism is open to question. The Society was certainly sufficiently pragmatic on such matters as to employ two Italians as instructors when setting up the gut string

---

[35] *A List of the Society for the Encouragement of Arts, Manufactures, and Commerce* (London, 3 July 1765).
[36] *A List of the Society for the Encouragement of Arts, Manufactures, and Commerce* (London, 6 June 1770).
[37] See Linda Colley's *Britons: Forging the Nation 1707–1837* (Yale, 1992), pp. 83–97, for an examination of the patriotic nature of commercial enterprise during this period.

project noted above. Similarly, when an examination is made of the repertoire and membership of the first years of the Catch Club, we will find it pursuing anything but a nationalistic agenda.

As is apparent from the present chapter, the singing of catches in organised musical circles remained largely a peripheral activity during the first half of the eighteenth century, restricted to an ancillary of an evening's serious musical entertainment or occasionally introduced into more general club life. One notable exception seems to have been Edinburgh, where although originally an offshoot of the city's music society, an independent catch club appears to have been established by at least the 1740s. According to a contemporary account 'some of the members of this society instituted a catch-club, which met after the concert'. Although the chronology is unclear, this catch club was obviously meeting before 1745–6, a period covered by the visit to Scotland of the Prince of Hesse, who, along with several of the nobility, was 'elegantly entertained by the Lord Drummore,[38] then governour of the musical society, and the gentlemen of the catch-club' during the course of his visit. There were apparently 'many excellent voices in the catch-club, who sung their part at sight; and the easy chearfulness which reigned in this select society, rendered their meetings delightful'. Like many eighteenth-century societies, the Edinburgh Music Society's catch club seems to have fallen victim to its own success: 'The selection of company, which, for some years, gave high spirit and repute to this joyous convivial club, by degree relaxed; it of course became numerous and expensive, and at last broke up.'[39]

Notwithstanding the evidence of such activity, few composers are known to have devoted themselves to the composition of catches during the second quarter of the eighteenth century, a period that apparently contented itself with singing an established canon of works by Purcell and other seventeenth- and early eighteenth-century composers rather than adding to the repertoire. A rare exception is Maurice Greene, whose membership of the Castle Concerts and the Academy of Vocal Music has already been noted. In the preface to his *Catches and Canons for Three and Four Voices* (1747), Greene not only draws attention to the neglect of the catch, but also suggests that it is widely acknowledged:

> The Reader need not be inform'd that the Singing of Catches and Canons is of late Years much less in Use, amongst us in England, than it has formerly been.[40]

The continuation of Greene's Preface implies that notwithstanding such neglect, his catches have been sung within his own circle of friends:

> As an Attempt therefore to revive a Practice, undeservedly growing obsolete, some partial Friends have prevail'd upon Me, to trust the following little Pieces to the Press; in hopes that the Novelty of the Performance at least, (for what

---

[38] Hew Dalrymple (Lord Drummore) (1690–1755), was a lawyer and member of a prominent Scottish family.
[39] Hugo Arnot, *The History of Edinburgh from the Earliest Accounts to the Present Time* (Edinburgh, 1779; 2nd ed. 1788), pp. 380–1.
[40] Maurice Greene, *Catches and Canons for Three and Four Voices* (London, 1747).

other Merit it may have, is submitted to the Candour of the Publick) might recommend it to the Acceptance, I won't say approbation of such of my Musical Acquaintance, as are Lovers of Vocal Harmony.

'Twas judg'd proper to publish this Work in Score, tho' in opposition to Custom, for many reasons: chiefly that the Contrivance of the Composer in the Aptness and Congruity of the several Parts, might be the more accurately understood; that if any Errors in the Printing occur, they may be easily observ'd and rectified; and that by a just and frequent Practice of these Pieces, a Readiness may be acquired of Singing out of Score; the usefulness of which I need not enlarge upon.

The Catches are to be begun by a single voice, and sung in the Usual Manner; when, to avoid Confusion, each singer is desir'd to take particular care, not to be too loud for the rest of his Company.

They are put in the Treble Cliff,[41] in order to be of more general use; many Persons having taught Themselves and Others to Sing, by Playing upon Treble Instruments. The Skilfull, I am well aware, need not this kind of Assistance; and for the Unskilfull, it was ever my Opinion, no assistance can be too much.

Greene's preface is also of interest for the insight he provides into performance practice and in explaining his decision to publish in score rather than parts, an innovative idea that has no precedent in earlier catch publications, which, as Greene suggests, are frequently error-prone. His words also emphasise the fact that catches were intended to be sung one voice to a part and that, contrary to an impression often given, care was needed in performance if they were to make their best effect. Greene's suggestion that his catches are suitable for instrumental transcription, thus being 'of more general use' may have been motivated as much by marketing considerations as having the didactic purpose of helping performers to teach themselves to sing.

The distinction of having one of the earliest club or clubs formed specifically for the performance of catches in England goes not to London, but to Oxford, already as we have seen, long established as a leading centre for music clubs. The opening of the Holywell Music Room in 1748 provided new impetus to music making in the city and while detailed information is tantalisingly scanty, the first known reference to an English club being denominated as a catch club comes in a letter written by Edward Fawkener, a Fellow of Merton, to his friend James Harris, himself later briefly a member of the London Catch Club. Dated 10 November 1752, it reads:

> I was last night at a Catch Club, of which Dr [William] Hayes and his son [probably Thomas], with other good performers were members, & was there very agreeably entertained.[42]

William Hayes now enters the scene as a principal player in the development of the catch and glee. Born in Gloucester in 1708, he was a chorister at Gloucester Cathedral and in 1731 became organist of Worcester Cathedral. Three years later he moved to Oxford as organist of Magdalen College, living in the city for the remainder of his life. A prime mover behind the attempts to provide Oxford with a

---

[41] An old word for clef.
[42] Donald Burrows and Rosemary Dunhill, eds, *Music and Theatre in Handel's World: The Family Papers of James Harris 1732–1780* (Oxford, 2002), p. 285.

dedicated venue for music making that resulted in the Holywell Music Room, Hayes was deeply involved in the musical life of the city for many years, his association with catch clubs still being recorded as late as 1775, just two years before his death. Hayes was also the composer of a number of catches and glees that were first issued in his *Catches, Glees and Canons for 3, 4, and 5 Voices* in 1757. Dedicated to the baronet Sir William Dolben of Finedon, Northants, the son of Sir John Dolben, Oxford University MP from 1768, and a member of the Society for the Encouragement of Arts, Hayes' preface, like Greene's ten years earlier, suggests that the publication was the result of promptings by friends 'who must have been disappointed in not seeing them earlier',[43] an indication that the contents had been composed some while ago. These friends were doubtless those who met 'under the happy Auspices of a most agreeable and well regulated Society that met weekly', doubtless the same club attended by Fawkener in 1752. While no venue is mentioned, that omission was repaired ten years later in the Supplement issued by Hayes, where he dedicates the contents to the 'Worthy Members of the Catch-Club, At the King's Head Tavern'.[44] Hayes continues by stating that the club had

> subsisted several Years, in very high Perfection, and which I found to be productive of the desirable Effects: viz. *Chearfulness* and *Good-humour, Friendship* and a *Love of Harmony*; not to mention how much it contributed to the *Improvement* of the younger Practitioners, enabling them to sing readily at Sight [...] and this not by Compulsion or Drudgery, but, by Allurement, and the Gratification of a Pleasure they found in it themselves [...] Thus much suffice as to the Utility and laudable Practice of frequently singing Catches, and other little detached Pieces of Vocal Harmony; and I cannot help wishing it may prove an inducement to others, my Brethren of Cathedrals especially, to encourage and promote such Societies as the above; well knowing it will contribute greatly to their own Satisfaction, the Improvement of those who may stand in need of their Assistance, and thereby, not a little, to the just Execution of *Church-Music*, or the Support of any *Choral Performance*.
>
> [...] I shall beg leave to add, that these little pieces produce an agreeable effect, when justly performed on such instruments; especially, if a convenient Number of them are selected, and properly ranged together. The Canons do well on three Violoncellos [...]
>
> Few I should imagine, need be informed, that the Manner of performing Catches [...] But I must beg leave to suggest, that, so often as it [the catch] is repeated, an Alternacy of *Forte* and *Piano* or *Loud* and *Soft*, in imitation of the *Chiaro Oscuro*, or *Light* and *Shade* in painting, has an agreeable effect; except in such, where the humour of the Subject requires a certain Jollity to be kept up throughout the whole, which the Performer will very easily distinguish. And if, amongst the following, any should be found worthy of being *pathetic*, or to have

---

[43] William Hayes, *Catches, Glees and Canons for 3, 4, & 5 Voices* (London, 1757).
[44] William Hayes, *A Supplement to the Catches, Glees and Canons, Lately published by Dr Hayes* (London, 1765).

any thing *delicate* in their *Taste* or *Construction*, I would recommend *Mezzo Piano* (at least sometimes under the full Tone of Voice) as being more expressive of Tenderness.

I shall hope for a Pardon from the *judicious Reader*, for having given these few Hints concerning the Manner of performing Catches, when I assure him, they were intended chiefly for the Information of *Novices* in the Art; and not to insult the better *Taste* and *Skill* of the Adept [...] For this Reason, I have been very sparing in arbitrarily prescribing Graces, and in putting Marks for Expression; being persuaded that a Redundancy of such Marks not only perplex the Performer, but if his *Taste* in the Executive Part be better than the Composer's (a very possible Case) will certainly give him disgust, tho' calculated with the utmost Care and Precision.

[...] As to this species of Composition, the CATCH in *Music* answers to the EPIGRAM in *Poetry*; where much is to be expresst within a very small Compass; and unless the Turn is neat and well pointed, it is of little Value: But, on the Contrary, if the Incidents are fully, tho' concisely expresst, and the Conclusion be spirited and striking, whether it be of the humourous, or serious kind, it is justly esteemed excellent.

[...] In the following Compositions, I have endeavoured to imitate that simplicity of Style which distinguishes the Works of those Masters who are allowed to have excelled in this Species of Music; particu'arly those of our Countrymen HILTON, LAWES, BREWER, FORD and others of the last Century; But above all, the famous PURCELL; whose incomparable Humour can never be outdone if equalled...

Here we find Hayes not only re-stating the fundamental catch club ethos of 'chearfulness, and good humour, friendship and love of harmony', but also reiterating the didactic uses of learning to sing catches, the advice in this instance specifically directed at cathedral singers, who Hayes suggests might with value form their own societies with the objective of enhancing their performance of church music. Later, and again like Greene, Hayes is at pains to stress that the performance of catches needs a careful approach. This, he makes clear, applies particularly to works of a delicate or pathetic character, a salutary reminder to those writers who would have it that an essential component of the catch is humour.[45] Also of note is the value Hayes places on his musical heritage, an appreciation he shares with many of the coming generation of catch and glee composers. Interestingly, Hayes' comparison with the painting term *chiaroscuro* and references to light and shade almost exactly mirror a passage in Charles Avison's *Essay on Musical Expression*, published four years earlier in 1753 and a work bitterly attacked anonymously by Hayes in his responding *Remarks*.[46] Hayes however transforms Avison by using the terms as an analogy for alternating *piano* and *forte* rather than Avison's applying them

---

[45] See for example David Johnson, 'Catch' in *The New Grove Dictionary of Music and Musicians*, second edition, ed. Stanley Sadie and John Tyrrell (London, 2001).
[46] William Hayes, *Remarks on Mr. Avisons's Essay on Musical Expression* (London, 1753). See Chapter 7 for further discussion of the aesthetics that lay behind the dispute between Avison and Hayes.

to concord and discord.[47] Hayes' subsequent analogy between the catch and the epigram again emphasises that he sees the catch as a serious, if miniature, form in which it is possible to say much within the context of a small framework. His regard for the canon of catch repertoire of the previous century marks him out as an antiquarian who advocated in the *Remarks* that in his ideal academy 'no Author whatever should be studied, unless deemed truly *Classical*. This, Hayes opines, might enable us 'to pay back with *Interest* what we have borrowed from foreign Countries at too large a *Premium*'. The national prejudice implied by his remarks is then made overt as Hayes continues with the hope that such a scheme 'might be productive of excellent Performers, and learned Composers in every useful Branch of Music, no less to the Honour and the Advantage of the Nation, in rivalling the haughty *French* and *Italians*, and saving itself vast Sums *annually*.[48]

It seems probable that Hayes is here thinking principally of church music, of which he ruefully observes elsewhere that 'the further we look back, the more excellent the Composition will be found'.[49] His ideal of an English music that owed at least something to the nation's 'truly Classical' tradition was about to be realised, founded not so much on sacred music, but on the kind of small-scale secular work that Hayes and Greene had themselves fostered.

---

[47] I am grateful to Pierre Dubois for drawing my attention to the similarity with Avison's original passage.
[48] Quoted in Simon Heighes, *The Lives and Works of William and Philip Hayes* (New York and London, 1995), pp. 17–18.
[49] Heighes, *Lives and Works*, p. 18.

Chapter 3
The Catch Club

On a November evening in 1761 a group of nine men gathered at a tavern in St James' Street, London. From their deliberations emerged what is generally known as the Noblemen and Gentlemen's Catch Club,[1] the first such club in London to have been formed with the specific purpose of performing catches and glees. The venue for this historic meeting is invariably cited as Almack's,[2] an ambiguous description requiring clarification. William Almack was probably a Scot originally known as Macall. He had risen from service as a valet to the Duke of Hamilton to become the duke's major domo and deputy steward, at a generous salary. By the middle of the century Almack had obviously accrued sufficient funds to become the owner of the Thatched House, which had developed from a small seventeenth-century inn to become a fashionable meeting place for wits and politicians.[3] Almack became a successful entrepreneur, in 1764 opening a club in Pall Mall known as Almack's (today Brooks'), an enterprise followed the succeeding year by Almack's Assembly Rooms, also located in St James' Street. Neither of the two institutions customarily referred to as Almack's therefore qualify as the first home of the Catch Club, which was in fact the Thatched House Tavern. Equally, there is no contemporary evidence to suggest that the founding fathers of the club ever used the grand appendage by which music historians universally refer to it today. The earliest references to the organisation consistently refer simply to the 'Catch Club', while the Minutes never deviate from the use of the terms 'the Club' or 'the Society'.[4] The earliest historical survey of the club and its institution, written by John Wall Callcott in 1801, is quite definite in its nomenclature. In the course of his manuscript essay *On the Catch Club*, Callcott, who himself had intimate connections with the club,[5] writes only that it was formed by 'a few of the English Nobility and Gentry' who 'in Nov. 1761 formed the design of establishing a Catch Club'.[6] The earliest use of the title Noblemen and Gentlemen's Catch Club discovered to date is on the title page of a collection of glees and catches by Joseph Baildon published in 1768.[7]

---

[1] The club remains in existence, today based at the House of Lords.
[2] See for instance: Herbert John Gladstone, *The Story of the Noblemen and Gentlemen's Catch Club* (London, 1930). Rep. *The Noblemen and Gentlemen's Catch Club* with additional material by Guy Boas and Harald Christopherson (London, 1996), p. 53; Emanuel Leo Rubin, Introduction to *The Warren Collection* (Wilmington, De, 1970), not page numbered; Rubin, 'The English Glee', p. 91.
[3] Robert Elkin, *The Old Concert Rooms of London* (London, 1955), p. 74.
[4] The Minutes of the Catch Club are held in the British Library, Add. H2788.rr-ss (1761–96). Writing in 1970, Rubin believed them to have been lost during World War II bombing.
[5] Callcott was elected as a privileged member in 1788, Minutes, H2788.ss.
[6] Callcott, 'Essays'. Callcott obtained his information largely from the Minutes, which were loaned to him by Samuel Webbe the elder, Warren's successor as secretary.
[7] Joseph Baildon, *A Collection of Glees & Catches for three and four voices, as they are performed at the Noblemen & Gentlemen's Catch Club. Never before printed* (London, 1768).

The nine men who founded the Catch Club that November evening were an interesting and disparate mix, but with one notable exception they could all be described as noblemen or gentlemen:

> John Montagu, fourth Earl of Sandwich (1718–92)
> Archibald [Alexander] Montgomery, tenth Earl of Eglinton (1723–69)
> William Douglas, 3rd Earl of March, later 4th Duke of Queensbury (1724–1810)
> Major-General John Barrington (1719–64)
> Lieutenant-General Robert Rich, later Sir Robert Rich (1717–85)
> The Honourable John Ward, later 2nd Viscount Dudley and Ward (1724 or 5–88)
> Hugo Menil (*recte* Meynell) (1735–1808)
> Richard Phelps (d. 1771)

The ninth member of the gathering was Edmund Thomas Warren (*c.* 1730–94), a man who would come to play a crucial role in the early history of the Catch Club.[8] How Warren came to be involved with this group is not clear, but it is more than likely that it was through connections with Sandwich, its most musically involved member. Sufficiently competent as a musician to compose a number of catches,[9] Warren was also a keen collector and musical antiquarian whose interests made him a natural candidate to become the Catch Club's first secretary, a position he maintained until shortly before his death. His diligent service to the club, which from the outset included not only the usual secretarial duties, but work as a copyist, would prove to be an invaluable asset, well recognised by the club. In May 1764 Warren was rewarded by a resolution to strike a medal to him as 'testimony to the Society's sense of his respectful attention to them', a distinction supplemented two months later (and in subsequent years) by 'a compliment of Twenty Guineas [...] to Mr Warren for his Extraordinary Trouble and Assiduity'.[10] In February 1763 a motion was passed to give Warren 'leave to inscribe a collection of Catches, Canons, and Glees to the Society',[11] thus inaugurating the remarkable run of publications now known as the Warren Collection, a series eventually comprising thirty-two volumes, their annual appearance halted only by Warren's resignation and death in 1794. The date that Warren was first granted leave to dedicate his collections to the Catch Club suggests that Rubin's conclusion that the cycle had commenced in 1762 is incorrect, a verdict supported by additional internal evidence to which we will return later.[12] Warren's exhaustive work as a compiler also bore fruit in several periodically issued

---

[8] In 1784 Warren received a Royal Licence enabling him 'to take the name and bear the arms of Horne, the name of his uncle Edmund Horne, sometime captain in the Royal Navy'. Quoted in Rubin, 'Introduction' to *The Warren Collection*. He subsequently took the name Warren Horne. He is referred to throughout this book as Warren.
[9] Several of Warren's own catches are included in the early collections he issued on behalf of the Catch Club. One was copied into the books of the Catch Club (vol. 2) and two are included in the books of the Canterbury Catch Club.
[10] Minutes, H.2788.rr., p. 79.
[11] Minutes, H.2788.rr., p. 7.
[12] Rubin, *The Warren Collection*. The dating in the exhaustive, if often inaccurate, list of glee publications in *Die Musik in Geschichte und Gegenwart* (DGG), would therefore in this instance appear to be correct.

supplementary volumes, probably issued from around 1765,[13] but his most ambitious project failed to reach print. This was intended as a testament to Warren's antiquarian interests in the form of a six-volume anthology of motets and madrigals of the Renaissance, a collection incorporating an extraordinarily diverse range of composers including Isaac, Josquin, Jannequin, Rore, Marenzio, Pierre de la Rue, and Wilbye.[14] The music books of the Catch Club also bear witness to Warren's devotion to 'old' music, many of the historic pieces included in the earlier volumes having been 'introduced by Mr Warren'.[15]

Of the original members Warren served as secretary, much the most influential was John Montagu, Earl of Sandwich, who was almost certainly the prime mover behind the foundation of the Catch Club and for many years its driving force. As William Weber has noted, his considerable musical interests and activities probably found fresh impetus during the 1750s after his naval career stalled.[16] However, Weber's suggestion that the musical and dramatic events staged at Sandwich's Huntingdonshire seat date from the end of this decade cannot be sustained.[17] His source, Joseph Craddock, is clear that 'the first attraction' at these events was Sandwich's mistress, the actress and singer Martha Ray, who was not born until 1745.[18] Sandwich's Hinchingbroke entertainments in fact almost certainly took place during the early 1770s, a decade during which his involvement in musical activity increased dramatically with his stewardship of the Festival of the Sons of the Clergy (in 1773),[19] and, crucially, as one of the founders of the Concert of Antient Music in 1776. While the full and significant role played by Sandwich in the musical life of the country remains to be investigated, it seems reasonable to suggest that his leading role in the foundation of the Catch Club represents his first significant participation in organised music making. It was an undertaking to which he was eminently suited. Of Sandwich's Hinchingbroke events, which included the singing of glees and catches after dinner, Craddock observed that 'all this was well conducted; for whatever his Lordship undertook he generally accomplished'.[20] In addition to organisational accomplishment, Sandwich was able to bring that conviviality of character that was the essence of club life. In the words of Charles Butler, he was 'the soul of the Catch Club, a man whose manners partook of the old court' and that 'he possessed, in a singular degree, the art of attracting persons of every rank to

---

[13] Gathered together in the single volume *A Collection of Vocal Harmony consisting of Catches, Canons and Glees [...] to which are added several Motetts and Madrigals composed by the Best Masters. Selected by Thomas Warren* (London, c. 1775).

[14] A set of proof sheets engraved for the first volume is all that remains of Warren's project. See BL K.7.i.12.

[15] Together with the Warren Collection, the Catch Club's twenty manuscript music volumes (now housed in the British Library as H.2788.p–z and aa–ii) represent the most important source of information regarding the repertoire of the Catch Club.

[16] Weber, *Musical Classics*, p. 147.

[17] Weber, *Musical Classics*, p. 149.

[18] Joseph Craddock, *Memoirs*, vol. I (London, 1828), p. 117. Martha Ray, a pupil of Giardini and Joah Bates, was famously shot dead by a spurned lover while leaving Covent Garden in 1779 after playing in Thomas Arne's *Love in a Village*. She was a subscriber to a number of catch and glee collection publications.

[19] *Lists of the Nobility, Clergy, and Gentry who have been Stewards for the Feasts of the Sons of the Clergy* (London 1853).

[20] Craddock, *Memoirs*, p. 117.

him... every one was at ease'.[21] The Leicester manufacturer and amateur musician William Gardiner, recording an event attended by his father, gives us another glimpse of Sandwich's ebullient conviviality on the occasion of a large-scale music meeting he organised in Leicester in September 1774. The Sunday before this event Sandwich and the 'London party' dined at Gumley Hall, the residence of Joseph Craddock.[22] 'On the cloth being drawn', Gardiner relates, 'his Lordship addressing himself to Mr. Warren, secretary to the Noblemen's Catch Club, said, "Tom, have you got the catch books here?" "Yes, my Lord", said Warren. "Then hand them to me"', replied Sandwich. The singing of a number of catches and glees followed during the course of which the ladies eventually retired, probably, thought Gardiner's father, 'driven away by the unrestrained conversation of my Lord'.[23] Within the more formal surroundings of the Catch Club, Sandwich appears to have exercised powers of attentiveness and discrimination. The dilettante musician and diarist John Marsh was told by his local Chichester MP Thomas Steele, a member of the Catch Club from 1780, that Sandwich was in the habit of showing his displeasure at poor performances by calling out at the end 'Very bad indeed, gentlemen'.[24] In May 1790 Marsh was taken to the club as a visitor by Steele, an occasion that suggests that at the age of 72 Sandwich had lost little of his natural ebullience:

> Mr Steele our Member, having offer'd to take me to the Catch Club at the Thatched House Tavern of which he was a member, on this day, I accordingly went a little before 4 to the Salopian Coffee House, where I met him & Mr Toghill & accompanied them to the meeting, at which I was much entertained, Lord Sandwich being president & joining with great good humour in some of the catches that were sung.[25]

None of the other founder members emulated the breadth of Sandwich's musical interests, although external evidence provided by subscription lists suggests that several were sufficiently musical to obtain their own copies of published collections of catches and glees. Four had only a relatively short relationship with the club. Hugo Meynell of Bradley in Derbyshire was High Sheriff of the county in 1758 and was successively MP for Lichfield (1762–68), Lymington (1769–74), and Stafford (1774–80).[26] He is one of three founder members whose name is to be found in the 1783 list of subscribers to the Italian opera at the King's Theatre, a connection that will be

---

[21] Quoted in Weber, *Musical Classics*, p. 149. Butler was never a member of the Catch Club, so must have based his impressions on attendance as a visitor.
[22] Craddock took a considerable interest in the glee and catch repertoire. He was the author of the words of Samuel Webbe the elder's famous prize-winning glee *You gave me your heart*, and was a subscriber to Webbe's third published collection, which appeared in 1775. Craddock also relates how he became involved at Garrick's house in a 'warm dispute' over the merits of a glee of Thomas Arne's. *Memoirs*, vol. IV, p. 127.
[23] William Gardiner, *Music and Friends* (London & Leicester, 1828), vol. 1, p. 6.
[24] Brian Robins, ed., *The Journals of John Marsh* (Stuyvesant, NY, 1998), p. 474. The strict conditions of silence maintained by Sandwich at the meetings of the Concert of Antient Music were also noted by Marsh.
[25] Ibid.
[26] Sir L. Napier and J. Brooke, eds, *The History of Parliament: The House of Commons 1754–1790*, 3 vols. (London, 1985). All subsequent parliamentary details are taken from this source.

further discussed below.²⁷ He vacated his place in March 1764, a departure closely followed by that of John Barrington, who died in Paris on 2 April. Mistakenly identified by Rubin as William Wildman Barrington, second Viscount Barrington, he was in fact the younger brother of the Viscount, a man who had pursued a distinguished military career culminating with his key role in the capture of Guadeloupe from the French in 1759. For this he was promoted to major general.²⁸ The other military man, Lieutenant-General Robert Rich, fought at Culloden in 1746, where he was so seriously injured that the *Gentleman's Magazine* reported his death. Later he became governor of Londonderry and Culmore Fort, and in 1768 inherited a baronetcy.²⁹ His short-lived membership of the Catch Club was by that time well in the past, since he resigned early in 1765, probably in connection with the bizarre incident recounted below. The Earl of Eglinton's association with the club was even shorter, since although he was named by Callcott as one of the two prime instigators of the Catch Club (along with Sandwich) he vacated his place in December 1764. Five years later he was killed on his Ayrshire estate during a stand-off with an excise man turned poacher, an incident that elicted a tribute from the Catch Club in the form of a three-part glee, *An Elegy on the late Earl of Eglinton*, written by no less distinguished a composer than William Boyce.³⁰

The three remaining founders enjoyed a rather longer membership. Little is known about Richard Phelps other than that he was under-secretary to Sandwich. The Minutes of the club show that he played an active role in the running of it during its early years, apparently acting as treasurer. A resolution of 10 May 1764 gave Phelps authority 'to take such measures as he shall think most conducive to the good of the Society for this purpose ('charge of the Reck'nings') and that his determination be final as well on the Members of the Society as Almack'.³¹ Interest in the club appears to have been more restricted in the case of the Earl of March, better known as the fourth Duke of Queensbury (a title to which he succeeded in 1786) or 'Old Q'. One of the most colourful figures of the age, March was notorious for his gambling, drinking and womanising. His lurid lifestyle has tended to obscure the fact he was known to be intelligent and, like Sandwich, the possessor of highly engaging manners. According to the tenor Michael Kelly, a frequent visitor to the Duke's Piccadilly home in his later years, he was 'passionately fond of music, and an excellent judge of the art',³² although it has been suggested that his patronage of the opera house had more to do with a desire to ogle attractive young women than an interest in the finer points of opera. March remained a member of the Catch Club until March 1779, when he was expelled under the club's non-attendance rules.³³

---

[27] I am grateful to William Weber for supplying me with this listing, which includes information culled from a variety of sources. The other founder members listed as subscribers to the King's Theatre are the Earl of March and the Hon. John Ward.

[28] Jonathan Spain, 'John Barrington' in *Oxford Dictionary of National Biography* (Oxford, 2004).

[29] Alastair W. Massie, 'Sir Robert Rich' in *Oxford Biography Dictionary*.

[30] The event is recorded in some detail in an unidentified local newspaper cutting held by the North Ayrshire Museum Association. Boyce's *Elegy*, dated 1770, is included in the fourth of the Catch Club's books.

[31] Minutes, H.2788.rr., p. 73.

[32] Roger Fiske, ed., *Michael Kelly: Reminiscences* (Oxford, 1975), p. 221.

[33] He was also a subscriber to Webbe's third published collection (1775).

John Ward, the final founding member, was descended from a Staffordshire family whose two titles were combined in 1763 in the creation of the title of Viscount Dudley and Ward. From 1754 until 1761 he was Tory MP for Marlborough, later becoming MP for the county of Worcester from 1761 until 1774, when he became second holder of the title on the death of his father. He had a home in Park Lane. The family appear to have taken a greater interest in music than many of the members of the Catch Club. Ward's father was a member of the Madrigal Society,[34] while his name can be found on several subscribers' lists for catch and glee publications.[35]

In his valuable, if somewhat disorganised survey of the Catch Club, Viscount Gladstone, writing without regard for historical context, notes that the early documentation makes no mention of any reason or motivation for its founding. 'There is', he concludes, 'no record to show how or why the Noblemen and Gentlemen's Catch Club came into existence.'[36] Callcott is more definite, stating explicitly that the club was formed with the intention of reviving 'the neglected music of that period [the great era of the English madrigal] & to encourage the efforts of rising talents'.[37] Both Gladstone's air of mystery and Callcott's explanation prompt questions that are not too difficult to answer. The founders of the Catch Club in fact needed neither reason nor motivation for its founding, since, as has been established in previous chapters, it represented not innovation, but the culmination of a musical movement that had been set in train a century earlier, and a social movement that was highly fashionable.

The foundation of the Catch Club was therefore entirely logical, the club itself simply one more specialised institution to add to the large number that had already proliferated and would continue to do so. For inspiration it had only to turn to the Society for the Encouragement of Arts and the Madrigal Society, both of which, as we have seen, included among their membership men involved in the formation of the new club.[38] Callcott, with the benefit of hindsight, was able to elucidate aims that were manifestly obvious by the time he was writing in 1801. He had himself greatly benefited from the encouragement given by the Catch Club to young composers. Callcott would also have been well aware of the inclusion of madrigals and catches by sixteenth- and seventeenth-century composers on the books of the society. The revival of such pieces was, however, well established by institutions such as the Academy of Ancient Music and the Madrigal Society by the time the Catch Club was formed, and the degree to which historicism was motivation for its foundation must remain questionable. While the Catch Club's early volumes include a healthy number of 'old' works, there was little alternative repertoire in the early days. The rapid establishment of a prize competition to encourage the creation of a contemporary repertoire suggests that the preservation of historic music was unlikely to have been a primary consideration. Once that new repertoire had been established, the proportion of earlier music dropped sharply to judge by both the Catch Club's books

---

[34] Stevens, *Recollections*, p. 11.
[35] Among them Samuel Webbe the elder's Third Book, (*c*. 1775), and Benjamin Cooke's op. 5 (1775).
[36] Gladstone, *Catch Club*, rep., p. 13.
[37] Calcott, 'Essays'.
[38] See above p. 25ff.

and Warrens's collections. By the 1780s, as Table 1 shows, the amount of historic repertoire performed by the club had dwindled to near-insignificance.[39]

Table 1
Proportion of 'Old' Music Included in The Catch Club Books & The Warren Collection

	1760s	1770s	1780s	1790s
Catch Club Books Average: 7%	18%	5.5%	2%	1%
Warren Collection Average: 6.13%	5%	5%	6.5%	3%

Without the personal enthusiasm for historic music of Warren and to a lesser extent Sandwich, the figures would certainly have been appreciably lower, as indeed they would have been in the early days had not a substantial number of Purcell's catches been included, particularly in the Catch Club books.

No more is heard of the newly established club until the spring of 1762. Early meetings seem to have been arbitrarily arranged, with a Monday or Tuesday the preferred choice until the latter emerged (by 1763) as the regular meeting day. During these meetings the club set about formulating its first rules, which unsurprisingly show that the society was founded on a framework similar to those of other such organisations. The first of these resolutions, passed in March, dealt with the all-important matters of the presidency and dining:

> Resolv'd that according to the above List [of founding members] Each Member shall take his turn to be President, and if not, shall pay a forfeit of one guinea unless out of the Kingdom / and the Presidentship to devolve to the next in turn who happens to be present.
> Dinner to be order'd for 12 at five shillings per head: the messages to be sent in the name of the President. Allmack [sic] to give notice every Saturday morning to the next President whose turn it is to serve whether in Town or Country.[40]

The use of forfeits would come to play an important role not only in the club's constitution but also in its finances. The onus placed upon Almack to notify the forthcoming president is in accordance with the widespread precedent of involving closely the landlord of the venue at which clubs held their meetings. During April two further resolutions were passed, the first of which followed familiar procedures by stipulating that membership should be limited. As we have already seen in the

---

[39] For the purposes of the survey in Table 1 'old' music is defined as works composed more than forty years previously.
[40] Minutes, H.2788.rr., p. 2.

instance of the catch club in Edinburgh, failure to do so often led to the ultimate demise of a club. In the case of the Catch Club the number was set at twenty-one 'and no more', a figure amended to twenty-four in 1768. For reasons that are not clear neither this rule nor its amendment was ever enforced, and it was almost immediately broken by the election of sixteen new members. By January 1764 the figure had already risen to twenty-seven, and there were further increases to thirty-one in November 1767 and thirty-three in November 1769.[41] Two related explanations may account for this obvious breach of rules. There is little doubt that the Catch Club rapidly became highly fashionable among parliamentarians and leading members of society, creating a constant demand for membership that may or may not have had an interest in music at heart. At the same time, that demand allowed the club to develop a stringent set of attendance laws that virtually ensured a rapid turnover of membership among a class of men whose way of life dictated that they were frequently involved in the affairs of state or away from the capital. As we have already seen, four of the founding members had already departed in one manner or another by early 1765 and of the sixteen who joined in April 1762 only William Gordon was still a member by 1770,[42] ten having resigned or been expelled for non-attendance within two years.

The new intake preserved the high social status and, in some instances, the low moral standards of the founder members. Among them were three peers of the realm, including the fourth Earl of Rochford, a notable dissolute in his younger days, but a later Secretary of State (from 1768); Viscount (later Lord) Weymouth, who emulated Rochford by progressing from a hard drinking, gambling youth to become Secretary of State in 1765; and four military men who included John Manners, Marquis of Granby, later the third Duke of Rutland and a future Commander-in-Chief of the army. The most interesting name to music historians is that of James Harris, the philosopher, writer, and friend of Handel, although Harris' interest in the Catch Club appears to have been peripheral and was certainly short-lived. The recent publication of his voluminous papers makes no mention of his membership of the club,[43] and on 22 December 1763 Harris was expelled for non-attendance. During the 1770s he did attend as a visitor several times, including one occasion in March 1770 as a guest of the Duke of Queensbury, an occasion on which he recorded in his diary that he heard 'many excellent catches and glees'.[44] A full list of members up until 1800 will be found in Appendix A, its most notable feature being the large proportion of parliamentarians. Of those who were not members of the aristocracy, who of course were automatically members of the House of Lords, some three-quarters have been positively identified as members of the House of Commons, a considerable majority of them government supporters.[45]

Over the course of the next two months the Catch Club made two far-reaching decisions that would determine its future. The first, enacted in April, was a resolution

[41] Minutes, H.2788.rr., pp. 2, 184, 202.
[42] He later became the Lord Gordon who was involved in a scandalous elopement with Lady Sarah Bunbury, the daughter of the Duke of Richmond.
[43] Burrows, *Music and Theatre*.
[44] Burrows, *Music and Theatre*, p. 586.
[45] The source is Napier & Brooke, *The History of Parliament*.

to invite professional musicians to be become privileged or honorary members of the club. By the second, introduced in the following month, the committee of the Catch Club took the most significant step in its history: the institution of medal prizes for the best catches and glees submitted annually to the committee.

The admission of privileged members represented a move that was sound common sense. Again it was hardly innovatory. A century earlier William Ellis' Oxford club had collapsed because its displaced professional members dispersed widely to take up new posts in the wake of the Restoration,[46] while in 1725 the Academy of Vocal Music had solicited the Gentlemen of the Chapel Royal and the members of St Paul's Cathedral choir in order to obtain expert vocal participation at its meetings.[47] The significance of the Catch Club's early resolution is a clear determination that from the outset its members were concerned not solely with conviviality, however important a role that may have been expected to play in its proceedings, but also with the high standards of performance expected by Sandwich. Since full members were expected to join the professionals in the singing of catches and glees, it also implied a degree of didacticism. The musicianship of the honourable gentlemen could not but help improve if they performed part songs with experienced professionals.

Privileged members were entitled to many of the same benefits and restrictions as full members. They were permitted to dine with them, but could be summarily expelled by the committee and their membership forfeited if they did not attend at least twice (later revised to five times) during the course of a season. The names of those who became members over the following twenty years or so suggest that privileged membership was highly valued, a notion supported by R. J. S. Stevens (1757–1837), who recalled that 'to be an Honorary Member of the Catch Club appeared to me at this time in my life to be a desirable thing for a young Musician'.[48] The initial group consisted of:

>   John Beard (1716–91)
>   Jonathan Battishill (1738–1801)
>   Thomas Arne (1710–78)
>   Gaetano Quilici (fl.1754–80)
>   Carl Friedrich Abel (1723–87)
>   ? Cowper or Cooper (?–?).
>   William Savage (1720–89)
>   Samuel Champness (d. 1803)
>   Felice Giardini (1716–96)

The list includes some of the most eminent men in contemporary London musical life. John Beard was the finest English tenor of his day. As a boy he was blessed with a strong and clear treble; he had been one of the Children of the Chapel Royal and sang in Handel's *Esther* (in 1732) and *Il Pastor Fido* (1734). A convivial man

---

[46] See above p. 10.
[47] See above p. 21.
[48] Stevens, *Recollections*, p. 43. Stevens was writing in 1782, the year before he was elected a member.

– during the 1740s he was a member of the famous Beef Steak Club – of handsome appearance and gentlemanly manners, Beard in 1739 married a society bride, Lady Henrietta Herbert, the daughter of the Earl of Waldegrave. Six years after her death in 1753, Beard married Charlotte, one the four daughters of John Rich, patentee and manager of Covent Garden, at the same time transferring his own services there from Drury Lane. After Rich's death in November 1761, Beard assumed active management of Covent Garden. He remained a member of the Catch Club until June 1767, when he was permitted to retire, a decision doubtless dictated by the onset of deafness that dated from the previous year.

One of the key figures in the history of the catch and glee, Jonathan Battishill was a former chorister of St Paul's Cathedral, and a pupil of William Savage, Master of the Choristers, a member of the Madrigal Society, the Beef Steak Club and another of the Catch Club's initial intake of privileged members. Like Beard, Savage had sung as a boy for Handel in several of his operas and oratorios, later developing what R. J. S. Stevens described as a 'pleasant [bass] voice' that stretched over two octaves, his singing also being notable for 'clear articulation' and 'perfect intonation'.[49] Savage also composed both sacred music and a number of songs, catches and glees, his humorous epitaph *Poor Ralpho lies* being included in the first of Warren's Catch Club publications. Savage was expelled from the Catch Club under its non-attendance rule, one of three professionals to have left under these circumstances by the end of the 1764/65 season.[50] His protégé Battishill's contribution was both greater and longer lasting. After completing his training, Battishill had appeared as a singer in Handel's *Alexander's Feast*, and in 1758 he became a member of the Madrigal Society.[51] Shortly before he joined the Catch Club, he was appointed harpsichordist at Covent Garden, an engagement that led directly to meeting his future wife Cecilia Davies, one of the leading sopranos of the day. In addition to a number of songs composed for the stage, Battishill collaborated with Michael Arne in a serious English opera, *Almena* (1764). In the same year he was appointed organist of the parishes of St Clement, Eastcheap and St Martin, Ongar, thereafter devoting much of his considerable talent to the composition of sacred music. In addition to a collection of his own,[52] ten of Battishill's catches and glees were included in Warren's collections. He had two stints as a privileged member, the first coming to an end in June 1767, when he was expelled for the same reason as Savage, only to be reinstated in late November of that same year 'upon promising to be constant in his attendance in future'.[53] At the end of November 1774 Battishill was again elected a privileged member, this time becoming a long-lasting and loyal servant of the club.[54]

---

[49] R. J. S. Stevens, 'The Life of Mr William Savage' Handwritten in Stevens' copy of Savage's works. Euing Library, University of Glasgow: MS Euing R.d.23.
[50] His expulsion, along with those of Abel and 'Cooper' is noted in the list of privileged members recorded on 19 May 1765. Minutes, H.2788.rr., p. 128.
[51] Battishill may have left the Madrigal Society by the time he became a privileged member of the Catch Club. The list of members who signed the rules between 1757 and 1765 (BL MadSoc.F2) has his name crossed out.
[52] *A Collection of Songs for Three and Four Voices* (c. 1775).
[53] Minutes, H.2788.rr., p. 184.
[54] During the 1776/77 season, for example, Battishill attended 27 out of a possible 32 meetings, a better record than that of any other privileged member. Minutes, H.2788.ss.

Thomas Arne is sufficiently well known as one of the leading English eighteenth-century composers to require little comment here. However, his significant contribution to the rise of catch and glee culture is less well documented and it is worth noting that in 1767 he was almost certainly the first composer to perform accompanied glees in a London pleasure garden, in this instance Marybone (Marylebone).[55] As previously noted, Arne was also a member of the Madrigal Society. His contribution to the Catch Club in his earlier years was considerable. Thirty-three catches and glees by him were included in the Catch Club books and twenty-nine found their way into Warren's anthologies. Arne was also a prize-winner of the annual competition for the best catches and glees on no fewer than seven occasions, including 1766 with two Italian-texted works, the glee *Già riede prima vera* and the canon *Ombré a mene*. Attendance records show that Arne was initially an enthusiastic privileged member. During the 1766/67 season he was present at 24 out of a possible 27 meetings and he maintained a good record until the 1770s, when renewed demand for his theatre works and increasing poor health doubtless combined to provide an explanation for more frequent absences.

Gaetano Quilici is first heard of as a member of a foreign burletta company that gave several performances at Covent Garden in the 1754/55 season, during which he sang in the first English performance of Galuppi's *L'Arcadia in Brenta*. According to Burney he was a bass and 'a good musician' who joined the roster of singers at the King's Theatre in 1759.[56] He is also recorded by Burney as having appeared in the pasticcio *Astarto, Re di Tiro* during the 1762 season. Thereafter the regularity of his appearances at the Catch Club suggest that Quilici spent much of his time in England, particularly after 1769, although he is noted as being abroad in 1767, and his absence from the list of privileged members during the 1770/71 season was doubtless for the same reason. When he was in England, Quilici seems to have been a keen privileged member, clocking up 17 attendances in 1769/70, 12 in 1771/72, 16 in 1772/73, nine the following season, and achieving high figures for most others, in particular 1776/77, when he appeared at 20 out of 32 possible meetings.

Two other names requiring little introduction are those of the émigrés Carl Friedrich Abel and Felice Giardini. The German-born composer and viola da gamba player Abel had settled in London in 1759 and was later involved in a famous series of subscription concerts in collaboration with Johann Christian Bach, the youngest son of J. S. Bach. His motivation in becoming a privileged member is not clear, since he appears to have contributed only a single catch to the club's books and is not known to have been a singer.[57] Possibly, as a relative newcomer to the London musical scene, he joined for social and career reasons – the opportunity to mix with some of London's social elite and leading musicians. He was certainly known as a convivial man who enjoyed his wine.[58] In any event, Abel's connection with the

---

[55] See below p. 108.
[56] Charles Burney, *A General History of Music* (London, 1776–89). Rep. 2 vols. (New York, 1957), vol. 2, p. 858.
[57] *Dolly's eyes* (Catch Club Collection, vol. 2).
[58] In May 1779 John Marsh professed himself disappointed that Abel was absent from one of the Bach-Abel concerts he attended on account of the gambist having gone 'on his annual jaunt to Paris to procure some of the best claret' (Marsh's underlining). Marsh, *Journals*, p. 197.

Catch Club was of short duration; in May 1766 he was one of the three privileged members noted as having been expelled for non-attendance.[59]

The violinist and composer Giardini arrived in London in 1750 during the course of a European concert tour, creating something of a sensation at his first public concert.[60] Thereafter he remained in England for much of the rest of his life. An outstanding violinist and another sociable man, Giardini was readily accepted into London's concert life and the higher echelons of society. In 1754 he took over the orchestra of the Italian opera at the King's Theatre, instilling it with a new discipline, while according to Burney his own playing was 'universally admired' for its 'great hand, taste and style'.[61] Burney was rather less complimentary to Giardini in a scurrilous article published in Rees' *Cyclopaedia* (1819), in which he describes the Italian musician's disposition as 'truly diabolical', adding that Giardini 'was constantly at war with favourites of every kind, public and private'.[62] Such characteristics are at odds with the warm friendship Giardini enjoyed with the painter Thomas Gainsborough,[63] but appear to find support in the circumstances surrounding Giardini's expulsion from the Catch Club, which were rather more dramatic than non-attendance. Page 4 of the first volume of the Catch Club Minutes reproduces in full a letter addressed to Lord Sandwich from Sir Robert Rich, one of the founder members. Dated 'Dublin 13 April 1765', it reads:

> My Lord
>
> I take the first opportunity of assuring your Lordship how much I am oblig'd to you, and the Members of the Catch Club for the early notice they have taken of the infamous libel publish'd against me, and for the just indignation with which they have resented so unprecedented an attack upon my character both as a Gentleman and an Officer.
> The Measures pursu'd by so respectable a Society and the ready concurrence of your Lordship give me room to hope that Giardini will meet with every discountenance which his atrocious behavior deserves, 'till such time as the Law prescribes a punishment adequate to the enormity of his crime.
> At the same time that I assure your Lordship of the sense I retain of your obliging behavior on this occasion, permit me in order to render my thanks more acceptable to the Club, to offer them with my best respects thro' your Lordship's channell.

The letter has its origins in an incident in which Rich, apparently the worse for drink, had identified a catch by Giardini as being by Orlando Gibbons. The humiliated Rich, known to be a disputatious man who was later embroiled in two

---

[59] See n. 50.
[60] The event was recorded by Charles Burney, who was present, in adulatory detail – *History*, vol. 2, p. 896. For a general survey of Giardini's London career see Simon McVeigh, *The Violinist in London's Concert Life, 1750–1784: Felice Giardini and his Contemporaries* (New York, 1989).
[61] Burney, *History*, p. 1012.
[62] Quoted in *Memoirs of Dr Charles Burney*, ed. S. Klima, G. Bowers, and Kerry S. Grant (Nebraska, 1988), Appendix B8.
[63] John Hayes, ed., *The Letters of Thomas Gainsborough* (Yale, 2001). See especially pp. 122–3.

serious family disputes,[64] apparently vowed to destroy Giardini. His chosen course was through the King's Theatre, where in 1764 Giardini, now running the theatre, had become involved in a legal dispute with some of the performers, who countersued him. When the violinist discovered that Rich was paying the legal costs of the employees he added Rich to the list of defendants. As the row intensified, press advertisements and pamphlets flew between the two sides, culminating in the publication of a pamphlet, 'Defence of F. Giardini' (1765), lampooning Rich and ironically dedicated to 'L[ieut] G[eneral] R[ich]', who had fought the dispute under the ill-disguised pseudonym 'Cacophron'.[65] It was this pamphlet that prompted the accusations of libel by Rich, who had resigned from the Catch Club by the time he wrote his letter to Sandwich on 13 April. By this time the club had obviously considered Giardini's actions sufficiently serious for his expulsion to have taken place in March when he was 'Expell'd by Order of the Society upon account of a Libel written against a late Member'.[66] Interestingly, Rich's letter suggests that he did not feel he had sufficient grounds to take legal action against Giardini, despite the 'enormity of his crime'. Many years later Giardini, then 64, was apparently considered by the Club to have expiated his sins, for on 14 November 1780 he was readmitted as a privileged member. He celebrated the event by composing at least three works for the Club, two glees and a round that were included in volume 20 of Warren's collections. Giardini was also the subject of an amusing, if possibly apocryphal, anecdote relating to his privileged membership of the Catch Club:

> At the first establishment of the Catch Club a rule was instituted (probably by oral convention) we are told, that any member who was named to sing, if he failed in his part either by mispronunciation of the words in singing the notes, or in any other way, was liable, at the direction of the president, to drink a half-pint bumper of wine. A nobleman [?Sandwich], celebrated for his conviviality, fined poor Giardini for his foreign accent so often that he seldom returned home sober. To obviate the effects of his lordship's jovial persecution, Giardini wrote *Beviamo tutti tre* [a glee published in the first of Warren's anthologies. It subsequently became enormously popular]. He had, it seems, obtained a faculty of sustaining a note upon the syllable be, and at the same time swallowing his wine without any manifest interruption of his tone... This feat was impossible to others, and as it was a component part of the glee, Giardini, by calling for *Beviamo* had his punishers in his power. Whenever they talked of fining him he threatened to produce his trio – and thus at length the musician was permitted to go home in his senses.[67]

The two remaining names can be dealt with rather more quickly. 'Mr Cowper' (or Cooper, as he is named in 1765) has not been positively identified, but he may be the

---

[64] Massie, 'Rich' in *Oxford Biography Dictionary*. The author makes no mention of Rich's connections with the Catch Club or Giardini.
[65] Curtis Price, Judith Millhous and Robert D. Hume, *The Impressario's Ten Commandments: Continental Recruitment for Italian Opera in London, 1763–64*, RMA Monographs, 6 (London, 1992), pp. 24–5. The authors suggest that Rich's action may have been motivated by an attempt to gain control of the King's Theatre, rather than retribution against Giardini.
[66] 'List of Privileg'd Members, May 19.' Minutes, H.2788.rr., p. 128 The record of Giardini's expulsion is appended to his name.
[67] *Euterpeiad, or Musical Intelligencer* (Boston, USA), 24 March 1821, Rep. from *The Musical Review*.

Cowper listed in Joseph Doane's 1794 *Directory* as an alto who sang at the Handel commemoration concerts, and was also a lay vicar at Lincoln Cathedral.[68] With Abel and Savage, he was among the first privileged members to forfeit his privilege, an event that had taken place by the end of the 1764/65 season.[69] Samuel Champness is known, being a bass who was a Gentleman of the Chapel Royal and who sang at the Covent Garden oratorios. He also enjoyed a career, if apparently a somewhat restricted one, on the London stage.[70] Although he does not appear to have tried his hand at composing catches or glees, he would prove to be a loyal and valuable servant to the Catch Club, consistently turning in a high attendance record throughout the 1770s and into the 80s.

R. J. S. Stevens' desire to join the Catch Club as an honorary member was in all likelihood spurred by the avid predilection for social climbing revealed in his *Reminiscences*. After winning a medal for his 'cheerful' glee, *See what horrid tempests rise*, in 1782,[71] his ambition was fulfilled the following year. It is Stevens who provided the most detailed eighteenth-century account of how an honorary member was elected. Following his prize success, Stevens attended a meeting of the club, probably some time during the autumn. After being 'very politely received by Warren Horne', who introduced him to Lord Sandwich ('very chatty'), Stevens continues:

> being a Stranger I was placed above the Secretary: the Duke of Hamilton, sat above me. One of the Nobility (who could not sing) called *I lov'd thee beautiful and kind*, a Round of Battishill's composition. I was called upon to sing a part, with David Wood, and my friend John Dyne,[72] both Gentlemen of the Chapel Royal. I was obliged to quit my seat, and go to them. These Veterans of the Catch Club made *me* lead this round, (which was not very pleasant to me as a visitor). I was a little abashed at the beginning, but I kept true to my part, and upon the whole it went very well. When I returned to my place, the Duke of Hamilton said to me, "You sing very well, Sir: why do you not come among us?" "I am so unfortunate" (replied I) "my Lord Duke, as not to know any member to propose me." With great condescension, and prompt nature, his grace immediately replied, "*I* will do it for you". I thanked him very respectfully for his politeness and kindness. He immediately proposed me to be an Honorary Member of the Catch Club, and Mr. Windham seconded his Grace.[73]

---

[68] Joseph Doane, *A Musical Directory for the Year 1794* (reprint, London, 1993). This impression is strengthened by the fact that 'Mr Cowper of Lincoln Cathedral' is listed as a subscriber to Samuel Webbe the elder's third published book of Catches and Glees (1775).

[69] Minutes, H. 2788.rr., p. 128.

[70] He created the role of the Vizier in Battishill and Michael Arne's *Almena*. Noting that an elaborate coloratura aria by Battishill was omitted in performance, Fiske claims that Champness 'would hardly have had the necessary technique' to sing it. Roger Fiske, *English Theatre Music in the Eighteenth Century* (Oxford, 1986), p. 314.

[71] Stevens's statement that the glee was published in Warren's twenty-first collection in 1782 would seem to support Rubin's dating of the Warren Collection. But see above p. 33 and below pp. 49–50 for my rejection of this theory.

[72] John Dyne had been an honorary member since 1772, David Wood since 1777.

[73] Stevens, *Recollections*, p. 43. The Duke of Hamilton had been a member of the Catch Club since 1777. No 'Mr Windham' is listed as having been a member during the 18th century. The custom of making guests 'sing for their supper' also disconcerted William Gardiner – see p. 59.

By the following spring Stevens, having heard nothing further regarding his nomination, wrote to the Duke, who again put his name forward. He was eventually elected at the end of the season on 27 May 1783.[74] Stevens thus gained his place as an honorary member as a result of impressing a full member during what looks suspiciously like a trial. There is, however, no evidence to suggest that this was the normal method of recruiting privileged members, who were more likely to be nominated by members on the basis of an established reputation, a reputation that Stevens at the age of 25 did not have at this stage in his career.

One further category of imported singer needs to be noted. While most catches and many glees were scored for alto(s), tenor(s) and bass, a smaller number called for a soprano voice on the top line. To cater for such pieces, the Catch Club from its inauguration brought in boy treble choristers, as did the Academy of Vocal (later Ancient) Music and the Madrigal Society earlier.[75] The accounts for 1763 include an entry 'To the singing boys a compliment £2. 2. 0',[76] a figure that doubled the following year. Later, in a move that has to date passed without comment, the Catch Club's privileged membership would also include a number of noted Italian soprano and alto castratos who would also have taken upper parts on the occasions on which they attended. The first castrato at the club was Tommaso Guarducci (*c.*1720–after 1770), who in 1766 became one of five new honorary members in an intake remarkable for the fact that it was all-Italian.[77] Guarducci, who spent two seasons at the King's Theatre (1766–68) during the course of which he sang in the premiere of J. C. Bach's *Carattico*, was to Burney 'one of the most correct singers I ever heard', despite the disadvantage of being 'in countenence ill-favoured and morbid'.[78] Later castrato singers associated with the Catch Club were the alto Gaetano Guadagni (1729–92), who joined in 1769, and was the creator of the title role in the original Vienna version of Gluck's *Orfeo ed Eurydice*; and the sopranos Giusto Tenducci, admitted in 1770 and re-admitted in 1781; Giuseppe Millico (1774); Francesco Roncaglia (1778); Gasparo Pacchierotti (1779); and Venanzio Rauzzini (1780), for whom Mozart in 1773 had composed his florid *Exultate, jubilate*, K165/158a. Thereafter no more castratos are numbered among new privileged members, the only other Italian singer to join subsequently being the bass Luigi Tasca (in 1786).

By any standard this is an impressive list, including as it does some of the greatest opera singers of the day. However, it must be noted that surviving attendance records suggest that few attended more than the odd meeting. With the exception of those like Tenducci and Rauzzini who had settled in England, the dates of joining show that many were made members during seasonal trips to England when they were engaged at the King's Theatre. Both Guarducci and Grassi, for example, are

---

[74] Stevens, *Recollections*, p. 46. As a mark of gratitude Stevens dedicated his first book of published glees (his opus 3) to the Duke.
[75] As already noted, R. J. S. Stevens sang at the Madrigal Society as a boy.
[76] Accounts, H.2788.rr.
[77] The other Italians admitted in 1766 were the bass Cristiano Tedeschino; the tenor Ercole Ciprandi; the composer Mattia Vento; and 'Sigr Grassi', who remains unidentified. He may have been either the father-in-law of J. C. Bach or possibly Andrea Grassi, who sang in J. C. Bach's *Catone in Utica*, (Naples, 1764). Of these Vento became a fairly regular visitor, his appearances between 1767 and 1776 at least partially filling the 'mysterious hiatus' noted in his *New Grove Opera* entry.
[78] Burney, *History*, vol. 2, p. 872.

noted as being 'abroad' in June 1767, and Pacchierotti never seems to have made a visit to the club. The distinct impression therefore emerges that famous visiting singers were invited to join (and they would have been encountered by those Catch Club members who maintained a close association with the King's Theatre) more for reasons of prestige – advantageous to both club and singer – than practical purpose. It is therefore likely that the Catch Club continued to use trebles, although no disbursements are noted after 1764 and there is evidence from R. J. S. Stevens that trebles were not always readily available. Meeting with jealousy from John Stafford Smith, a noted glee composer and an honorary member since 1777, over his first gold medal triumph noted above, Stevens diplomatically suggested that although Smith's *Flora now calleth forth* was the better piece, it had 'suffered in effect in performance, for want of two Soprano Voices'.[79]

As Smith's jealousy suggests, the awards for prize-winning pieces were highly prestigious. When the competition was first established in May 1762, a resolution was passed to award a premium of a gold medal of ten guineas in value in each of the three categories that formed the repertoire of the club – catch, canon, and glee – with a runner-up medal worth half that amount. In addition to English, entries of works with Italian, French and, in the instance of canons, Latin texts would be permitted. In inaugurating such a competition, the Catch Club was thus following the lead of the Society of Arts, whose own competition was noted in the previous chapter. While the rules of the competition gradually evolved (as did those of the Society of Arts), many of the principles were similar to the earlier example. Secretary Warren was duly instructed to announce the new prize competition in the daily papers 'from time to time', plans for the initial competition being set in train early in 1763. On 31 January the committee passed a number of resolutions relating to the forthcoming contest, including one that James Harris should make a preliminary examination of the entries for the catches and 'give his opinion how far they are consistent with the rules of composition and counterpoint',[80] the only occasion on which a single person appears to have been given such a responsibility. Later a committee of professionals was given the task of weeding out from the anonymous entries those works that failed to conform to the rules of the contest or were musically inept. The performance of entries was in the hands of privileged members and the odd imported professional, who were adjured 'to make themselves perfect' in the performance of prize catches in order that they could be heard to the best advantage.[81] Strict controls to ensure impartiality were maintained, professionals who had examined or sung entries being strongly recommended 'not to give their Opinion on the Merits of any of the Prize Catches', while at the same time Warren was directed not to give out copies of any entry 'without express orders of the Society'.[82]

The closing date was set for the first meeting in March, after which groups of works were tried in committee. On 10 March, fourteen canons (a category soon to be

---

[79] Stevens, *Recollections*, p. 41.
[80] Minutes, H.2788.rr., p. 4.
[81] Ibid.
[82] Minutes, H.2788.rr., p. 7.

restricted to being in no more than four parts),[83] were tried by 'Messrs Quilici, Zirgoni,[84] Champness, Cowper and Warren' at the Earl of Eglinton's home, being graded according to five codes. They were followed by five catches and four glees at Rich's on the 17th, all seemingly three-part works, since the singers involved were Arne, Champness and Warren. A week later another meeting at Rich's decided on the best four glees, at this stage the smallest category, after hearing them sung by Arne, Champness, Warren and two boys. The glees chosen included two by the Italian Cristiano Lidarti (1730–93), *Treman gli spirti* and *Che viva San Martino*; Hayes' *Melting airs*, a work that would achieve lasting popularity, and *On softest beds* by George Berg (?1730s–75), the organist of St Mary-at-Hill, and like Hayes shortly to become an honorary member of the Catch Club. To Berg went the honour of being the first composer to win a Catch Club medal for glees. Interestingly, *Treman gli spirti* was termed a canon at the trials on 10 May, a reminder that nomenclature still remained somewhat arbitrary. The substantially larger number of catches and canons entered took longer to assess and it was not until 23 April that the committee reported back with its choice.

The stage was now set for the final judging, which in 1763 took place on 5 May. For this event attendance and voting was mandatory for all full members of the club, who were subjected to a substantial fine of half a guinea for not doing so, no letter of apology being accepted.[85] In the catch and canon classes Hayes, made up for his disappointment of being placed second for his glee with an eight-part canon, *Allelujah*, while the award for the best catch went to the highly suggestive *When is it best?* by Joseph Baildon (c. 1727–74), the organist of St Luke's, Old Street, and All Saint's, Fulham.[86]

Preparations for the following year's contest were soon set in motion, the following announcement appearing in newspapers during June:

> Advertisement
> June 7 1763
> The Members of the Catch Club at Almack's give notice, that they have Order'd the following Premiums for the year 1764.
> Three Gold Medals of Ten Guineas value each, to be given to the Author or Authors of the best Catch Canon and Glee, set to English words. The same Prizes to be assigned to the three best compositions of the same kind set to Italian or French words, with this difference, that any composer who chuses to make use of the Latin tongue instead of the Italian or French, in the Canons only, is at liberty to do it.
> The Candidates are desir'd to send in their compositions to Mr Warren Secretary to the Society, in Great Queen Street, Lincoln's Inn Fields, on or before the first day of March next ensuing, as none can be receiv'd afterwards:

---

[83] Still later canons at the octave were banned, 'it being the most inferior stile of that species'.
[84] 'Zirgoni' is almost certainly Giovanni Battista Zingoni, a member of a travelling opera company that arrived in London in 1761. He was not a privileged member and was therefore obviously brought in as a professional to help assess the prize entries. During this same year he sang in small roles in J. C. Bach's *Orione* and *Zanaida*.
[85] Minutes, H.2788.rr., p. 26. By 1793 the fine had been increased to a guinea. (Revised Penal Laws included in Minutes, H.2788.ss., pp. 145–7.)
[86] Baildon's catch is included as No. 167 in *The Aldrich Book of Catches*.

The Decision to be finally made at the first meeting in the month of May following.
Every Candidate to be careful to conceal his Name, 'till he is call'd upon to declare it, as he will lose all his claim and pretensions if he discovers himself to be the author of any Composition so sent in, 'till after the prizes are adjudg'd.[87]

The notice was translated into French and Italian and also inserted in unidentified foreign papers. The awarding of separate medals for English and foreign language entries continued until after the judging in 1766, when it was resolved that 'to prevent the great multiplying of Prize Medals, which must naturally tend to lower their Estimation', the number of prizes was to be reduced to three gold medals annually 'to the author or authors in the three different species of Catch, Canon and Glee'. Entries from composers of all nationalities were to be admitted and they were 'allow'd to make a choice of words either in the English, Latin, Italian, Spanish or French languages'.[88] Two years later the number of awards was raised again to five, which were awarded for catches in English and Italian, and a canon, while the glee prize was to be awarded for both a 'serious' and a 'cheerful' glee, recognition of the genre's ever increasing popularity. By 1770 the Italian catch had been dropped and a format of four awards established that would remain in force until the prize competition was discontinued in 1794.

In general the competition appears to have worked well, but inevitably the odd problem arose. In 1771 the 'serious' glee category was won by *Applaud so great a guest*, an epitaph on Purcell purportedly by Mary Hudson (d. 1801), the daughter of the tenor and future master of the Children at St Paul's, Robert Hudson (1730–1815). At the time Mary, later the first organist of St Olave, Hart Street, was a girl of about 13. A Minute of 25 January 1772 tells the rest of the story:

A motion was made that the said Glee be not entitled to the Prize, the said Rob't Hudson being employ'd as a singer on that occasion and who acknowledges that he did correct and was assisting in putting the parts of the said Glee together and that he sent in at the same time a composition of his own. The question was put and carried by a majority. A motion was made that the Medal be given to the author of the Glee which stood in competition being How sleep the Brave.[89]

It appears that some doubt had been raised in the immediate aftermath of the competition, Warren having been instructed as far back as 11 June 1771 to withhold the medal from the claimant until the club had reached a decision. The glee finally awarded the prize, another epitaph, was by Benjamin Cooke, who had been a privileged member since 1767. Both his and Mary Hudson's glee were included in Warren's tenth annual collection, with Cooke's identified as the winning entrant. Here, then, is positive evidence that Rubin's assignation of dates to the Warren Collection is inaccurate,[90] since by his reckoning volume ten belongs to 1771, an

---

[87] Copy included in Minutes, H.2788.rr., p. 38.
[88] Minutes, H.2788.rr., p. 126.
[89] Minutes, H.2788.rr., p. 275.
[90] See also above p. 33.

impossibility given that Cooke's glee was not finally declared the winner by default until late in January 1772. Leaving aside poor Mary's disappointment and her father's obvious embarrassment, the incident indicates that the Catch Club scrupulously adhered to its rules.

A problem of a rather different nature arose directly as a result of the increasing popularity of the prize competition. Many composers were now making multiple entries, a situation that reached its peak in 1786, when the extraordinarily prolific Callcott reputedly submitted no fewer than 120 compositions.[91] The committee decided the time had come to call a halt to such practices, which involved the membership in having to provide extra funding,[92] instructing Warren to write to all contestants informing them that in future no composer would be allowed to enter more than three compositions in each class, since multiple entries not only occasioned 'much additional expence, but bring on such difficulty in the trial of the several pieces, that if continued, it will frustrate the intention of the Club, to hear and determine on them with judgment and impartiality'. Doubtless the number of entries hastily prepared for submission by some composers accounted for the second paragraph of Warren's letter, which goes on to admonish those putting in entries that in many instances were 'scarcely legible, and in a very rough state'.[93]

Copyright on prize-winning entries seems to have become another problem, particularly in the case of the works published by Warren in his annual collections. Evidence suggests that copyright was not in force in the earlier years of the contest. For example, Joseph Baildon's glee *When gay Bacchus* won the glee prize in 1766 and was duly included in Warren's fifth collection the following year. This did not preclude the glee also being included in Baildon's own *A Collection of Glees and Catches for Three and Four Voices*, which appeared in 1768. In 1774 the prize for the serious glee was won by John Stafford Smith's *Let happy lovers fly*, which subsequently appeared in Warren's thirteenth book (1775) and Smith's own collection of c. 1776. Although no record of a change in the rules exists, the question of copyright had apparently become an issue a few years later. In 1789 R. J. S. Stevens could be found grumpily complaining that he would not allow Warren to publish any of his glees that year because the secretary had attempted to establish copyright in his *Sigh no more, ladies*, a claim Stevens considered 'perfectly unjust'.[94] It would appear that Stevens was not the only composer to be aggravated by the question of copyright. Two years later a group of composers including Stevens, all of them honorary members of the Catch Club, took the step of issuing *The Professional Collection of Glees*, a publication that seems to have been launched in direct competition to Warren's annual compilation.[95] Although the anthology apparently irritated the Catch Club, the six composers involved obviously found it was not a viable proposition, only a single issue being produced.

[91] Volume 24 of the Warren Collection (1786) reflects Callcott's industry. No less than a third of its contents, including three prize-winning works, are by him.
[92] See below p. 62.
[93] The whole of Warren's letter is reproduced in R. J. S. Stevens, *Recollections*, p. 58.
[94] Stevens, *Recollections*, p. 67. Stevens' attitude is doubtless responsible for the fact that a larger proportion of his works appears in the Catch Club books (3%) than in Warren (1.5%).
[95] Stevens, *Recollections*, p. 68. The other composers involved in the venture were Robert Cooke (the son of Benjamin), John Hindle, John Danby, Samuel Webbe the elder, and John Wall Callcott.

In June 1793 the rules of the prize competition were changed, possibly at Warren's behest, to require composers to relinquish copyright in prize submissions for a period of two and a half years. Among other changes made at the time was a reduction in the number of gold medals to three, the canon being dropped, as were works composed to French or Spanish texts. The number of submissions allowed was now curtailed to one for each category. The changes were detailed in a letter sent out by Warren, its contents so infuriating Stevens that he resolved not to write any more music for the Catch Club.[96] In fact the new rules can in retrospect be viewed as a harbinger of the future. The following March the committee decided to call a halt to prize competitions on the grounds that 'it is the opinion of this Committee that in consideration of the large of stock of music of which the Club is now possessed, it is deem'd expedient to discontinue the prize medals for the present'.[97] The matter had apparently been previously discussed with Warren, the Minute proceeding to record that the long-standing secretary had 'signified that it would no longer be an object to him to continue in his office' should such an eventually come to take place. Warren's resignation duly took place on 10 June, on which date he was replaced by Samuel Webbe the elder, who had applied for the post and was appointed at a salary of 30 guineas instead of the honorarium voted annually to Warren.[98] Warren's departure from the club seems to have been conducted on amicable terms, since by a Minute of 24 May it was determined that in recognition of his many years of service he 'continue on the books of the Society as a Privileg'd Member' without being subjected to the Rules of the Club regarding non-attendance. Warren had little chance to enjoy his special dispensation. By the end of the year he was dead, having meanwhile produced the last issue of his anthologies, No. 32.

The resignation and death of Warren, together with the cessation of the prize competition, which was not reinstated until 1811, coincided with the latter days of the great period of the 'pure' unaccompanied glee. As early as 1768 the musician and publisher John Arnold had noted that the premiums awarded by the Catch Club 'have of late Years been productive of a great Number of the most excellent Compositions of the Kind that ever existed'.[99] Over the next thirty years that number came to be swollen by hundreds of compositions that owe their existence to the competition, while there can be no doubt that it was directly responsible for initiating the big upsurge in the glee's popularity and the creation of a substantial part of the glee and catch repertoire.

As is evident from the number of foreign musicians who became privileged members, nationalism played no part in the early days of the Catch Club. Indeed, all the evidence suggests the contrary, and that attempts to pigeonhole the catch and glee repertoire in a narrow, national context belong to subsequent observers rather the founding fathers of the club.[100] The first foreign full member to be admitted was the Duc de Nivernais, who joined in January 1763 under the exceptional circumstances of being elected without ballot, a distinction subsequently accorded

---

[96] Stevens, *Recollections*, p. 91. The full text of Warren's letter is reproduced on the same page.
[97] Minutes, H.2788.ss., p. 150.
[98] The date of 1784 given in the entry for Webbe in the revised *New Grove* is incorrect.
[99] John Arnold, comp., *The Essex Harmony* (London?, 1769).
[100] See especially Chapter 8.

only to the Prince of Wales in 1786. A distinguished soldier, diplomat and man of letters, Nivernais was a great-nephew of Cardinal Mazarin. He had come to London as French Ambassador in the course of the same year that he was elected a member of the club to negotiate peace following the Seven Years War, having previously served as ambassador at Rome and Berlin. From 1787 to 1789 he would be a member of the Council of State. During the Revolution he remained in France, losing all his money and being imprisoned in 1793. Following the fall of Robespierre, he was released and died in 1798 at the age of 82, still a member of the Catch Club.[101]

The events surrounding the unusual invitation to Nivernais, a national of a country recently at war with Britain, remain a mystery, but it is possible that it was connected with the presentation of a collection of French canons to the club. A minute of 8 March 1763 orders that 'the Thanks of the Society be given to Monsr D'Angeul'.[102] In the margin is added 'for a collection of French canons presented by the Duc de Nivernais'. The club obviously felt sufficiently indebted to D'Angeul to select some of the 'best pieces belonging to the club and that Mr Secretary Warren do copy them and have them handsomely Bound at the expence of the Society as a present'.[103] It is difficult to imagine that Nivernais was not also responsible for Rameau sending to the club a copy of his *Methode pour faire les canons*, an offering for which a Minute of 22 March records thanks.[104] It seems likely that the duke and Rameau were acquainted through their mutual association with Le Clerc de la Bruère, the young nobleman who provided Rameau with the libretto for *Dardanus* in 1739, and in the 1750s became secretary to Nivernais during his period as ambassador to Rome. Following a report on the *Methode*,[105] the club decided to make a fair copy and translation, a task undertaken at a cost of £21, to which was added a further two guineas for each task for producing fifteen copies.[106] By the end of 1764 much of the outlay had been recouped as a result of eleven recorded sales.[107]

No other foreign member was to play such a significant role in the Catch Club's history. Indeed up to 1810 only two other European aristocrats were elected: the Marquis Carraccioli in 1764 (he resigned in December 1766) and in 1784 Godefroy-Charles-Henri La Tour d'Auvergne, Duc de Bouillon, a former Grand Chamberlain of France.

As noted the Catch Club was from the outset happy to include émigré and visiting privileged foreign members among its numbers, a third of the initial intake being foreign musicians. The prize competition from its inception solicited entries in Italian and French, while the tradition of Latin canons was also maintained. As we have

---

[101] General biographical details from www.academie-francaise.fr/immortels/base/academiciens.
[102] Minute, H.2788.rr., p. 17. The identity of 'Monsr D'Angeul' has not been established, but he may have been the French political economist Plumart D'Angeul.
[103] Minute, H.2788.rr., p. 35.
[104] The *Methode* has not been identified as a separate work. The famous *Traité de l'harmonie* (1722) contains several pages on the subject and includes two of Rameau's own canons as examples. Rep. ed. P. Gossett, (New York, 1971), pp. 369–73. However it is unlikely that this was the source of the Catch Club's *Methode* since the relevant Part 3 of the *Traité* had been available in English since 1737. There would therefore have been no need for the translation the club undertook.
[105] Minute, H.2788.rr, p. 37.
[106] Accounts, H.2788.rr.
[107] Ibid.

seen, the committee went so far as to translate its newspaper insertions for publication in the foreign press. In May 1766 it was decided that 'composers of all Nations be admitted as candidates',[108] while adding Spanish to the lists of languages that could be employed. Although French and Spanish language submissions were dropped in the final revision of rules in June 1793, Italian and Latin language entries were still permitted, the latter by implication confined to canons. Further evidence that the club took not only an active interest in foreign repertoire, but also in its early years took positive steps to encourage a foreign glee and catch repertoire is provided by Minutes of May and June 1764. On 10 May a resolution extended the club's thanks to the Earl of Rochford 'for the Music he has transmitted and that his Lordship be requested [...] to procure some original Spanish Compositions whereby the Society may be enabled to judge of the true Taste of the Nation as their intent is to do justice to every Stile of writing'.[109] The following month it was decided that a copper medal be presented to William Hamilton (later Sir William), the minister in Naples, 'to produce it among the Italian Professors in order to excite an emulation and to convince them of the regard paid by this Society to merit'.[110] The result of this initiative is not recorded, but there is little evidence to suggest that beyond the confines of the Catch Club foreign composers showed serious interest in cultivating either the glee or catch, the early case of Lidarti being an exception.

As with all aspects of the Catch Club's repertoire, it is difficult in the absence of detailed programme records to be precise regarding the exact proportion of music by foreign and immigrant composers that was performed. The Catch Club books and the Warren Collection are the only sources, but notwithstanding such a caveat, the two may safely be assumed to provide a fair indication of trends.

As Table 2 (in which the term 'foreign composers' is taken to include all those born outside Britain) clearly shows, the inclusion of works by non-British composers declined steeply after the main thrust of the Catch Club's positive espousal of foreign participation in the prize competition during the 1760s, the same decade in which it was most actively inviting foreign performers to be honorary members. The decline in the 1780s and 90s is in fact near total if Giardini's brief reappearance on the scene in 1780 and Warren's inclusion of works by such long-dead composers as Marenzio are discounted.

Table 2
Proportion of Works by Foreign Composers in the Catch Club Books & the Warren Collection

	1760s	1770s	1780s	1790s	Average
Catch Club Books	19%	4%	1%	2.5%	6.5%
Warren Collection	5%	3.5%	2.5%	2%	5.75%

---

[108] Minutes, H.2788.rr., p. 126.
[109] Minutes, H.2788.rr., p. 73.
[110] Minutes, H.2788.rr., p. 79.

Foreign composers fared poorly in the prize competitions, winning not a single prize medal for a glee or a catch. The first Continental composer to win a medal was not, as might be expected, Italian or French, but a Spaniard, the *maestro de capilla* of Figueras (Catalonia), Juan Bautista Bruguera y Morreras. How Bruguera came to enter the competition in 1765 is not known, but he gained his success with *Beatus vir*, a canon for nine voices.[111] Subsequently two immigrant composers, the Italian Gioacchino Cocchi and the Dutchman Peter Hellendaal won prizes, the latter for *Glory be to God*, the winning canon in 1769.[112] The previous year Cocchi, one of the few foreign composers to enter into print with a book of catches and glees, had won the catch category with his *Quando, quando*.[113]

Such singular lack of success, despite the best efforts of the Catch Club committee during the 1760s, may at least in part account for the dramatic decline in foreign participation during the following decade, a period when Samuel Webbe the elder, Benjamin Cooke and John Stafford Smith (to name just the leading lights) firmly stamped their ascendancy on the repertoire. By the end of the 1770s both the catch and the glee had become almost the exclusive province of British composers, a position challenged solely by Giardini. By the time Callcott wrote his essay on the Catch Club in 1801, the first precepts of the Catch Club were long forgotten. 'Every nation', he believed, 'had cultivated a style of music peculiar to the temper of its inhabitants; & if the splendid compositions of Italy and Germany have sufficient excellence to excite the curiosity and the attention of several neighbouring countries, yet there will always be found some particular bias towards a national music in whatever form it may appear. England, in this respect, may claim some degree of pre-eminence [...] The social pleasures of our own vocal compositions the Catch or the Glee fully interest the friends of harmony [outside] of the British Islands.'[114] Here, then, is a view diametrically opposed to that expressed thirty years earlier by the anonymous writer quoted at the start of this book. Far from having 'no musick but Italian', Callcott is of the opinion that the English have created a national music in the form of the catch and glee. Moreover, he believes, it is a music that has the potential to be appreciated as a national style beyond the confines of Britain, a music peculiar to native composers, but at the same time exportable. Callcott's observations are of particular interest for being among the first to express pride in a native repertoire and they can be viewed as a blueprint for later, more overtly nationalistic, claims made for the 'Englishness' of the catch and, more particularly, the glee made by commentators during the course of the nineteenth century.[115]

By the time Callcott came to write his 'Essay on the Catch Club', the organisation had enjoyed a successful existence stretching back forty years. It had a season that ran from late November until the Tuesday after the birthday of George III on 4 June. During the eighteenth century both venue and meeting day changed on several occasions. The first such alteration took place at the start of the 1763/64 season,

---

[111] Bruguera's *Beatus vir* was included in the fourth volume of the Warren Collection.
[112] A five-part canon included in the Warren Collection, Book 8.
[113] Cocchi's *Twelve Italian Glees for two or three voices after the manner of the Catch Club* was published in London, *c.* 1770.
[114] Callcott, 'Essays'.
[115] See Chapter 8.

when it was decided to change the day of meetings from Tuesday to Thursday on 'account of the Opera',[116] not only a reflection the wider interests of members, but also a measure that would avoid the loss on club nights of privileged members who were involved in performances at the opera. As already noted, three of the eight founding members have been identified as subscribers at the King's Theatre, but the degree to which general membership of the Catch Club overlapped with subscribers is not completely clear. It seems likely to have been less than might be supposed. Of the 21 men who were elected members of the club between 1782 and 1784, only four are listed on the subscribers list for 1783.[117] Overall, of the 195 men on the subscribers list, 30 were at one time or another members of the Catch Club, although others doubtless subscribed at other times. Given the fact that both drew largely from the same class of men, even these limited figures imply that the two organisations attracted patronage that differed to a considerable extent. It is possible therefore to make the tentative suggestion that the lines of demarcation that existed between many English musicians and the Italian opera were to some extent reflected in the relative lack of contiguity between membership of the Catch Club and the patrons of the opera.

Before the beginning of the following season further change took place. For reasons that are not clear, the committee had obviously decided to move from the Thatched House, undertaking an examination of 'all the different Taverns in the proper part of Town' that resulted in them moving to the St Alban's Tavern as being the only one with a 'proper Room suited to the Society'. Situated in St Alban's Street, Pall Mall, the St Alban's Tavern was highly fashionable and the haunt of wealthy young men about town. It was also very conveniently placed for the King's Theatre, situated just round the corner in the Haymarket. At the same time the meeting day had to be changed to Monday, the only night other than Tuesday that the desired room was available.

By April of the 1766/67 season the committee evidently decided that increasing membership (standing at twenty-seven in June 1767) dictated a further move, the room at St Alban's 'having been found inconvenient for the number of Members, Strangers and others who assist at the Weekly Meetings and it having been represented that there is a very Spacious room at the Thatched House in St James Street Resolv'd that for the future the Society do hold their Weekly Meetings at the Thatched House... and that their first meeting there will be held upon Monday next the 13th instant'.[118] Doubtless the committee had been keeping a close watch on the development of Almack's empire. In 1764 he had opened Almack's Club in Pall Mall, and the following year large Assembly Rooms in King Street, St. James'. In 1814 (by which time they were known as Willis' Rooms) they would themselves become the next home of the Catch Club. Mention of 'a very spacious Room' at the Thatched House suggests that it had also been improved since the club's departure, although there is no record of any alteration during this period.[119] By mid-May members had

---

[116] Minutes, H.2788.rr., p. 43.
[117] See n. 27 and Appendix A.
[118] Minutes, H.2788.rr., p. 161.
[119] London Survey Committee, *Survey of London*, vol. 30: *The Parish of St James', Westminster, Pt. 1*, pp. 466–8.

decided they found it wanting and a committee was formed to consider the matter. By 23 May it had decided that the room 'is by no means convenient for the meeting, and that the room below is the only one that can answer the purpose'. Almack's lettings dictating that the only days available to the club for this lower room were Tuesday or Wednesday, the choice naturally fell on Wednesday as not clashing with the opera, although curiously a year later Tuesday was readopted as the night of the meeting.[120] And there matters finally rested until the 1814 move mentioned above.

As would be expected, the constitution of the club gradually evolved during its early years. In March 1767 a codified collection of rules and regulations, subsequently known as the Digest, was produced from the existing Minutes. This stood the club in good stead until April 1793, when an amended set of 'Penal Laws' was introduced.[121] These two sets of laws, taken in conjunction with the extant Minutes, enable us to reconstruct the week-to-week activity of the Catch Club in considerable detail. Following the first intake of members, vacancies were filled by balloting on proposed candidates, the ballot having to be conducted by a minimum of twelve (later eight) existing members. The result was determined by the blackballing method. Members were each given two balls, one white, one black, his choice then being dropped into a hat. Three black balls – two when there were only eight voters – led to rejection. Given that there was always a waiting list, blackballing did not necessarily imply that the candidate was undesirable. It was far more likely that he had simply failed to attract sufficient support from existing members and those rejected were frequently later admitted. The minutes show that Lord Chesterfield, for example, was blackballed on no fewer than four occasions (in January 1777, February 1777, January 1778 and July 1778) before finally achieving success in December 1780. A survey of the lists of candidates during the later half of the 1770s reveals that the numbers blackballed gradually diminished, probably at least in part because of the unusually large intake of twelve new members in both 1779 and 1780. By the 1790s blackballing appears to have been all but eliminated, with no instance of a candidate being blackballed recorded between 1791 and 1795.

Once over the ballot hurdle a new member was obliged to pay a five-guinea joining fee (from December 1763) and to attend the weekly meeting. Failure to do so without a written excuse led to a penalty of half a guinea, while going four successive meetings without notifying the club resulted in expulsion. The first member to be dismissed under the ruling was the Earl of Orford, who was ejected in May 1763.[122] It appears that Orford, who was replaced by the Duke of Queensbury, was less than happy with his treatment since he immediately registered for a future vacancy and was re-elected on 12 January 1764. Most of those expelled obviously no longer wished to attend, although in 1776 one Mr Douglas, probably Archibald Douglas, the MP for Forfarshire, was reinstated after the postmark on his letter of apology showed that it should have been in the hands of the club in good time.[123]

---

[120] Minutes, H.2788.rr., p. 195. No explanation for the change is given, but it possibly supports the idea that membership of the Catch Club did not overlap with subscribers to the opera to any significant degree.
[121] Minutes, H.2788.ss., pp. 145–7.
[122] Minutes, H.2788.rr., p. 31. Orford had been elected in April 1762.
[123] Minutes, H.2788.ss., p.11.

In common with virtually all eighteenth-century clubs and distinct from music societies such as the Concert of Antient Music, women were precluded from becoming members or attending meetings as guests. Peter Clark quotes an eighteenth-century source which noted that for many, 'the ad libitum part of the entertainment at clubs was considered as the most pleasant part of the evening's entertainment',[124] a feature that would necessarily be far more restrained in the presence of ladies. As will be seen in the next chapter, the demise of the Anacreontic Society would be a direct result of the incursion of women into such a male-dominated world.[125] The barring of women in fact carried none of the misogynistic connotations it would in today's world. Indeed, women were the subject of toasts at the Catch Club and an annual ladies' night, held at the close of each season, was an innovation that was certainly established by May 1768,[126] when Lady Mary Coke recorded in her journals that a Mr Morris came to her: 'His business was to invite me to a dinner at the Catch Club. The Duke of Queensbury, Ld March, Ld Sandwich, & two or three more he named that I have forgot, & said that none of the Lady's were such as I should object to.'[127] Since Lady Mary declined the invitation, we are sadly denied her likely account of such an evening, purely social events at which no business was transacted. One of the few mentions of these annual evenings occurs in May 1775, when it was ordered that a compliment of 5 guineas be paid to Benjamin Cooke for composing an ode for the ladies' dinner.[128] This apparently set a precedent that was followed in subsequent years. Women could therefore be toasted and entertained, but were not permitted to play any part in the normal functioning of the club.

In common with most clubs, meetings of the Catch Club were conducted by the president and vice-president for the night, offices shared on the basis of rotation. Both positions carried important duties at meetings and both were subjected to fines of a guinea for the president and half a guinea for the vice-president if the incumbents failed to attend a meeting at which they were due to officiate. In addition both were subject to a further fine for leaving the table before the formal proceedings were concluded. A minute of 22 February 1785 records that while serving as vice-president, Sir Henry Gough, the MP for Bramber, fell foul of this rule, 'having quitted the Chair at 26 minutes past 7 o'clock, before the toasts were gone round, and for leaving the Society without permission of the President, or appointing another person to officiate for him'.[129] Sir Henry was duly fined half a guinea.

Proceedings got under way with the commencement of dinner. There appears to be no record of the time it started in the first years, but after reverting to meeting at the Thatched House in 1767 the club 'Order'd that for the future the dinner be

---

[124] Clark, *British Clubs*, p. 122.
[125] See below p. 75.
[126] The introduction of ladies' nights does not appear to have been minuted.
[127] *The Letters and Journals of Lady Mary Coke*, vol. II (Edinburgh, 1889), p. 267.
[128] *'Tis beauty calls*. Autograph score in the Royal College of Music, London, 814.01.
[129] Minutes, H.2788.ss., p. 78. Sir Henry appears to have been a man of independent spirit who apparently attended parliament irregularly and was not attached to any political party.

serv'd up exactly at half past four,[130] and the Master of the house be inform'd, that he shall incur the highest displeasure of the Society, if he does not punctually comply with this article'.[131] This was a more authoritarian attitude than societies generally adopted toward their host, upon whom, as previously noted, they were frequently dependent for mutual benefits. Once dinner was served, the president, flanked by the vice-president, took his seat at the head of the table. He was then expected to examine letters of apology for non-attendance, and make up the book of fines. Forfeits due were payable immediately after dinner.

The most vivid and detailed extant account of a Catch Club evening is that provided by William Gardiner. Although the exact date is not given, its place in Gardiner's recollections suggests that it must have been some time around 1812. Although this is beyond the remit of the present study, there is no reason to believe that in essence the account would not have applied to the eighteenth-century activities of the Catch Club.

> I had the honour of being introduced to the Noblemen's Catch Club at the Thatched House Tavern by Temple West, Esq.,[132] who was president of the evening, and I sat next to him in the chair of the Duke of Argyle,[133] who happened to be absent. On my left was Lord Dunstanville, Sir George Warrender, the Earl of Oxford, and Sir George Bamfield. On the right was Lord Clinton, Sir Gore Ouseley,[134] Lord Blessington, the Earl of Fortescue, and Lord Lonsdale. Besides these noblemen, and many other distinguished persons, there were not less than twenty professional gentlemen, eminent as vocalists; Mr William Linley, the brother of Mrs Sheridan, holding the office of vice-president ...[135] These convivial meetings commence on the opening of parliament, and continue every Tuesday, with a splendid dinner at four o'clock, immediately after which the grace, Non nobis Domine,[136] is sung by the whole company. After the cloth is drawn the chairman recapitulates some of the ancient laws of the society, namely – "If any honourable member has come to a fortune or estate, he shall pay a per centage upon the same; or he may commute the same for ten pounds. If any nobleman, knight, baronet, or esquire, shall have taken unto himself a wife, he shall pay into the treasury a fine of twenty pounds, in sterling money." Those who visit these meetings cannot but be

---

[130] The most fashionable time for dinner during this period was 5 o'clock, although between 3 and 4 was more usual. See Liza Picard *Dr. Johnson's London* (London, 2000), p. 193 (2001 ed.).

[131] Minutes, H.2788.rr, p. 173. In December of the same year, Fleet, the landlord, was informed that a guinea fine would be levied for failing to conform with this condition.

[132] Temple West was elected a member of the Catch Club in 1799. His home was Mathan Lodge, Worchestershire. An amateur singer, he was famed for the music parties he gave in Bath and London (*The Piozzi Letters: Correspondence of Hester Lynch Piozzi, 1784–1821* [Delaware, 2003], p. 269).

[133] A member from 1807.

[134] The father of the composer Sir Frederick Arthur Gore Ouseley. He was a distinguished amateur musician in his own right.

[135] William Linley (1771–1835) was a member of the famous family of musicians. He occupies a unique place in the annals of the Catch Club, being, for reasons that are not clear, the only instance of a professional being elected (in 1809) as a full member. Both he and his father, Thomas Linley the elder, composed a number of glees. Mrs Sheridan was formerly Elizabeth Linley, who before her marriage to Richard Brinsley Sheridan was a noted singer. She died in 1792 at the age of 35.

[136] The grace *Non nobis Domine* was frequently sung at club meetings where a dinner was involved. See also pp. 6–7 and 73.

surprised at the audible manner in which these rules are pronounced from the chair; and still more to see the bank-notes laid on the table before the president, by the secretary, for the fines of the previous week. Lord Clinton addressed me, and said, "It was one of their rules that the visitor next the chair should give the first toast, and appoint the first glee, in which he was expected to take a part." I replied, "Had I previously known the conditions, I doubted whether I should have had courage enough to accept the high honour of the invitation."[137] I had dined before with Mrs. Salmon, who delighted me with her exquisite singing, and I gave her as a toast. In this I learnt, afterwards, that I had not complied with the true etiquette, which a subsequent conversation will explain. Upon the table were five or six little wagons, filled with books, that could readily be wheeled about, and one of these moveable libraries was sent up to me that I might make choice of a glee. I confess it required something more than ordinary courage to fix upon one that would show my taste and I could get through with credit. However I ventured to choose that beautiful composition of Webb's [sic] – *If love and all the world were young*[138] […] Lord Clinton asked me what part I should like to sing and I chose the bass. He then said, "You will please to call up, from the lower end of the table, those professional gentlemen you should like to join you in the glee." "My Lord", I replied, "I could soon make my selection, but I cannot put a face to call up such eminent vocalists to join their voices with mine." "Who, Sir, then", said his Lordship, "would you like for the alto?" "Mr Knyvett" […] He then asked me to name the tenor; I chose Mr Vaughan. "And who for your second tenor, Sir?" "I would prefer Mr Greatorex, my Lord."[139] Upon this, they all three left their places, and came to the head of the table […] With these three masters, standing at my back, we began the glee, and I did my best to sustain the part. I was pretty alert, or I should have had my heels tripped up by the tasteful liberties they took in performing it. However, on its being finished, I received a slight tap of approbation from Mr Vaughan, who whispered in my ear, "You are a scientific performer, Sir." More than ordinary applause followed, and I was complimented upon my choice by one or two noblemen, who said they had never heard it before.

We had many glees afterwards, which were finely sung by the professional gentlemen […] I learnt afterwards, that, had I been the man of consequence I was then taken for (to have followed strict etiquette), I should have given, as a toast, the Duchess of Rutland, or some such titled lady in my county…[140] About nine o'clock the servants brought the cloths of several gentlemen, to dress for the opera, but such was our growing hilarity, after the professors had

---

[137] As we have seen, this custom had also disconcerted R. J. S. Stevens. See above p. 45.

[138] Included in Webbe's Seventh Book (*c.* 1790) and a number of popular collections. The words are by Sir Walter Raleigh, not Christopher Marlowe as Gardiner later erroneously states.

[139] Gardiner had certainly chosen an eminent trio. Charles Knyvett the younger (1773–1859), organist of St George's, Hanover Square, was a former pupil of Samuel Webbe the elder. He became an honorary member in 1792, his brother William, also an alto, two years later. An honorary member since 1805, Thomas Vaughan (1782–1843) was a former Gentleman of the Chapel Royal, and held appointments at both St Paul's Cathedral and Westminster Abbey. Thomas Greatorex (1758–1831) was also an eminent organist. In 1793 he had succeeded Joah Bates as the conductor of the Concert of Ancient Music. With the Knyvett brothers and James Bartleman he had revived the Vocal Concerts in 1801. He had been an honorary member since 1798.

[140] In Gladstone's day the toast was made to 'a living professional lady singer', a custom he asserts was a tradition from the first days of the club – Gladstone, *Story*, p. 22. Gardiner appears to contradict such an assumption. An order of 2 February 1767 states that 'no Member for the future do drink to any person or persons present and that any member offending herein shall forfeit half a crown to be applied to the general fund of the Society'.

left (for we got into a complete vein of singing), that the opera was given up, and I continued with the noble guests till one o'clock in the morning.[141]

Gardiner's concluding paragraph clearly suggests that a Catch Club evening was not an event for the fainthearted. The members had gathered around 4 in the afternoon, many apparently remaining until the early hours, a continuous period of some nine hours! Bearing in mind also that some who had left had gone on to the opera only serves to increase admiration for the endurance of the club's members. It is also noteworthy that the club was at this time apparently a sufficient attraction to detain potential opera-goers. At 7 p.m. further sustenance in the form of Welsh rarebit and anchovy toast washed down with porter was provided on a side table for those who wished to partake of it.[142] The consumption of copious amounts of alcohol doubtless assisted the staying power of those present. Charge of the wine provided for members was one of the duties of the vice-president. A resolution of 28 February 1767 tells us 'that the Vice-President should be directed for the future to take an Account of the Wine which is drunk at dinner, and to order that to be returned which remains after dinner upon the Side-board, and is returnable. And that he do likewise enter into a book prepar'd for that purpose the number of bottles of every sort which are us'd during that days sitting'.[143] In May of the same year and concurrent with the move to the Thatched House Tavern, the club decided to lay in its own stock of wine rather than purchase from its hosts. A committee was formed to buy claret 'of the best sort', any cost beyond £48 per hogshead to be paid for by the members,[144] and on the 28th a claret recommended by Lord Buckingham was chosen and subsequently bottled and sealed. In June 1771 a stock of claret amounting to 798 quart bottles was supplied to the club by Anderson and Colvil. Non-alcoholic drinks such as tea and coffee were frowned upon, members requiring such 'unnatural mixtures' being under strict orders not only to pay for them themselves, but also to carry them to a 'distant table with a due sense of the society's indulgence'.[145]

Alcohol also played its part in the penal laws. During the first round of singing anyone performing found to be singing out of tune or time, or who stopped before his part finished (this applied particularly to catches), was ordered by the president to drink a glass of any type of wine currently on the table. This rule was doubtless the origination of the Giardini anecdote recounted above. An alcoholic 'penalty' was also levied for breach of a rule forbidding the discussion of politics or religion while the club was in session. In December 1782 the president himself, William Ward, was found to be in breach of this rule and was fined a bumper for talking politics. Since Ward himself and many other members of the club were politicians, it seems unlikely this was anything like an isolated incident. Neither were such rules uncharacteristic of club life. As has been noted the excessive drinking associated with such organisations carried with it risks of disorderly conduct: 'A stream of orders excoriated and

---

[141] Gardiner, *Music and Friends*, vol. 2, p. 513ff.
[142] Stevens, *Recollections*, p. 43.
[143] Minutes, H.2788.rr., p. 151.
[144] Minutes, H.2788.rr., p. 173. A hogshead is a cask generally containing about 50 gallons.
[145] Quoted in Gladstone, *Story*, p. 25. Taken from the Rule Book of 2 March 1767.

prohibited swearing, cursing, immoral or controversial speeches, indecent songs, betting, and the like'.[146]

Most penalties, however, were financial. The revised penal laws of April 1793 list no fewer than fifteen different transgressions for which a member could be fined, including penalties for not paying penalties. Among a number of the sometimes convoluted rules, perhaps the most fascinating to a contemporary observer is that which Gardiner describes as being pronounced from the chair at the meeting he attended. The rule that a levy should made on members who had increased their fortune by means of inheritance, marriage, legacy, or preferment was by no means unique. It appears to have been borrowed from the Dilettanti Society, which had ordered that every member increasing his wealth by such means should pay a half per cent of his augmented income or face a fine of ten pounds.[147] The Catch Club modified this by offering members the alternative of a 'Compound of Ten Guineas', at the same time looking forward to a substantial increase in funds 'particularly by the laudable spirit of matrimony which now prevails among us',[148] doubtless partly a reflection of the club's predominantly youthful membership. Among those who paid such levies we find: the Earl of Sandwich, who paid 9s. on receipt of an annuity of £90 and £10 on the occasion of his appointment as Secretary of State in 1770; Hans Stanley, Tory MP for Southampton, who paid 10 guineas on the occasion of his appointment as Governor of the Isle of Wight in 1770; and the assiduous music collector, Sir Watkin Williams Wynn, who contributed a guinea from a Lottery win of £50. Fines and levies came to make up a large part of the Catch Club's income, which rose from a total of £35 14s. (17 out of 19 members paying two guineas each) during the inaugural 1762/3 season, to an average of around £230 in the 1770s. While full accounts are not listed in the surviving documents of the club, Table 3 provides a summary of the existing data.[149] Although fragmentary, this data shows clearly that by the 1770s income from fines and levies outstripped that being received from fees, a proportion amounting to 58% during the four seasons between 1771 and 1775. The fluctuating annual membership fee was geared to the state of the club's overall finances. In the event the committee felt that the balance in hand was becoming too low it simply levied an extra charge on members, a prerogative possible for a self-governing body whose membership was by definition well-heeled. The combination of a marginally lower membership and a below average income from fines and levies in the 1774/75 season resulted in a very modest balance for the end of the year.

---

[146] Clark, *British Clubs*, p. 250.
[147] Clark, *British Clubs*, p. 258. Evidence that the Catch Club to some extent modelled its rules on those of the Dilettante Society also comes from a resolution of 5 April 1763. This requires Richard Phelps 'to inform the Society at their next meeting of the method observ'd in the Dilettante Society relative to the exclusion of the non-attending members' – Minutes, H.2788.rr., p. 25.
[148] Minutes, H.2788.rr., p. 233.
[149] In Table 3 total income includes the initial 5 guinea joining fee for new members. Discrepancies are accounted for by members who for one reason or another had not paid; for example, the accounts for 1763/4 note two members 'abroad', one 'out' and one 'not paid'. For the sake of clarity figures have been rounded to the nearest pound.

Table 3
Income of the Catch Club 1763–1765

Season	1763/4	1764/5	1769/70	1770/1	1771/2	1772/3	1773/4	1774/5
No. of members	27	27	n/a	24	27	26	26	25
Income fees [Membership fee]	£120 5gns	£201 7gns	£196 n/a	£126 5gns	£56 2gns	£109 4gns	£109 4gns	£79 3gns
Fines etc.	-	£29	n/a	n/a	£163	£137	£131	£117
Total Income	£120	£289	n/a	£250	£222	£259	£240	£222
Balance	n/a	£91	£98	n/a	n/a	n/a	n/a	£27

On 23 March the following the year a Minute was passed determining that the committee 'find it necessary that every Member should contribute Three Guineas and one half in order to make good deficiencies of Forfeits etc. and that the Secretary who collects the same should ask every Member whether he has had any increase of income, by Inheritance, Marriage, or Preferment since Lady Day 1775'.[150] The clear implication in the last part of this Minute is that members were not always prepared to be forthcoming in admitting to changes in their fortune. Similar action was also taken in April 1787 and April 1791, on the former occasion arising partly from 'the extraordinary number of compositions sent in for the Prize Medals', but also because receipts from fines and levies were £57 less than they had been the previous year. Since this left £121 to be raised for the season then nearing its end, the committee resolved 'that each Member do contribute Six Guineas to make good the Deficiencies for the Season, and that the Secretary do immediately collect the same.'[151] By adopting such practices the Catch Club therefore ensured that unlike many eighteenth-century clubs and societies it never ran into financial difficulties.

During the earliest years of the society, there are few detailed records of how the Catch Club spent its income. The bulk of its expenditure must have been on the hire of rooms, advertising, the purchase of music, and (from 1767) wine. A continuing expense must also have been the fees paid to Warren for copying music into the club's books; it is specifically mentioned twice in the early years, although it is not possible to determine the exact amounts, since in both instances the figure is included in a more general sum, an item of £34 1s. 6d. to 'Mr Warren's Bill for copying music' and making Disbursements in 1763/64, and in the following season £30 7s. 10d. 'for copying and advertising costs'.[152] At the end of 1796, the year after Samuel Webbe the elder took over as secretary, we do find a statement of the

[150] Minutes, H.2788.ss., p. 6.
[151] Minutes, H.2788.ss., p. 97.
[152] Accounts, H.2788.rr.

accounts for the latter part of 1795/6 season, which reveals that the club was then paying 15s. per night for the hire of the room at the Thatched House Tavern. Dated Monday 6 June 1796, the full details are as follows:

To the House the Allowance of 15s every Club Day from The 12 March last and Deficiencies in Reckoning as per Bill	£ 32. 4. 2d.
Two volumes consisting of Nine Books each vol. of Mr Webbe's glees [153]	£ 9. 9. 0d.
Binding 1s 5 each	£ 1. 10. 0d.
Paging & Indexing	£ 2. 2. 0d.
Paid to Mr Rbt Cooke	£ 1. 1. 0d.
Binding 3 Books No. 20	£ 1. 16. 0d.
Salary	£ 31. 10. 0d.
Extra	£ 2. 2. 0d.[154]

There is no indication as to why Benjamin Cooke's son Robert was paid one guinea, but the 'Salary' was of course the annual amount paid to Webbe in his capacity as secretary.

Following the choice made by the president, the selection of repertoire performed at club meetings was left to the membership, who selected the pieces to be sung in strict rotation. Members were permitted either to introduce a new catch or glee or choose a piece from the club's books. Following the performance of a new work, a member could ask for it to be entered by permission into the books and many such pieces give the name of the member responsible for the addition. The remaining pieces included in the club's books are those submitted for consideration in the prize competition, such entries being noted as having been obtained 'By advertisement'. By these means the Catch Club was able to build a large repertoire of its own that was copied by Warren into a series of bulky volumes (as we have seen from Gardiner's testimony, at meetings they were wheeled around on the table by means of small trolleys) which by 1794 had run to nineteen complete books and an incomplete twentieth book containing in all 1,185 different works.

As early as 1780 the club was finding that earlier volumes were being neglected. A resolution was therefore passed on 27 May that year determining that in addition to the usual rotation the president of the day should name three pieces 'beginning with the first volume in our Collection, by which means many valuable pieces will be reviv'd which have been for some time buried in oblivion'. The resolution continues: 'When the club is of the opinion that all the pieces in the first Volume which deserve attention have been heard, it will be proper to go on to the second Volume and so progressively on thro' the whole collection.' It was also decided that the secretary should keep a list of the pieces chosen. This list is extant,[155] revealing that the exercise lasted ten years, by which time volume fifteen (dating from 1787) had been reached, the three-year gap now apparently considered small enough for the club to feel it had mined its earlier repertoire in sufficient depth.

---

[153] Samuel Webbe's nine published books of glees appeared between 1764 and c. 1795.
[154] Audit, H.2788.ss., p. 167.
[155] Catch Club Collection, BL H.2788.ccc.

Not surprisingly, the selections Warren made for his own volumes published under the auspices of the club drew heavily, but far from exclusively, on its own collection. Nearly three-quarters of the works he included are also found in the Catch Club books and there is an obvious pattern to the way Warren worked after his first book, where only eighteen out of the seventy-six pieces (mostly catches and canons) he included also appeared in the club's books. Thereafter his annual publications conform closely to individual volumes in the club's series, Warren volume 2, for example, draws most of its material from the club's volume one. Notwithstanding such a pattern, the analysis in Table 4 reveals surprising discrepancies between the contents of the two series.[156]

While both the Catch Club books and Warren provide evidence of the increasing popularity of the glee at the expense of the catch, Warren suggests this process occurred at a considerably slower rate than do the club's books. Indeed, in stark contrast to the latter, his collections during the 1770s continue to give precedence to the catch, possibly due to an understandable desire to maintain a balance in publications that were designed as a commercial venture. Moreover, catches in general being much shorter than glees, more could be included within an allotted number of pages, a consideration of little interest to the club.

Table 4
Proportion of Glees, Catches & Canons Included in the Catch Club Books & the Warren Collection

	1760s	1770s	1780s	1790s	Overall
Catch Club Books					
Glees	25%	56%	64%	50%	49%
Catches	56%	32%	28%	19%	34%
Canons	14%	7%	8%	7%	9%
Warren Collection					
Glees	27%	32%	48%	48%	39%
Catches	54%	40%	24%	31%	37%
Canons	18%	10%	7%	11%	12%

The same concerns may also account for Warren's inclusion of a greater number of canons, which were usually religious in nature and therefore less appropriate to a gathering whose main purpose was to meet in a convivial spirit. For these reasons it seems reasonable to suggest that the Catch Club's books are more likely to provide an accurate guide to what was sung at the club than Warren's publications. Nevertheless, the latter not only provides an unparalleled guide to the most popular

---

[156] Works that fail to conform to any category account for percentage discrepancies in Table 4.

glees, catches and canons, but was also influential in spreading the repertoire to the numerous clubs that emerged in London and across the country in the wake of the Catch Club. John Marsh tells us that the catch club he founded in Chichester was the recipient of a set of Warren, a gift of the local MP Thomas Steele,[157] while the Bristol Catch Club is also recorded as having owned a set.[158]

The resignation and death of Warren obviously brought to an end his own annual publications, but also coincided with the final regular entries in the Catch Club's own books. Henceforth, the club seems to have purchased published volumes of composer's works, the first being Samuel Webbe the elder's, of which two sets, presumably of all eight books, were obtained by an order of 19 May 1795. In December of the same year a motion proposed by Lord Grey de Wilton that 'the last Publication of Dr Cooke be procured for the Club' was also carried.[159]

The most striking change demonstrated by Table 4 is the replacement of the catch by the glee as the dominant form of the repertoire. Several reasons may be advanced for such a development. The first and most obvious has already been touched upon. When the Catch Club was first formed there was no glee repertoire to speak of. Indeed, the club has the distinction of almost single-handedly having fostered the creation of a new genre. There are, however, other factors behind the gradual demise of the catch's influence, some musical, others social. Infinitely more restricted than the glee both as to musical form and possible range of text, the catch was ill-suited to compete with a form capable of encompassing the changing spirit of the times so effectively. That spirit may be best summed up by two words – 'politeness' and 'sentiment', both – especially sentiment – much changed in meaning since the eighteenth century. As John Brewer has observed, 'The ideal of politeness became well-established during the course of the eighteenth century, and its language and values permeated every aspect of cultural life.'[160] Politeness was therefore not just a matter of good manners, although this entered into it, but a philosophy of behaviour affecting literature, the fine arts and music. Above all it was a social phenomenon, in Brewer's words, 'a complete system of conduct embracing every aspect of manners and morals'. As he points out, 'the home of politeness was in company, and the place of company was in the institutions that lay at the heart of urban culture'.[161] Sentiment may in some ways be viewed as a corollary of politeness; a recognition that while man harboured strong passions, these must be harnessed and expressed in a refined, controlled manner that precludes the gross or the vulgar. The glee, with its close fusion of music and verse, can be seen as the perfect vehicle for what we might term the English sentimental style, a form perhaps summed up by William Hogarth,[162]

---

[157] Marsh, *Journals*, p. 526. Steele's gift was also used by the local subscription concerts, which took over the volumes following the demise of the Chichester Catch Club.

[158] Graham Hooper, 'A Survey of Music in Bristol with Special Reference to the Eighteenth Century' (MA. Diss. University of Bristol, 1963), p. 201.

[159] Cooke's *Nine Glees and Two Duets (Never Before Printed)* was published during the course of 1795. Lord Grey de Wilton is listed as one of the subscribers to the volume.

[160] John Brewer, *Pleasures of the Imagination* (London, 1997), p. 100. His succeeding pages provide an admirable introduction to the topic.

[161] Brewer, *Pleasures*, p. 103.

[162] As noted on p. 21 above Hogarth had sufficient interest in music to have been a member of the Academy of Vocal Music in 1729.

who noted that the glees of Benjamin Cooke were 'remarkable for natural and graceful ease of melody, great simplicity and yet much art in the disposition of parts, and fine expression'.[163]

If the glee may in general terms be thus considered a manifestation of politeness, the catch was far from it. This is not to ignore the fact that some glees had ribald texts, or conversely to suggest that all catches dealt with such subject matter. But it was the catch that came increasingly to be viewed as an unruly misfit that breached the rules of polite society. As society became increasingly 'polite' during the last decades of the eighteenth century, so attacks on the 'rudeness' of catches increased in ferocity. In 1757 William Hayes could still express the view that a well-constructed catch might be 'justly esteemed excellent'.[164] Ten years later the *Monthly Review*, in considering a publication of the texts of some of Arne's catches and glees, could chide the 'namby-pamby' words of the glee *Fair the op'ning lily blows*,[165] but by 1787 Charles Dibdin could be found bitterly complaining about the uncharitable treatment meted out to Arne's impoverished widow, while sarcastically suggesting that 'his catches and glees had caused half the drunkenness and disorder that pervaded their [the Catch Club's] convivial meetings'.[166] Such changing perceptions of the catch and glee found many echoes during the last decades of the century. In 1771 the same *Monthly Review* that had ridiculed Arne for composing a glee to 'namby-pamby' words was able to inform its readers that the recently published *Songsters Companion* contained 'none of those indecent, ribaldry pieces [...] by which other collections have been disgraced';[167] while some four years later Samuel Webbe the elder (himself not averse to composing the occasional bawdy catch) sought to tap into the increasingly refined market by announcing *The Ladies Catch-Book, Being a Collection of Catches, Canons and Glees the Words of Which Will Not Offend the Nicest Delicacy*. That Webbe should trouble to incorporate such assurances into the title of his publication confirms that by the mid 1770s the question of 'delicacy' was a live issue and it continued to gather force in the succeeding decade. In 1781 the London publisher Joseph Vernon issued a broad collection of songs, ballads, catches, and glees in which the editor's preface 'begs leave to observe that the Reader will find in the following choice selection [...] that humour and decency go hand in hand together, and that obscenity and ribaldry are entirely excluded, as being foreign to the nature of innocent mirth and good humour'.[168] It is difficult to be sure how much of Vernon's Preface was dictated by commercial considerations, but he appears to be trying to encompass as broad a market as possible, playing to the gallery of fashionable

---

[163] Quoted in Rubin, 'Introduction'.
[164] William Hayes, Preface to *Catches, Glees and Canons for 3, 4, 5 Voices* (1757).
[165] *Monthly Review*, vol. 37 (July 1767), p. 58. *The New Oxford Dictionary of English* (Oxford, 1998), suggests that the term 'namby-pamby' is a fanciful derivation from the name of the English poet Ambrose Philips (d. 1749), whose pastorals were mocked by Carey and Pope. The glee was included in volume three of the Warren Collection. The full text of the lines quoted by the journal runs: Fair the op'ning lily blows/Sweet the fragrant citron grows/Which perfumes the eastern grove:/Say, can ought with these compare?/Oh, much fairer, sweeter far,/Bloom the charms of her I love.
[166] Charles Dibdin, *The Musical Tour of Mr Dibdin* (Sheffield, 1787), p. 162.
[167] *Monthly Review*, vol. 44 (January 1771), p. 174.
[168] *The New London and Country Songster; or A Banquet of Vocal Music* (London, 1781).

'politeness', while at the same time not excluding the convivial atmosphere associated with singing.

One of the most trenchant attacks on the catch (and the Catch Club itself) came from the pen of William Jackson (1730–1803), the Exeter composer, writer, and one-time friend of the painter Thomas Gainsborough. For his own compositions he stressed that his ambitions lay only in setting verse of the highest quality to melodies of a national character, while his often-acerbic writings reveal deeply conservative views that allowed little merit in modern music. Jackson's *The Four Ages*, published in London in 1798, lashes out in a variety of directions, the targets including gentlemen composers 'who amuse themselves in making a succession of chords and call them Glees' [169] – a clear indication that the glee had already become debased currency by the end of the century. But Jackson reserves his greatest opprobrium for the catch. Having castigated the era of Charles II, a time when 'real music was in its infancy' and a reign that 'carried every kind of vulgar debauchery to its height',[170] he goes on to describe the catch and lament its revival in modern times:

> The harmony of a catch is nothing more than the common result of filling up a chord. – There is not contrivance enough to make it esteemed as a piece of ingenuity. "What! They are all canons!" So is every tune in the world, if you will set it in three or more parts, and sing these parts in succession, as a catch – but a real canon is not easily produced[...] The excellence in the composition of a catch consists in making the breaks and filling them up properly. The melody is, for the most part, the unimproved vulgar drawl of the times of ignorance.
> Let us attend next to the manner of performance. One voice leads, a second follows, and a third &c. succeeds, unaccompanied by any instrument to keep them together. The consequence is, that the voices are always sinking; but not equally, for the best singers will keep nearest the pitch, and the others depart farthest from it. If the parts are doubled, which is sometimes the case, all these defects are multiplied. To this, let there be added the imperfect scale of an uncultivated voice, the departing from the real sound by way of humour, the noise of so many people striving to outsing each other, the confusion of speaking different words at the same time, and all this heightened by the laughing and other accompaniments of the audience – it presents such a scene of savage folly, as would not disgrace the Hottentots indeed, but it is not much to the credit of a civilised people.
> As the catch in a manner owed its existence to a drunken club, of which some members were musicians; upon their dying, it languished for years, and was scarce known except among choir-men, who now and then kept up the spirit of their forefathers. As the age grew more polished, a better style of music appeared[...]
> Now, if this were speculation only, is it credible that taste should revert to barbarism; and yet contrary to experience in every other instance, we have gone back a century and catches flourish in the reign of George the third. There is a club composed of some of the first people in the kingdom, who meet professedly to hear this style of composition: they cultivate and encourage it with premiums. To obtain which, many composers, who aught to be above such nonsense, become candidates, and produce such things[...]

---

[169] William Jackson, *The Four Ages; together with Essays on Various Subjects* (London, 1798), 'Essay on Gentlemen Artists'.
[170] Jackson, *Four Ages*, Letter X – 'On Catches', p. 63.

> I confess that I never heard a catch sung, but I felt more ashamed than I can express. I pretend to no more delicacy than that of the age I live in, which is very properly too refined to endure such barbarisms – I was ashamed for myself – for my company – and if a foreigner was present – for my country.[171]

To Jackson the catch was specifically associated with a former age of musical immaturity, an unenlightened era that had yet to attain refinement or politeness. Its continued existence at the end of the eighteenth century represented nothing less than an affront to sensibility, the crude and bawdy offspring of a form that had no place in modern society. It seems unlikely that Jackson ever attended the Catch Club and he made no true contribution to either the catch (for obvious reasons!) or glee repertoire, instead writing accompanied part songs that he preferred to designate 'elegies' (op. 3), 'epigrams' (op. 17), or 'quartets for voices' (op. 11). By 1801 even Callcott, one of the mainstays of the Catch Club and himself the composer of numerous catches, felt sufficiently awkward about 'the difficulty of performing Catches & the other causes which prevent their more general use' to 'pass over them lightly'.[172]

Jackson's preference for accompanied part songs automatically precluded the inclusion of any of his compositions in either Warren or the Catch Club books,[173] since there is no evidence that any music performed at the club during the period in question was ever sung other than unaccompanied and with single voices per part. Callcott was quite specific about this, stating unambiguously that the glee was 'designed to be sung without instrumental accompaniment'.[174] The Catch Club seems to have fiercely protected the 'purity' of both catch and glee well after the accompaniment of glees had become an accepted convention elsewhere. Neither were other genres admitted to the club's entertainment, a small group of works that falls outside the description of catches, glees or canons consisting largely of Elizabethan and Jacobean madrigals. William Gardiner's account of his visit to the club around 1812 has already been quoted at length, and also includes a pertinent anecdote on this subject:

> My Lord Blessington had brought with him the humourous Mr Matthews, and he called upon him for a song; upon which Mr [William] Linley, the vice-president, arose, and addressing the chair, said, "It was contrary to the rules of the society for a song to be introduced at their meetings. Their object was to give encouragement to a species of composition peculiar to the English, catches and glees, in which style of music this country has excelled all others".[175]

---

[171] Jackson, 'On Catches'.
[172] Callcott, 'Essays'.
[173] Rubin's 'The English Glee', includes Jackson's three opuses in his listing of published glees. None of his works appear in Warren or the Catch Clubs Books.
[174] Callcott, 'Essays'.
[175] Gardiner, *Music and Friends*, vol. 2, p. 513ff. There is no evidence that the MS volume of songs and keyboard pieces included in the Catch Club collection in the British Library (E.1858.dd.) has any association with the Catch Club.

Linley's words not only represent a clear reiteration of the Catch Club's original purpose, but also equally once more draw attention to the overt nationalism that had been attached to the catch and glee by the early years of the nineteenth century.

The cynic might be tempted to find the purchase of the elder Webbe's published collections of catches and glees immediately following his appointment as secretary rather more than a coincidence, but there is no doubt that over a twenty-year period he had established a widely recognised pre-eminence in the field.[176] This is clearly illustrated in Table 5, where analysis of the works included in the Catch Club books and the Warren Collection reveals Webbe to be substantially the most represented composer in either.

Table 5
Composer Representation in the Catch Club Books & the Warren Collection
The Table shows the number of works and % of whole to nearest percentage point.

	Catch Club Books	Warren
Samuel Webbe the elder (1740–1816)	145 [13%]	68 [11%]
John Wall Callcott (1766–1821)	115 [9%]	47 [7%]
John Danby (1757–98)	62 [5%]	22 [3%]
Benjamin Cooke (1734–93)	52 [4%]	35 [5%]
John Stafford Smith (1750–1836)	39 [3%]	32 [5%]
Earl of Mornington (1735–81)	37 [3%]	23 [4%]
Thomas Arne (1710–78)	33 [3%]	29 [4%]
Francis Hutcheson (Ireland) (1721–80)	31 [3%]	10 [2%]
Luffman Atterbury (? –1796)	29 [3%]	27 [4%]

The table shows that despite the large number of composers involved in the composition of catches and glees, the bulk of the repertoire during the most important phase of both genres was the product of a relatively small group. When anonymous productions are eliminated from the Catch Club's books, we find that around 36% of the works included came from the pens of the first five listed composers. It should also be noted that both anthologies include a substantial number of anonymous compositions, 11.5% in the case of the Catch Club's books, 10.5% in the Warren Collection, the percentages given in the table being inclusive of such works. With the notable exceptions of Cooke and Smith, pupils of Pepusch and Boyce respectively, both of whom therefore came through traditional channels of musical training, one of the striking features of the careers of the composers listed in Table 5 is that all were either autodidacts or amateurs. Two, Garret Wesley, 1st Earl of Mornington and his fellow Irishman Francis Hutcheson would remain musical amateurs throughout their lives, Mornington for the obvious reason that he was a

---

[176] See below p. 105 for the observations of a connoisseur like James Harris.

member of the nobility (and the father of the Duke of Wellington). Hutcheson was a physician who was consultant to a number of Dublin hospitals. Although happy to appear as an amateur violinist under his own name, he adopted the pseudonym of Francis Ireland for his compositions. He also appears to have sought anonymity for printed works, many of his submissions to the Catch Club being published by Warren without credit, a factor that accounts for the substantial proportional discrepancy between his share of works in the Catch Club manuscript books and Warren's editions. Luffman Atterbury might also essentially be considered an amateur, being (like Callcott's father) a builder or carpenter by trade who was a member of the Society for the Encouragement of Arts and only later developed a second career as a composer and singer, becoming a musician-in-ordinary to George III in 1775.

The backgrounds of Webbe and Callcott are remarkably similar. Both were Londoners who were largely self-taught musicians, receiving only rudimentary instruction on the organ. Webbe's gift for languages (he is reputed to have taught himself German, Greek and Hebrew) would later be mirrored by Callcott, a prodigy who in addition to having been a brilliant classics scholar also taught himself to play the clarinet and oboe. The long-established connection between the catch, the glee, and the church was maintained by both Webbe, a Roman Catholic who in 1775 was appointed organist of the Sardinian Embassy Chapel, and Callcott, who with Charles Evans was joint organist of St Paul's, Covent Garden from 1789. In addition Cooke,[177] Danby, a pupil of Webbe's and also a Catholic who was organist of the chapel of the Spanish Embassy, and John Stafford Smith, a Gentleman of the Chapel Royal and from 1802 one of its organists, also had links with the church.

Two other factors link the nine leading composers. The first is not surprising, since we would expect their lives to interact and cross paths institutionally. With the exception of the two Irish amateurs, who for obvious reasons would not have been capable of regularly attending London events, all were active honorary members of the Catch Club, Webbe being appointed as its secretary in succession to Warren, as already noted. As will become apparent in the following chapter, most of the names reappear as members of the London clubs and societies that formed in the wake of the Catch Club. Several, such as Arne and Cooke, have already been identified as members of organisations such as the Academy of Ancient Music and the Madrigal Society, while both Webbe and his son, also Samuel, were frequent visitors to the latter in the early 1800s.

The connection between catch and glee composers and the Madrigal Society brings us to a second point of contact: a widely shared interest in 'old' music. In the case of John Stafford Smith, it amounts to considerably more than a passing interest, since like Edmund Warren he was an antiquarian who amassed a collection that included such priceless items as the *Old Hall Manuscript* and the *Ulm Gesangbuch* of 1538. In 1812, Smith issued his *Musica Antiqua*, an anthology of carefully edited works from his own collection and other available sources dating from the twelfth to the eighteenth centuries, and including music by such composers as Ockeghem,

---

[177] Cooke was Master of the Choristers at Westminster Abbey (from 1757), organist of the Abbey (from 1762) and organist of St Martin-in-the-Fields (from 1782).

Obrecht, Wert and Morales.[178] Another keen collector of historic music was Benjamin Cooke, whose personal library of 33 volumes included extracts from the *Fayrfax Manuscript*, and music by John Bull and Clemens non Papa.[179] While our remaining composers evinced less overt interest, historicism is implied in a number of their compositions. Callcott appears to have developed such an interest; one of his later works was a six-part Italian madrigal, *Padre del ciel*, composed in 1800 in deliberate imitation of Renaissance style. Several of Mornington's works, including *As it fell upon the day* and *Come shepherds come* (both *c.* 1778), were designated as madrigals, the latter specifically composed 'In Imitation of Matthew Locke', while *Flora now calleth forth*, one of John Stafford Smith's most famous works, also carried the rubric 'madrigal'. Further evidence of interest in the past from a more general selection of glee composers comes from a popular sub-species of the glee, the epitaph or elegy. Among a number of epitaphs dedicated to prominent composers of the past we find tributes to Thomas Tallis in Benjamin Cooke's *Interr'd here doth lie* (1768), his son Robert's epitaph on William Lawes, *Concord is Conquered* (*c.* 1788), Robert Hudson's *On the Grave Stone of Dr William Child in the choir at Windsor*,[180] and his daughter Mary's *Applaud so great a guest*, a tribute to Purcell, and the subject of the disputed prize mentioned above.

The extent to which such interest in antiquarianism influenced the generality of glees composed for the Catch Club is a topic beyond the remit of the present study. Certainly, it is also reflected in the large number of historic texts drawn upon by the glee composers, but this may be part of the more general trend to revive interest in the Gothic.[181]

To conclude, it seems certain the Catch Club progressed far beyond the original convivial intentions of the founder's aristocratic membership. By means of the prize competition, a positive encouragement to composers to devote themselves to the catch and glee was established, thus creating not only a large corpus of works that increasingly came to be seen as the foundation of a truly national repertoire, but in essence creating in the glee a new genre that formed the core of that repertoire.

---

[178] John Stafford Smith, *Musica Antiqua, a Selection of Music of This and Other Countries* (London, 1812).
[179] Cooke's collection is now housed in the Royal College of Music.
[180] The organist and composer William Child (1606–97).
[181] See Chapter 7 for discussion of how texts mirror the aesthetic approach of the glee composers.

Chapter 4
The Expansion of London Catch Club Culture

The social cachet of the Catch Club, with its permanent waiting list for membership, and its success in reviving the catch and establishing the glee, inevitably inspired emulation. Some notion of the spread of catch clubs during the following years can be gained from the preface to *The Essex Harmony*, a collection compiled by John Arnold and first published in 1769.[1] 'That Part Songs and Catches, Canons and Glees, were never held in greater esteem in this Kingdom than at present', wrote Arnold, 'is evident by the great Number of Catch-Clubs which are now established both in Town and Country.' He goes on to cite specifically the Catch Club, later also mentioning Oxford as a place with a catch club. Frustratingly from the point of view of the modern historian, he then contents himself with '&c.', believing that 'it would be giving both myself and the Readers too much trouble, to give a succinct Account of them all, some held weekly, some once a Fortnight, and some of them once a Month'. Tantalising though Arnold's words are, they make clear the widespread expansion that had taken place during the 1760s, not only in London, but also in the provinces.

One of the earliest and most significant London imitators was the Anacreontic Society, founded in 1766. Detailed records of the membership and rules of the club have not survived, the only information relating to it being derived from contemporary observers. According to R. J. S. Stevens, it was run by a committee of eleven gentlemen members,[2] while the oboist and composer William Parke (1761–1847) noted that it met once a fortnight during the winter season.[3] As in the case of the Catch Club, it was founded by a group of noblemen and wealthy amateurs, mostly, according to the tenor Michael Kelly, 'bankers and merchants',[4] and, like the Catch Club, employed the services of leading professional musicians as honorary members. It took its name from the Greek lyric poet Anacreon, famous for his celebration of love and wine. The earliest meetings of the society were held at the London Coffee House on Ludgate Hill, a venue noted by James Boswell in 1772 as having a clientele mainly composed of 'Physicians, dissenting clergy and masters of academies'.[5] The repertoire initially consisted exclusively of catches and glees, but by the early 1770s it had been expanded to include choral and instrumental music. Like the Catch Club, which almost certainly inspired its formation, the Anacreontic Society rapidly became extremely fashionable, although far from exclusive. In 1773 the young John Marsh found no trouble not only in gaining admission when invited by a Mr Bowen ('who played a very good fiddle' and was presumably a member), but

---

[1] Arnold, *The Essex Harmony*.
[2] Stevens, *Recollections*, p. 25.
[3] William T. Parke, *Musical Memoirs*, 2 vols (London, 1830), vol. 1, p. 80.
[4] Kelly, *Reminiscences*, p. 225.
[5] Quoted in *The London Encyclopaedia*, ed. Ben Weinreb and Christopher Hibbert (London, 1993), p. 484.

in taking his place as a violinist during the instrumental part of the proceedings. After this was concluded, Marsh relates, 'we sat down a pretty many of us to supper in another room after which catches and glees were perform'd, in which a Mr Webster,[6] a young man with a very fine bass voice much distinguished himself. The *Anacreontic Song* was also sung by him, in the last verse of which we stood hand in hand all round the table...'[7] The *Anacreontic Song*, ritually performed at all meetings of the society, had been specially composed by members of the society under the direction of John Stafford Smith to words by the lawyer Ralph Tomlinson, for a number of years the president of the Anacreontics, and described by R. J. S. Stevens as 'very much of a Gentleman, and a sensible, sedate, quiet man'.[8] Today the tune of the song is better known as *The Star-spangled Banner*.

Finding its quarters at the London Coffee House too small for a membership for which Parke tells us 'noblemen and gentlemen would wait a year', the society moved at some point after Marsh's visit in 1773 to the Crown and Anchor Tavern. Situated at the top of Arundel Street in the Strand, this was for many years also the home of the Academy of Ancient Music, and a future venue for meetings of the Glee Club. The society was certainly established at the Crown and Anchor by 1777, where its meetings were held in the large ballroom. R. J. S. Stevens was regularly attending its meetings at this time, his account providing us with a detailed description of its proceedings:

> The Evening's entertainment began at seven o'clock, with a concert, chiefly of instrumental music: it was not very uncommon to have some Vocal Music interspersed with the Instrumental. Mr Sabbattier was the Manager of this department, and generally stood behind the person who was at the Piano Forte. At ten o'clock the Instrumental Concert ended, when we retired to the Supper rooms. After Supper, having sung *Non nobis Domine*, we returned to the Concert Room, which in the meantime had been differently arranged. The President, then took his seat in the center of the elevated table, at the upper end of the room, supported on each side, by the various Vocal performers. After the Anacreontic Song had been sung, in the chorus of the last verse of which all the Members, Visitors, and Performers joined [...] we were entertained by the performance of various celebrated Catches, Glees, Songs, Duettos, and other Vocal, with some Rhetorical compositions, till twelve o'clock.[9]

At midnight the president left his chair and the evening continued on a more informal basis, described by the sober-minded Stevens as proceedings 'that were very disgraceful to the Society; as the greatest levity, and vulgar obscenity, generally prevailed. Improper Songs, and vicious compositions were performed without any shame at all.'[10] The scheme outlined by Marsh and Stevens was one that would be reflected in the constitution of many provincial catch clubs, who unlike the Catch

---

[6] Anthony Webster. According to the gossipy Michael Kelly he later eloped to Dublin with the wife of Jonathan Battishill, singing there at the Smock Alley Theatre. Kelly, *Reminiscences*, p. 6.
[7] Marsh, *Journals*, pp. 115–16. *The Anacreontic Song* ('To Anacreon in Heav'n').
[8] Stevens, *Recollections*, p. 25.
[9] Ibid.
[10] In 1808 Stevens burned a number of 'obscene' catches he had been 'silly enough to compose' for the Catch Club's competitions. *Recollections*, p. 156.

Club, and later the Glee Club, rarely devoted an entire evening to the singing of catches and glees. Conversely, this juxtaposition of instrumental concert repertoire and the performance of catches and glees would find new impetus as the two vocal forms infiltrated the public concert.[11] One notes, too, the typical club arrangement for the second part of the evening's entertainment, with the chairman at the centre of a raised dais, and, as with the Catch Club and many imitators, the sheer length of an evening that concluded with the informal 'levity' that so outraged Stevens. A significant difference between the Catch Club and the Anacreontic Society was the much later time of meetings, almost certainly a reflection of a membership that included professional men in addition to a largely leisured class.

Like the Catch Club, the Anacreontic Society attracted many of London's leading professionals as honorary members, both to the orchestral and vocal parts of the evening's entertainment. According to Parke, an honorary member during the 1780s and 1790s, during the first part of the evening 'all the flower of the musical profession assisted as honorary members',[12] an assertion supported by John Marsh, who on another visit to the society in 1781 noted the presence of the leading violinist William Cramer as leader, the cellist James Cervetto, and 'young Westley', who was either Charles or Samuel Wesley.[13] Two years later, in November 1783, Marsh again visited the society, an occasion on which he was 'highly pleased, particularly with the concert before supper', at which in addition to Cramer's leadership, he noted the renowned double-bassist Stefano Gariboldi among the principal performers. Another prominent player mentioned by both Marsh and Stevens was the composer Samuel Arnold (1740–1802), who directed from the keyboard for the instrumental half of the concert and according to Stevens had pretensions to the presidency. This ambition was scathingly dismissed by Stevens, who considered Arnold to have 'neither consequence, ability or understanding enough to conduct such a popular Musical Society'.[14] The vocal performers listed by Stevens, and termed by Parke 'some of the finest vocalists in the country', also testify to the eminence of those who assisted in the performance after supper. They included: Benjamin Cooke; Samuel Webbe the elder; either William or Stephen Paxton; the alto singer and organist Charles Knyvett the elder; the tenor John Hindle; the tenor Samuel Harrison; a Linley (probably Thomas Linley the elder); John Danby; the singer and composer John Percy; Jack Smith; John Stafford Smith; the tenor and composer Joseph Vernon; the outstanding bass Charles Reinhold; and Stevens himself.

During the course of its existence, the Anacreontic Society was served by six presidents. On his death Ralph Tomlinson was succeeded by George Bellas, who in the view of Stevens 'conducted the Society with great spirit, had gentlemanly manners and was an admirable Chairman'. Bellas appears to have held the presidency for some ten years, after which he was succeeded by Edward Mulso, who was probably a lawyer, and a composer of catches himself. He was noted by Kelly as having 'a good tenor voice' which he employed to sing the Anacreontic Song (the performance of which was by this time apparently the duty of the president or his

[11] See Chapter 6.
[12] Parke, *Musical Memoirs*, vol. 1, p. 80.
[13] Marsh, *Journals*, p. 253. Philip Olleson suggests Samuel, who was 15 at the time, as the more likely.
[14] Stevens, *Recollections*, p. 25.

deputy) 'to great effect', but he was less charitably dismissed by Stevens as 'a convivial man: frothy, vain and silly'. Mulso died in 1782, when he was succeeded by Jack Smith. In the final years of the society the presidents were Sir Bernard Taylor; James Curtis, later possibly a member of the Catch Club;[15] and Sir Richard Hankey, a former military man who had served in the American war and was an accomplished amateur musician who 'performed admirably on the oboe'.[16]

By the early 1790s the Anacreontic Society had become more flourishing than ever, an important part of London's concert scene and an attraction to which eminent musical visitors were taken. On 12 January 1791 the recently arrived Joseph Haydn was a guest of the society; on entering the concert room he was received by Sir Richard Hankey 'with great civility'.[17] It would be a rather less welcome visitor who would bring about the sudden demise of the Anacreontic Society. According to the account by Parke, the incident was caused by a request from the Duchess of Devonshire to attend privately. The committee duly invited her, having rigged up a lattice to hide the Duchess and her entourage (women obviously not being permitted to attend the latter half of the evening under normal circumstances). Some of the repertoire not being intended for the ears of ladies – although given her reputation one suspects the Duchess probably enjoyed it – the singers apparently performed in an unusually inhibited manner. This displeased many of the members so much that they resigned en bloc, leaving the society to be dissolved at an ensuing general meeting.[18] The incident is so curious and the reaction of the membership apparently so extreme that the lack of further accounts is to be regretted. On face value, however, it illustrates clearly how closely societies protected their right to meet convivially in exclusively male company.

From the Minutes of the Catch Club in 1774 we learn of the formation of the New Catch Club, an organisation almost certainly inspired by the long waiting list for membership of the original club, which appears to have been happy to welcome the newcomer. The first mention comes in a Minute of 18 January, ordering that Edmund Warren should have 'permission to supply The New Catch Club with any Musical Pieces they shall choose out of their [the Catch Club's] collection'.[19] The following year a series of reciprocal visits was inaugurated, the Catch Club hosting the newcomers on 14 March. The Minutes record the visit of 'The Catch Club at St Alban's Tavern', the former home of the Catch Club, although Callcott also mentions the fashionable Star and Garter in Pall Mall as its meeting place.[20] The new club replied in kind, the Catch Club noting a week later that it had accepted an invitation to visit its emulator on 30 March, a date that suggests the new club met on Thursdays. The following year the exercise was repeated, when it was noted that the visitors included Sir Henry Gough, the independent MP for Bramber from 1774; Lord Calthorp; Edward Gibbon, the author of *The Decline and Fall of the Roman*

---

[15] A James Taylor was elected a member of the Catch Club in 1808.
[16] Parke, *Musical Memoirs*, p. 83.
[17] H. C. Robbins Landon, *Haydn Chronicle and Works: Haydn in England, 1792–1795* (London, 1976), p. 41. The quotation comes from an account in *The Times*, 14 January 1791.
[18] Parke, *Musical Memoirs*, vol. 2, p. 83.
[19] Minutes, H.2788.rr.
[20] John Wall Callcott, 'Plan of General Dictionary of Music', BL Add. MS 27693, fol. 5.

Empire, who had entered Parliament in 1774; Lord Brownlow, the lawyer and MP for Grantham; and the lawyer and future MP James Adams. It is significant that all these men were present or future politicians, enhancing the impression that the membership of the New Catch Club was an overspill of the original Catch Club. It also seems probable that the club acted as a kind of 'waiting room' for membership of the Catch Club; of this group all but Gibbon later achieved membership of the original club. For the meeting of the two clubs in 1776, Benjamin Cooke composed a new glee, *Welcome friends of harmony*. Such mutual exchanges between the two clubs took place annually until 1783, after which there is no further mention of the New Catch Club, and no other documentation relating to it has come to light. Callcott suggests that the club 'did not last probably more than four or five years'.[21]

In 1779 R. J. S. Stevens became involved with a club known as the Friendly Harmonists. Unusually, it met not at a public house, but at Anderton's Coffee House in Fleet Street. It appears to have been more of a private club, the members, all of whom were singers, meeting at 9 pm, when they partook of a cold supper before singing glees, catches, duets and songs. According to Stevens it was under the direction of Theodore Aylward (1730–1801), Professor of Music at Gresham College, and future organist and Master of the Choristers at St George's Chapel, Windsor. Himself a composer of glees and catches, Aylward was an enthusiast whom we will shortly also encounter as a founder member of the Glee Club. His name appears on the subscription lists of several glee and catch publications, including Benjamin Cooke's op. 5 and the ninth book of Samuel Webbe the elder's glees. Aylward directed proceedings from the piano, but this may have applied only to the songs and duets; Stevens gives no indication whether or not the glees and catches were accompanied. Among others he listed as members are: Edward Mulso, already encountered as a president of the Anacreontic Society; Howarth, a lawyer whose death in a boating accident was described by Stevens as a 'great loss to all Musical men, and an irreparable one to the Society of Friendly Harmonists'; the countertenor Dowding; James Blake, a bass who sung at the Handelian Society; George Pearce, probably the same person who had been at St Paul's as a boy chorister with Stevens; and several others, among whom were several friends of Stevens.[22] With the exception of Aylward, Mulso, Pearce, whose name is linked to the later and similarly named Harmonists Society,[23] and of course Stevens himself, none of the names associated with the society occur elsewhere in the annals of catch and glee culture, leading to the conclusion that it was more an intimate gathering of like musical minds than a formal club.

In addition to its meetings, described by Stevens as 'very pleasant', the society also held an annual dinner, to which each member was allowed to bring a guest. The Friendly Harmonists however proved to be short-lived, it being one of the many examples of clubs that disintegrated following what Stevens terms a 'ridiculous and nonsensical' dispute between Aylward (whose irascibility was noted by John Marsh on more than one occasion) and one Dinwoody, apparently one of four members attached to the Excise Office. By this, Stevens writes, 'we forfeited our right to our

---

[21] Ibid.
[22] Stevens, *Recollections*, pp. 32–3.
[23] See below p. 83.

title, for we were neither Friendly nor Harmonious'. The Excise members sided with Dinwoody and seceded, leaving the unfriendly Harmonists to 'at last expire very quietly' some time around 1780 or 1781.[24]

Of greater significance than the Friendly Harmonists is a club that has its genesis in a gathering that took place in December 1783. It consisted of a group of professional and amateur enthusiasts and was the first of a series of musical evenings held at the home in St Paul's Churchyard of Robert Smith, a gentleman dilettante who had been a boy chorister at St Paul's and was a member of the Academy of Ancient Music.[25] Among those involved in these meeting were three further gentlemen members of the Academy: John Roberts; James Heseltine; and Dr Thomas Bever. Bever, already encountered as a member of the Madrigal Society, is a particularly interesting example of the enthusiastic amateur collector. He was a magistrate of the Cinque Ports and fellow of All Soul's College, Oxford, and owned a large and rare collection of historic music, his name frequently turning up as a subscriber to editions of old music.[26] Bever's collection was placed at the disposal of the new meetings, which, after a dinner, performed motets, madrigals, glees, catches and canons. Both the interests of the assembly and this repertoire suggest that 'old' music played a large part in its proceedings.

For four years this company continued to meet informally in each other's homes, but in 1787 decided to form itself into a society styled the Glee Club, involving both amateur and professional members.[27] The inaugural meeting was held at the Newcastle Coffee House on Saturday 22 December 1787. From the outset the constitution of the membership was very different from that of the Catch Club or the Anacreontic Society, the organisation relying not on aristocratic or political support, but that of gentlemen enthusiasts and professional musicians who were also eligible to serve as officers of the club. As would be expected, the names of those who originally attended Robert Smith's informal meetings are to be found among the founder members.[28] Smith himself was named 'Father of the Club', in addition to serving as its first treasurer and steward, while the names of Bever, Heseltine, and Roberts are also included. Thomas Dupuis (1733–96), the organist of the Chapel Royal, was named as conductor, with Callcott as his deputy, the latter also being appointed secretary. The first president is not identified in the listing, but he was in fact Samuel Arnold, who thus achieved that to which, according to R. J. S. Stevens, he had unsuccessfully aspired at the Anacreontic Society. The vice-president was one of the gentlemen members, Charles Wright, perhaps the same Mr Wright who subscribed to Samuel Webbe the elder's ninth book of catches and glees. The indefatigable Webbe was also involved with the new club, becoming its librarian, a post he retained along with his later secretaryship of the Catch Club until his death in 1816. In 1796 he also succeeded Dupuis as conductor. Among other by now familiar names who initially joined as subscribing members we find those of Luffman

---

[24] Stevens, *Recollections*, pp. 32–3.
[25] Details from 'The Glee Club Register', which appears as an appendix to *The First Volume of Poetry […] compiled by Richard Clark, One of the Gentlemen of His Majesty's Chapels Royal* (London, 1824).
[26] Weber, *Musical Classics*, p. 162.
[27] 'The Glee Club Register'.
[28] Details from 'The Glee Club Register'.

Atterbury, already identified as a leading composer of catches and glees and as a privileged member of the Catch Club; Theodore Aylward, whose membership lasted under a year; and Thomas Linley senior.

The earliest extant list of rules and membership dates from 1797, the rules including twenty-three resolutions signed by the secretary, the tenor John Page, and dated 2 December 1797.[29] In a number of respects these resolutions follow rules similar to those of the Catch Club. There were to be twelve meetings in a winter season, commencing in November, and held on Saturdays. Dinner was served at four, before which any business was transacted with 'proper Notice inserted in the Summons'. A committee of eleven officers conducted the society's business, five (the president, vice-president, treasurer, conductor, and the secretary) being permanent appointees. The remainder were elected from the membership on an annual basis. Membership was limited to thirty (a rule introduced in April 1788 following the influx of a number of new members during the first few months of that year), the figure at which it stood in 1797. As vacancies occurred, a ballot of the existing membership elected new applicants by the blackballing scheme, two black balls excluding the potential member. At 5 guineas, a figure seldom exceeded by the Catch Club, the membership fee was comparatively high. In addition new members were charged an admission fee of 3 guineas that was put into a general fund for music and other expenses. In contrast to many clubs, penalties, already noted as a major source of income for the Catch Club,[30] are not mentioned either in the 1797 resolutions or those dating from 1824. This is not, however, to say that such penalties were not levied, and it is difficult to see how some of the rules could have been enforced without some kind of penal code. It is not clear whether the membership included the cost of dinner, but it was included for guests, who might be introduced by members up to a maximum of four times in a season at a cost of 15s. for each meeting. In February 1801 John Marsh declined an invitation to visit the club on the grounds that it was 'rather too much to pay for dinner'.[31] As with the Catch Club and the Anacreontic Society, dinner was always immediately followed by the singing of the canon *Non nobis Domine*. From 1790, the Glee Club also had its own official 'anthem', *Glorious Apollo*, written for the club by Samuel Webbe the elder and subsequently performed as the opening glee at all meetings. Notwithstanding the fact that it is considered by most commentators to be one of Webbe's less successful glees, it also became widely popular on the concert platform.[32]

In common with the Catch Club, the Glee Club instituted an honorary membership list of professional performers to assist with the singing, such members being 'in all respects, upon an equality with the Subscribing Members'.[33] Their numbers were also restricted, in this instance to thirteen, the number listed in 1797. Early honorary members included a number of names familiar from the Catch Club.

---

[29] 'Glee Club, Crown and Anchor Tavern, Strand. Eleventh Subscription for 1797'. BL 1879. cc. 13. (58).
[30] See above Table 3, p. 62.
[31] Marsh, *Journals*, p. 730.
[32] See Chapter 6.
[33] 'Glee Club Register', Resolutions for the Formation of the Glee Club, Rule VII.

Among them were Page; Danby;[34] John Dyne, an alto appointed a Gentleman of the Chapel Royal in 1772, the year in which he also became an honorary member of the Catch Club; John Hindle, a lay vicar at Westminster and an honorary member of the Catch Club since 1783; and two leading London singers, the bass James Bartleman and the tenor Samuel Harrison,[35] both of whom were honorary members of the Catch Club and would also become members of the Concentores Society, which is discussed below.

In addition the president, conductor, and deputy conductor were permitted to introduce professional honorary guests to any meeting. The appointment of a 'conductor' and his deputy is highly unusual and it is possible that the word was not used here in the modern sense, but to describe an accompanist. While there are no surviving records of the repertoire performed by the Glee Club, if the description is taken in the literal sense it would suggest that the practice of performing the old polyphonic repertoire continued after the formal institution of the club, the performance of catches and glees hardly being in need of the services of a conductor. There is no evidence that instrumental music was performed at the club during the eighteenth century.

In addition to the subscribing and honorary membership, the club also admitted a small number of 'perpetual visitors', who like honorary members enjoyed the same privileges as full members, with the exception that they were not allowed to vote at membership elections. In 1797 there were four such 'perpetual visitors', including the publisher Francis Broderip, who had resigned as a subscribing member in 1795; William Linley; and the alto Charles Knyvett.

While the honorary members of the Glee Club continued to enjoy dual professional membership with the Catch Club over the following years, there were remarkably few subscribing members who joined both organisations. Only three have been identified, all politicians. Gerard Noel Edwards, elected a member of the Catch Club in 1786 and of the Glee Club in 1795, was a Tory MP for Maidstone and later Rutland, who tried to form a third party independent of both William Pitt and Charles James Fox. His interest in the catch and glee repertoire extended to subscribing to Benjamin Cooke's opus 5. Charles Shaw Lefevre (elected in 1799 and 1800 respectively) was a barrister who later became Tory MP for Newport, Isle of Wight, while George Hardinge (1790 and 1793) was a poet and another Tory who sat for Old Sarum from 1784 to 1802. Such a small overlap, taken in combination with the strong parallel membership with the Academy of Ancient Music, offers grounds for the tentative suggestion that the ethos of the Glee Club was quite different to that of the Catch Club, with arguably a greater number of members whose prime interest was musical rather than social.

The new club rapidly became successful. By May 1788 nineteen more subscribing members and four new honorary members are recorded as having joined. Among the former one notes the names of Edmund Ayrton, a Gentleman of the Chapel Royal and royal lutenist, and Broderip, while the intake of honorary members included the composer Robert Cooke, the son of Benjamin, the alto Israel Gore, a member of

---

[34] See above p. 70.
[35] Harrison, with Charles Knyvett, also founded the Vocal Concerts. See Chapter 6.

both the Chapel Royal and St Paul's Cathedral choirs, and the leading bass John Sale, who was appointed deputy conductor in 1795 and in 1812 succeeded Webbe as conductor. It was doubtless this influx that persuaded the committee that its room at the Newcastle Coffee House was insufficient for its needs; as early as 8 March, less than three months after its foundation, the Glee Club removed to a more spacious room at the Freemasons' Tavern in Great Queen Street, part of a site today occupied by the Connaught Rooms. By October of the same year renovation to the Freemasons' necessitated a further move, this time to the Crown and Anchor Tavern. In February 1790, the club moved back to the Freemasons', but eighteen months later returned to the newly rebuilt Crown and Anchor, 'there being no room at the Freemasons' so convenient for their accommodation', at the same time 'acknowledging the excellent treatment and great attention they had received from Messrs. Richold and Mollard', presumably the landlords of the Freemasons' Tavern.[36] Also in 1790, a Ladies' dinner was instituted, being held at the end of the season in May, another development that parallels the Catch Club.[37] Later notable eighteenth-century honorary members include: Charles Knyvett (from 1789); the bass Thomas Bellamy (from 1790); Jacob Cubit Pring, one of the leading 'second generation' glee composers (from 1796); the tenor and ballad composer Charles Dignum (from 1797); and two other prominent 'second generation' glee composers, James Horsfall (from 1798), and Reginald Spofforth (from 1799).

Contemporary accounts of the Glee Club are regrettably few, but we can again call on R. J. S. Stevens for anecdotes of a couple of visits he made, although remembering that Samuel Arnold was no friend of Stevens', the first is likely to be somewhat coloured. In the spring of 1797 Stevens was invited to visit the club by Robert Smith, whom he would have known as a fellow chorister at St Paul's. 'Dr. Arnold', recalls Stevens, 'was the President: the room was very full. After a number of glees had been performed, some of them very indifferently; I sent my Compliments to the Doctor, saying, that I had two Manuscript glees in my pocket and should be happy to exhibit them whenever it was convenient for him to call upon me, as I had friends with me who could perform them.'[38] Stevens waited with mounting impatience until 7:30, when he called a waiter to ask if his message had been delivered to Arnold. On being informed that it had, Stevens took offence and walked out of the club. He met with rather more success on a further visit in March of the following year, when he was invited by the Revd Matthew Raine, a member since January 1794. Although Arnold was again in the chair, Stevens notes 'that this was a very different kind of attention from what we experienced at the Glee Club last year. My friend Samuel Webbe [...] was particularly kind to me, and assisted me very much with his opinion and advice in what I had to exhibit; and informed me which of the Performers would be proper to call upon to sing with us.'[39] Stevens had taken with him an alto by the name of Carter,[40] with whom and other unspecified singers

---

[36] 'Glee Club Register'.
[37] See above p. 57.
[38] Stevens, *Recollections*, pp. 107–8.
[39] Stevens, *Recollections*, p. 109.
[40] The identity of Carter is not clear. The J. Carter listed in Doane's *A Musical Directory* (1794) was a bass, whereas Stevens earlier lists this one as an alto. It was not unknown however for a singer to

two of Stevens' glees were sung. The method of choosing performers was thus similar to that exercised by the Catch Club, with the introducer naming the singers he wished to participate in the singing of the selected work.

The Glee Club would continue in existence until 1857, when it was dissolved and its library disposed of. In the nineteenth century some instrumental works were performed, Samuel Wesley, an honorary member from 1816, being recorded as playing Bach fugues at meetings in addition to playing keyboard extemporisations based on glees.[41]

To William Parke we owe knowledge of the existence of another club that confusingly also called itself the Glee Club. Founded in 1793, it appears to have been a small and informal meeting – Parke calls it 'select' – held on Sunday evenings at the Garrick's Head Coffee House. Among those who attended Parke lists William Shield (1748–1829), the house composer at Covent Garden and the composer of a number of glees for stage works;[42] Johnstone, who may be the Covent Garden tenor listed by Doane;[43] the bass theatre singer Charles Bannister; the tenor Charles Incledon;[44] C. Ashley;[45] and Parke himself. The connection between these men was friendship formed through the theatre. As Roger Fiske has noted, Parke, Incledon, and Shield at one time shared lodgings,[46] while all those named were connected with either Covent Garden or Drury Lane, thus forming a link between the theatre and the glee that is further explored in Chapter 6. At the club, Parke relates, 'we amused ourselves by singing the works of the old and modern masters, after which we sat down to supper, and passed an agreeable hour or two'. He also states that several glees, probably written by Shield, were composed for the club, 'which were afterwards given to the public and experienced a flattering reception'.[47]

A club apparently founded as a direct result of the success of the original Glee Club was known as the Graduates Meeting. As the name suggests, this was an elite and strictly professional body consisting of members who had graduated as doctor or bachelor of music at Oxford or Cambridge. Its formation was described by Callcott:

> Wm Parsons Esq. Master of the King's Band & T. S. Dupuis Esq. organist & composer to His Majesty having taken the accumulated degree of Bachelor & Doctor of Music June 1790, the small number of musical graduates was honourably increased. – At that time Drs Arnold, Ayrton, Burney & Cooke

---

encompass both ranges. Another possible candidate is the Irish composer and singer Thomas Carter (1769–1800), who is not be confused with Thomas Carter (1735–1804), his better-known compatriot and the composer of the immensely successful *The Rival Candidates* (1775).

[41] John Parry, 'The Glee Club', *Musical World*, 1 March 1838. I am grateful to Philip Olleson for providing this information.

[42] The existence of a second Glee Club has led to frequent confusion. The article on Shield in the revised *New Grove* states that he 'helped found the Glee Club', whereas Shield never had a connection with *the* Glee Club. See Chapter 6 for a discussion of Shield's operatic glees.

[43] Doane, *A Musical Directory*.

[44] Doane lists him as an alto, a reflection of a remarkable range that included a falsetto that was 'rich, sweet and brilliant'. Quoted in Roger Fiske, *Theatre Music*, p. 271.

[45] Either Charles or Charles Jane Ashley, both members of a prominent family of London musicians.

[46] Fiske, *Theatre Music*, p. 629. Doane gives different addresses for the three in 1794.

[47] Parke, *Musical Memoirs*, vol. 1, p. 175.

with Messrs Bellamy, Callcott, Guise & Andion were the only graduates resident near London.[48]

At an accidental visit paid to J. Beard Esq. at Hampton in August 1790 by Dr Arnold, Dr Dupuis, Messrs Callcott & Hudson the conversation happened to turn on the late establishment of the Glee Club and the rapid success which an institution barely three years old had found the number of candidates exceeding that of the thirty members.

Dr Dupuis who had been a principal in the formation of the Glee Club & who had given to the Society the name it now bears,[49] suggested the idea that the Musical Graduates were sufficiently numerous to constitute a select party & which might be held alternately at the house of each member at equal distances of time throughout the year.[50]

The idea was 'gladly received' and a preliminary meeting held at Dupuis' home at the beginning of November. Callcott relates that it was attended by all the graduates, 'with the exception of Benjamin Cooke, who having lost the situation he held for many years at the Academy of Ancient Music by the appointment of Dr Arnold, felt himself so much dissatisfied that he declined being considered as a member'.[51] However, Callcott continues,

the high respectability of his [Cooke's] character & the great opinion generally entertained by his ability made his absence no small cause of regret to several members who thought it a most desirable object that "Brethren should be well together in unity" & to the acute observation of Sir W. P. and his extensive knowledge of the world we owe the subsequent attendance of Dr Cooke to who invitations were regularly sent & whose irritated passions were cooled by the respect continually shown.[52]

On 5 January a second meeting was held at the home of Richard Guise, while subsequent gatherings are recorded by Callcott as having taken place at the homes of Edmund Ayrton, the Master of the Children at the Chapel Royal (on 16 February); Charles Burney's lodgings at Chelsea (11 May); and the Shepherds Bush home of William Parsons (22 June). On 8 July there was a distinguished accession to the number of Graduates. On that day Joseph Haydn, who had arrived in London in January, had a doctorate conferred on him by Oxford University, an honour that Charles Burney had been instrumental in obtaining. Haydn was naturally invited to the next meeting, held at Callcott's home at Kensington Gravel Pits on 3 August. Much to Callcott's disappointment, Haydn was unable to attend and it was 28

---

[48] This was Richard Guise, B. Mus., a tenor who was a member of the choirs of the Chapel Royal and St Paul's. He was Master of the Boys at Westminster Abbey. Andion has not been identified and does not seem to have become a member of the Graduates Meeting.

[49] It is not clear whether Callcott is here referring to the Glee Club or the Graduates Meeting. If the former, it seems unlikely since Dupuis was not one of the principal founders of the Glee Club.

[50] Callcott, 'Plan', BL Add. MS 27693 (fol. 6).

[51] The events surrounding Cooke's replacement are related in Andrew Pink, 'Benjamin Cooke (1734–93)'. MA. diss. (Anglia Polytechnic University, 2000), Part I, p. 40.

[52] Callcott, 'Plan', BL Add. MS 27693 (fol. 6). Sir W. P. is Sir William Parsons, a privileged member of the Catch Club since 1785. He doubtless knew Cooke well, since he had served under Cooke as a chorister of Westminster Abbey.

October before he finally made an appearance at a meeting held at Thomas Dupuis' house at Grosvenor Gate, 'the presence of the new member being highly gratifying to all'.[53] The following term brought three new members and on 14 December a meeting at Benjamin Cooke's home was attended by fourteen (including Haydn), 'the most numerous party... that ever has yet been invited'.[54] Of these no less than nine were at one time or another members of the original Glee Club, a figure that underlines the strong link between the organisations. While no records of the repertoire performed by the Graduates Society are extant, it must be assumed to have been similar to that of the organisation it sought to emulate. Before he left England, Haydn was able to repay the hospitality of the members of the society by hosting his own dinner for them. Because his own quarters were too small, it was held at Parsloe's Coffee House in St James Street on 20 June 1792, an occasion on which Johann Peter Salomon, the impresario who had brought Haydn to England, was admitted 'partly as the intimate friend of Dr. Haydn, partly as in interpreter, Dr. Haydn having not made sufficient progress in the English tongue'.[55] This is the last recorded meeting of the Graduates Society and there are no further records to suggest how long it existed.

By the end of the 1780s the glee had become firmly established among amateur musicians, its entry into the domestic sphere of music long established.[56] Its fashionable status also created a desire among amateurs to emulate more professionally constituted clubs. In London this led to the foundation of a club named the Harmonists Society. According to his own account, the principal mover behind the new club was R. J. S. Stevens, who at the start of 1794 was approached by 'a few Musical Amateurs' who expressed to him a desire to have an occasional meeting at which they would 'dine together and have vocal music afterwards'.[57] Stevens lists his co-founders of the Harmonists Society as his one-time apprentice and Drury Lane oboist George Arnull, George Pearce, his old acquaintance from the Friendly Harmonists, and Robert Tomkins, whom Stevens later describes as 'a very old acquaintance' and the possessor of 'one of the best Ears to Music that I ever knew...'[58] The first meeting of the society was held on 24 January 1794 at Will's Coffee House in Cornhill,[59] but this venue being found to have insufficient accommodation, meetings were moved to the New London Tavern in Cheapside.

Initially the society consisted of twenty-four members, the number increasing to thirty-two by April 1796 and forty by October 1798. Originally twelve meetings a year were held, but by 1798, in inverse proportion to the growth in membership, this had been reduced to six. Concerts were directed from the keyboard by Stevens, who was assisted by the young composer Thomas Attwood, best remembered today as a pupil and friend of Mozart. Stevens also provided the Harmonists with their 'house'

---

[53] Callcott, 'Plan', BL Add. MS 27693, fol. 6.
[54] Ibid.
[55] Ibid.
[56] See Chapter 6.
[57] Stevens, *Reminiscences*, pp. 95–6.
[58] Stevens, *Reminiscences*, p. 209.
[59] The second London coffee house to bear this name. The first, situated in Bow Street, dates from the 17th century and was patronised by Dryden. It closed around the middle of the 18th century.

glee, *Sober lay and mirthful glee*, and acted as librarian. In common with many societies, the Harmonists introduced an annual Ladies' Concert, first given on 10 April 1795, an occasion on which five of Stevens' own manuscript glees were performed. The inclusion of *O strike the harp*, which has upper parts designed for sopranos, leads Mark Argent to suggest that women singers may have taken part at these ladies' nights, for which Stevens always held special rehearsals.[60] In 1806 the opening meeting of the society's season was attended as a visitor by Samuel Wesley, who Stevens relates 'after dinner, being perfectly collected, and not in the least flushed with liquor (his usual practice at this time of his life), he played on the Piano Forte, some of the most astonishing and ingenious Combinations of *Harmony*, that I ever heard. By way of Finale, *to his extemporary*, he took the burthen of, *O strike the harp*, and made as simple and pleasing a movement on its subject, that we were all delighted.'[61] The format of six concerts with an additional ladies' night at the New London appears to have continued until 1808, when a move was made to the City of London Tavern following a disagreement with Lewis, the landlord of the New London, who had apparently received complaints about his wine and retorted that the 'members of the Society, did not know good wine, when they had it before them'. Stevens pithily noted against his account of this episode, 'Not a little impertinent'.[62] He is our sole source of information on the Harmonists Society, remaining its conductor until 1825, when he resigned both the directorship and his membership. By that time the society had moved again, this time to the Albion Tavern in Aldersgate Street.[63]

Stevens' close involvement with the Harmonists Society doubtless formed at least part of the reason why he declined a direct invitation to become a member of the last of the London societies to concern us in this chapter. Formed in June 1798, the inspiration for the Concentores Society (or Sodales Concentores, as its members called it following the suggestion of Samuel Webbe the elder) was a desire among leading professional musicians to meet, in the words of Callcott, one of its founder members, 'for their own amusement to sing madrigals, glees, canons, catches &c.'[64] In fact the Society had a rather more serious purpose than Callcott's words suggest, since its objective was not only to perform part songs, but also to inspire new compositions of a similar kind, composer presidents being expected to produce new compositions for performance during the course of evenings on which they officiated. In addition, the first rule of the Society laid down that every member must be capable of 'writing correct counterpoint', or at least be able to take part 'in any composition offered to him'.[65] The precepts of the Concentores thus accorded more closely with those of the original Academy of Vocal Music than with catch clubs formed with the prime objective of providing members with conviviality and sociability. There are no further clues as to the objectives of the new society, but it is

---

[60] Stevens, *Reminiscences*, p. 98. n. 36.
[61] Stevens, *Reminiscences*, p. 150. This of course parallels Wesley's already noted extemporisations at the Glee Club.
[62] Stevens, *Reminiscences*, p. 156.
[63] Clark, *First Volume of Poetry*, Preface.
[64] Callcott, 'Plan', BL Add MS. 27693 (fol. 5).
[65] 'Papers of the Concentores Society, Rules and Minutes', Guildhall Library, London, MS 8593c. Unless otherwise stated all references to the Society are taken from this source.

tempting to speculate that it may have represented some kind of attempt to revert to the 'pure' unaccompanied performance of the glee repertoire after a decade during which it had been transformed on the concert platform by the addition of instrumental accompaniments.

The first meeting of the Concentores took place at the Buffalo Tavern in Bloomsbury on 9 June 1798. It was attended by six men, including in addition to Callcott, the alto James Horsfall, who took the president's chair at the first meeting; Robert Cooke (1768–1814); Samuel Webbe the younger (1768–1843), Jacob Cubitt Pring (1771–99); and William Horsley (1774–1858). It was Horsley who may have been the moving spirit behind the Society, since he is named in the minutes as having formulated the rules. With the possible exception of Horsfall, whose dates are unknown, this group is notable for its youthfulness. Although his name has already become ubiquitous in this study, Callcott, the oldest, was still only thirty-one, while Pring and Horsley were still in their twenties. Such a founding membership might suggest some form of deliberate grouping by the younger generation of glee composers, but the invitation issued by the founding members to two of the most respected senior figures in the musical establishment to join the new organisation contradicts such an idea. As already noted, Stevens declined the offer, doubtless on the grounds of his other activities, although he attended as a guest on several occasions. Samuel Webbe the elder did however accept the invitation to join his son, soon becoming established as one of the pillars of the society. In addition to the new works expected from the presiding member, Callcott suggested at the first meeting that members be encouraged to write or bring a canon to be sung after dinner. This is the only mention in the Minutes of dinner, which as usual preceded the musical part of the proceedings.

Such an intimate society bound together by the familiarity of its members apparently found little need for the kind of complex rulebook we have noted other societies introducing. Membership was restricted to a maximum of twelve (a figure never attained during the period for which the Minutes are preserved) (Rule 1), with meetings being held monthly throughout the year. The president served on the customary rotational basis, a fine of half a guinea being imposed for not taking the chair on the allotted night (Rule 7). Other fines were modest, absentees having to contribute only 2s. 6d (Rule 6). Professional visitors were admitted, at least one visit being a precondition for application for subsequent membership. Those who did apply were expected to supply an entrance composition, or, in the case of non-composing members, be recommended by at least three members (Rule 10). From the outset, the Concentores took seriously the objective of collecting the music that was performed at its meetings, new works presented by the president of the evening remaining the possession of the society, which also undertook to publish periodically its own collections. The first, which included glees by Callcott, Robert Cooke, Horsley, Pring, Clement Smith, Reginald Spofforth, William Linley and both Webbes, appeared under the imprint of the London publisher Francis Broderip, who paid the society 20 guineas for the rights in the spring of 1801,[66] while a second was produced during the course of 1805.

---

[66] Minute of 18 February 1801.

By the time of the second meeting, on 23 June, the Concentores had gained the accession of three more members. Two, Reginald Spofforth (1769–1827) and William Linley, were composers who conformed to the essentially youthful character of the society, while the third was the bass James Bartleman, already encountered as an honorary member of both the Catch Club and the Glee Club. The programme for the evening, held under the presidency of Callcott, established a pattern that would remain unbroken for as long as existing records document. In addition to the canon, *Not, unto us, O lord*,[67] the members performed at least two other glees of Callcott's, *Go, gentle gale* and *Hark how the nightingale*, both of which may also have been manuscript works composed for the Concentores.[68] Typically, an evening's programme consisted of the after-dinner canon, and some six or seven glees, mostly the work of the president, sometimes supplemented by a couple of madrigals or a motet. It is notable (and doubtless a reflection of how times had moved) that there is no evidence that the singing of catches played any part in the society's agenda. But there appears little doubt that the encouragement to its members to provide new music resulted in the Concentores being responsible for additions to the glee and canon repertoire in numbers exceeded only by the Catch Club. In particular one notes several glees of Samuel Webbe the elder that appeared in none of his published volumes, among them *When Phoebus was amorous*, almost certainly written for the society and frequently performed there.

By the time of the July meeting, the Buffalo 'being shut up' (whether permanently or temporarily is not recorded), the society moved its meetings to the Queen's Head Tavern in Holborn, a large inn shown on Roque's famous 1738 map of London and the subsequent venue for meetings while records exist. The evidence of both the Minutes and the notes in Callcott's 'Plan' suggests that in addition to singing, members also engaged in learned discussion. At the fourth meeting, held on 14 August 1798, the minutes report 'some conversation arising on the subject of Musical Canons', the members 'differing in their ideas' on the topic. At the suggestion of Samuel Webbe senior, it was agreed that at the next meeting members should produce a written definition of 'canon', from which one should be chosen for the benefit of the society. At the following meeting, held on 19 September, Callcott, Cooke, Horsley, Pring, and Horsfall duly arrived with their definitions, which Webbe, who gives the distinct impression of having emerged as a 'father figure', was asked to adjudicate on in time for the next meeting. This he apparently did, although the author of his choice is not named. From Callcott we learn that at an unidentified meeting 'a cannon [*sic*] was particularly noticed for its uncommon modulation, from the major to the minor harmony',[69] again suggesting some form of debate on the works introduced and performed.

A notable feature of the Concentores was an unusual degree of stability in the membership. While the group lost members for such reasons as the untimely early death of Pring in 1799 (an event commemorated by William Horsley's glee *Softly drops*

---

[67] The familiar *Non nobis Domine*. Whether or not the use of English implies a new setting is unclear.
[68] Neither appears in Rubin's catalogue.
[69] Callcott states in his 'Plan' that the meeting was 'the first of the season' and that it was held on a Thursday, also noting that the presidency of the next meeting would be held by Bartleman. Such details accord with no minuted meeting.

the pensive tear), the removal to Liverpool of Samuel Webbe the younger,[70] and William Linley's departure for India in 1801, all six remaining members who had been present at the first musical evening of the society on 23 June 1798 are listed as having attended the meeting on 4 July 1805, the last to be recorded in the Minute Book. During the course of those seven years the membership was enhanced by two more notable London singers, Samuel Harrison and Thomas Greatorex, while another promising young composer, Michael Rock, was also admitted. The rigid rule of admitting only practising composers and singers was tested as early as January 1799, when John Spencer, who would have been known to a number of the Concentores from his membership of the Glee Club, was refused on the grounds 'that the Society should be confined to professional men'. The Minutes show that from November 1798 the society also welcomed a number of guests, among them such figures as William Knyvett and Samuel Wesley, whose attendance on 27 November 1800 was marked by the performance of two of his glees. Although the Minutes are no longer recorded after July 1805, the Concentores Sodales appears to have been active until around 1812, when it was discontinued following a period of decline. Five years later it was revived at the instigation of a group including such former members as Horsley, Spofforth and William Linley, strengthening further the professional qualification by allowing as members only composers capable of writing vocal compositions in at least four parts. In this form the society remained in existence until 1847, when it was finally disbanded.

---

[70] The date of 'around 1798' usually given for the younger Samuel Webbe's move to Liverpool seems likely to be too early given his involvement with the Concentores at this time.

Chapter 5
Provincial Catch and Glee Clubs

The increasing urbanisation of England during the course of the eighteenth century represents one of the most important defining characteristics of the period. Just how dramatic the change that took place may be illustrated by a single statistic. In 1700 it is estimated that around 7.5% of the population lived in provincial urban centres, a proportion that rose to some 20% over the next century.[1] Along with the growth in both the number and size of towns, the period also witnessed a significant parallel expansion of the establishment of a social structure that bound such communities together. Assemblies, clubs, lending libraries, theatres and public concerts may be counted among the numerous activities that contributed to the creation of modern civic unity. For the greater part such institutionalisation followed a predominantly middle-income course, expanding access to cultural pursuits that had previously been the preserve of the wealthy, while still leaving many educational and leisure pursuits falling beyond the financial means of the less well off.[2]

Roy Porter has drawn attention to the manner in which London fashions and institutions were taken as models by provincial towns,[3] so it is hardly surprising to find that following the establishment and widespread popularity of the aristocratic Catch Club and its emulators, the following decades witnessed the emergence of catch clubs in many cities and towns throughout Britain. Indeed, it is even possible that the earliest catch clubs may have been located in the provinces, their presence in Oxford already noted at the end of Chapter 2. Elizabeth Chevill has cited the existence of a music society meeting at the Mermaid in Carfax as early as the last decades of the seventeenth century.[4] Boasting some forty members, including James Brydges, later Duke of Chandos, the club met between 5 and 10 pm on the last Thursday of each month. Its organisation followed the pattern adopted by most clubs, the membership taking it in turns to act as steward whose responsibilities included collecting a shilling admission charge and maintaining quiet during performances. A significant feature was the large number of clergymen who were members, establishing a precedent found in many provincial catch clubs, particularly, if predictably, those located in cathedral cities. Chevill's research into musical clubs in Exeter, Hereford, Lichfield, Salisbury and York revealed no organisation that could be specifically identified as a catch club during the period covered (1700–60),

---

[1] Peter Borsay, Introduction, p. 5 in Borsay, ed., *The Eighteenth Century Town: A Reader in English Urban History 1688–1820* (London, 1990).
[2] Brewer, *Pleasures*, is an outstanding general survey of the spread of cultural activity in eighteenth-century England. See also T. C. W. Blanning, *The Culture of Power and the Power of Culture: Old Regime Europe 1660–1789* (Oxford, 2002) for an account of how the broadening of cultural parameters led to popular critical opinion becoming an arbiter of taste.
[3] Roy Porter, 'Science, provincial culture and public opinion in Enlightenment England', p. 252 in Borsay, ed. *The Eighteenth-Century Town*.
[4] Elizabeth Jane Chevill, 'Music Societies in Musical Life in Old Foundation Cathedral Cities 1700–1760' (Ph.D diss., University of London, 1993), p. 5.

although she notes that the singing of catches not infrequently brought an evening's entertainment to a convivial and probably rowdy close.

Further, if indirect evidence that catch singing was practised in the provinces around the time of the establishment of the Catch Club comes from a publication that appeared in Liverpool in 1763. Thomas Hales' *Social Harmony* is a substantial publication that in addition to including Masonic songs also incorporated a large number of part songs and catches ranging from two to five parts, a number of which subsequently appeared in glee collections.

For clues in the hunt for evidence of catch singing activity in the provinces we can also return to *The Essex Harmony*, from which John Arnold's 1769 preface was quoted at the beginning of my previous chapter. In addition to the catch clubs that Arnold states had been established in 'both Town and Country', he goes on to inform his readers that catches and other part-songs are 'sung by many Country Choirs &c. and in some places are given gratis, by Gentlemen, a Silver Cup, &c to be sung for by Country Choirs, on Holidays at some Inn, or Publick House; and in many places, Publicans themselves have put up Gold Rings &c. to be sung for in like manner'. Competitions such as those noted by Arnold also awarded cash prizes, as is clear from the singing contests held at local Oxfordshire inns (and doubtless elsewhere) during the 1770s. One such event held at the Crown Inn in Thame at the end of May 1775 (Whit Week) accords in almost exact detail to Arnold's description. The prize, a silver cup valued at £4, was offered by the landlord, George Stevens for a competition between sides who were each to sing three songs in two or three parts in addition to a catch or a glee. Competing teams were expected to provide an umpire 'to decide disputes'. Those intending to compete were required to hand in their names by midday and dine at the inn prior to the contest.[5]

Arnold also takes up Hayes' didactic theme,[6] extending it to the view that the cultivation of singing in country areas would serve a social purpose: 'it would not only prevent the many Accidents, Mischiefs, and other bad consequences, generally attending those Diversions of Heroism, Cudgeling, Football Playing &c. but would be a means of encouraging the practice of one of the greatest of Sciences'. 'What', he continues, 'can be more agreeable or commendable for Country Choirs, than to meet [...] and thereby entertain themselves and Friends, with such harmonious and inoffensive Mirth; which may not only introduce Peace and Tranquillity in a Neighbourhood, but the Practiceing of Part-Songs and Catches, which will be a means of greatly improving several Country choirs in their Knowledge of Musick.'

Both Hayes and Arnold had clearly alluded to the precedence of Oxford in the formation of provincial clubs. Notwithstanding Arnold's reportage of the widespread formation of clubs, no evidence of other provincial catch clubs being formed during the 1760s has to date emerged.[7] However, the next three decades witnessed a major expansion of catch club culture, both in London and the provinces, where the existence of clubs in historic urban centres such as Canterbury; Salisbury; Chichester; York; Lincoln; Norwich; Lichfield and Bristol; spa cities like Bath; and the newer,

---

[5] *Jackson's Oxford Journal* (27 May 1775).
[6] See above p. 30.
[7] My own research in this area has concentrated on detailed enquiry through city and county record offices.

fast-growing industrial conurbations of Nottingham, Liverpool and Manchester has been established. There can be small doubt others await discovery. One of the particular difficulties of uncovering detailed information on the organisation and activities of clubs is the lack of newspaper advertising and reporting. Unlike concert promoters, who obviously needed to make the public aware of their activities, the organisers of private clubs rarely needed to advertise their regular activities in the press. We are therefore largely reliant on a few extant records and personal observations. The most comprehensive records to have survived are those of the Canterbury Catch Club and the Bath Harmonic Society, and there is also a useful account of the Bristol Catch Club.[8] In addition a set of Rules exists for the Lichfield Cecilian Society (founded in 1772), although the document on which they are preserved is damaged and in part illegible.[9] For personal accounts of the activities of provincial catch clubs, we are hugely indebted to the indefatigable John Marsh, who was not only a member of clubs in Salisbury, Canterbury and Chichester (which he founded in 1787), but also recorded in his diaries anecdotal comments on catch clubs in Bath and Nottingham. It is therefore the clubs in Bath, Canterbury (established in 1779), Salisbury (before 1776), Chichester and Bristol (by 1774) that are the principal source for this chapter.

The inspiration for the formation of provincial catch clubs was, as already noted, almost certainly the example of the Catch Club, and the part it played in elevating the glee to a popular indigenous form. We have already seen how the clubs in Bristol and Chichester owned copies of Warren's annual anthologies, issued under the auspices of the Catch Club.[10] However, the provincial clubs could not (and did not) seek to emulate their grand London progenitor in certain major respects, most notably in terms of membership, structure and the participation of top-ranking professional singers. The Catch Club was a highly selective organisation that could afford, with the assistance of some of the best London singers, to adopt the purist stance of admitting only the performance of unaccompanied catches, glees and – particularly in its earlier days – canons. Provincial clubs necessarily took a more pragmatic line, invariably diversifying to include instrumental music and solo songs during the course of their evenings' entertainment. Details of instrumentalists exist for both the Canterbury and Bath clubs. Around 1785 the Canterbury club employed an orchestra of around 14 players (3 violins, 1 viola, 5 (!) 'basses', 3 oboes, and 2 horns).[11] When the club was re-formed in 1802 following dissolution, a quite separate orchestral committee of fourteen members was elected.[12] The catalogue of the Canterbury Catch Club collection, now housed in the library of Canterbury Cathedral, includes a substantial number of instrumental works, among them the 'complete' orchestral works of Handel and an extensive list of modern symphonies by such composers as Abel, J. C. Bach, and Haydn. John Marsh has left us with a

[8] Hooper, 'A Survey of Music in Bristol'.
[9] Lichfield Record Office, Add. MS. D127.
[10] See above, p. 65.
[11] Pencilled on the inside of vol. III of the Canterbury Catch Club collection, c. 1785. The full collection consists of nine original manuscript volumes of catches, glees, duets and songs. Vols 5, 6 and 9 are missing. Apparently commenced around 1785 (the year appended to Vols 1 & 3), entries in the same hand extend well into the 19th century. They are supplemented by later additions.
[12] 'Minutes of the Canterbury Catch Club', 1802. Canterbury Cathedral Library, CC/W7/1.

detailed account of the Canterbury Club that includes a description of the kind of programme he encountered when he first attended in November 1783:

> The plan of this club was as follows. About half past 6. an overture was played by the band (in a small orchestra railed off at one end of the room) after which follow'd a glee; then a quartetto, trio or concerto; after which follow'd another glee & then a catch, which constituted the first Act; the second of w'ch after a short cessation began with another overture, next to w'ch Mrs Goodban generally made her appearance & sung a song, after which another glee & a catch or chorus concluded the concert. The generality of the audience & performers however comonly remained 'till 11 or 12 o'clock, smoking their pipes (which they did all the time of the concert, except during Mrs Goodbans song, imediately preceding w'ch the company were always desired by the president to lay down their pipes) during which time single songs were sung, as called for by the president.[13]

Marsh's mention of the extremely unusual presence of a female singer at a catch club meeting calls for a brief digression on the subject of the place of women in clubs. As made clear in previous chapters, such institutions were normally exclusively the preserve of men. One exception in the provinces was general music societies, which are frequently difficult to distinguish from concert series and often admitted mixed audiences. Chevill, for instance, notes that women were somewhat controversially admitted to the New Musick Club in York as early as 1728, their presence causing one local observer to note that 'Filthy smoking, muddy Ale and Wine are now all forbid during Musick Time'.[14] The greater openness of musical societies constitutes a paradigmatic difference between them and the entire catch club culture, which was dependent upon the basic tenets of male conviviality – drinking, smoking, and male companionship. As we have seen, the risqué nature of many catches made them unsuitable for performance in front of 'polite', or mixed society. However, as we have seen women did have a restricted role within the broader parameters of catch club culture. The initiative of the Catch Club and other London clubs in introducing an annual Ladies' Night by the early 1770s was emulated in Canterbury, where Marsh informs us that he attended 'the annual Catch Club for <u>ladies</u> [Marsh's underlining] at Goodban's (of which there was always one as soon as the regular season was over)' in May 1785.[15] Rule XXVII of the Lichfield Cecilian Society states 'That the Lady-Patroness have a Ticket to the Concert on the Festival-Night [the celebration of St Cecilia's Day on or near 22 November] conveyed to her, with particular Compliments from the Stewards.'[16] Nevertheless, Marsh's stress implies that such events were sufficiently unusual to require special emphasis and there is no record of them being hosted in Salisbury, Chichester, Bath or, until 1810, in Bristol. Mrs Goodban's participation at the Canterbury club can almost certainly be attributed to the fact that she was the wife of the landlord of the Prince of Orange, the venue for its meetings.

---

[13] Marsh, *Journals*, p. 302.
[14] Chevill, 'Music Societies', p. 78.
[15] Marsh, *Journals*, p. 344.
[16] Lichfield, 'Rules'.

The fashionable status of Bath was probably responsible for its Harmonic Society following the lead of the Catch Club in appointing honorary professional members, both vocalists and instrumentalists. Four instrumentalists are appended to a list of club members dating from 1799, among them the cellist Alexander Herschel (the brother of the famous astronomer, William[17]) and one of the Mahon brothers (probably John), both of whom were eminent clarinettists. Article XI of the Rules of the society implies that this small number were used only for the purpose of accompanying vocal music at meetings, for which members were expected to be assembled 'before the Abbey clock strikes seven':

> The President shall be absolute during the Meeting, *consistent with the Rules and Orders of the Society*. On his taking the chair the MUSICAL PERFORMANCE shall commence, which shall consist of *Catches, Glees, Chorusses, Songs &c.* which shall continue until nine o'clock [...] a cold supper, at *Four Shillings* each (Port Wine and Sherry included) shall then be placed upon the table; before which the grace of *"Sodales Caenantes"* shall be sung, the whole Society standing up; and in like manner the Canon of *"Non nobis, Domine!"* shall be sung [...] Three Toasts only shall be given [...] after which such Catches, Glees, or Songs shall be sung as may be called for by the PRESIDENT or VICE-PRESIDENT. At eleven o'clock the bill shall be brought in, when the PRESIDENT shall quit the chair.[18]

The singing of grace and toasting was a common feature of formally constituted clubs, both musical and otherwise, though most would have found the Bath society's limitation to three distinctly on the parsimonious side.

Although detailed records are lacking, a collection of *Duets, Rotas* [rounds], *Canons and Glees* issued by the Bristol organist and composer Robert Broderip in 1795 and 'respectively inscribed To the Members of the Bristol Catch Club, and Cecilian Society' suggest that Bristol followed Bath in restricting its repertoire to vocal music. This impression is supported by a surviving Ladies' Night programme dating from March 1810, when only glees, catches, and songs were performed.[19] Bath and Bristol thus differ in this respect from Salisbury, Canterbury, Chichester, and Lichfield, where members were able to hear both vocal and instrumental music. As we have seen, in Canterbury the two were interspersed, while in Salisbury and Chichester the instrumental music preceded the singing of catches and glees, a format closer to that of the London Anacreontic Society.[20]

Whatever degree of incursion instrumental music did or did not make into club meetings, its role naturally remained secondary to the main objective of the entertainment – the singing of catches and glees supplemented by drinking and (in most instances) some form of supper. The singers who took part in these performances ranged from the eight professionals retained by the Bath club (three of whom also appeared in Bristol) to the near total dominance of vicars choral in clubs based in cathedral cities. In Norwich, the Harmonic Society, a catch club formed in

---

[17] William Herschel was also a composer, the author of the popular 'Echo' Catch.
[18] *A Selection of Favourite Catches, Glees, &c. as Sung at the Bath Harmonic Society with the Rules of the Society, and a List of Members. Second edition with considerable additions* (Bath, 1799).
[19] Hooper, 'Music in Bristol', p. 205.
[20] Marsh, *Journals*, p. 149 (Salisbury), p. 419 (Chichester).

the city in 1784, was established by singers from the cathedral,[21] while in Salisbury all four principal singers in the club – Joseph Corfe, John Goss, a Mr Barrett and Francis Wellman – were prominent members of the cathedral choir. Corfe, who was also a Gentleman of the Chapel Royal, played a major role in Salisbury's musical life over a long period, being appointed leader of the subscription concerts on the death of James Harris in 1780 and twelve years later succeeding his bitter rival Robert Parry as cathedral organist. During the period Marsh was there (1783–87), the Canterbury Catch Club could boast among its principal singers Israel Gore, a vicar choral who subsequently became a member of the St Paul's Cathedral choir and, like Corfe, a Gentleman of the Chapel Royal. Gore was also a privileged member of the Catch Club from 1785. In Chichester Marsh could also draw upon the services of four cathedral vicars choral, Moses Toghill, John Moore, Bartholomew Middleton, and Mr Webber. Toghill had what Marsh considered one of the finest countertenor voices he had ever heard, while on a visit to Chichester in 1781 the diarist Sylas Neville was much impressed by his 'most powerful & at the same time melodious bass voice',[22] (it was not unusual to sing both countertenor and bass). Webber was also a countertenor, considered by Marsh to be the possessor of a 'fine, clear voice'.[23] Another noted founding member of the Chichester Catch Club was Theodore Aylward, previously encountered as a founder member of the Glee Club and a member of the Academy of Ancient Music.

The participation of such men tempts the speculation that performance standards in the provinces were often fairly high, if hardly likely to have been on a level with those of the Catch Club and other leading London societies. Such a notion, however, must be tempered with the fact that this was a period during which it is widely recognised that the standard of singing in cathedrals was generally poor. Contemporary clues to the levels attained are scarce. With the exception of the comments quoted above on the Bath society, even that acute observer John Marsh rarely passed judgement on the quality of performance he heard other than to castigate the hapless Mrs Goodban of Canterbury for 'screaming' the top notes of Stephen Paxton's popular glee *How sweet, how fresh*, an observation that supports an impression that the best performances of catches and glees were generally achieved by adult male ensembles. Outside the confines of the clubs, William Gardiner recalled that during his boyhood (the 1780s) the church musicians of Sheepshead (Shepshed) in Leicestershire 'were in the habit of singing the best of our English glees, with a taste and expression rarely equalled in a country village'.[24] While assessment of general performance standards must therefore remain conjectural, it does seem entirely reasonable to propose that the expectation that both glees and catches should be performed with a degree of attention and refinement similar to that outlined by William Hayes in the 1760s remained unchanged.

The known repertoire of provincial clubs was to some extent predictably modelled on that of their grand London progenitor, and as previously noted in at least two instances, Bristol and Chichester, clubs owned the volumes produced

---

[21] Trevor Fawcett, *Music in Eighteenth-Century Norwich and Norfolk* (Norwich, 1979), p. 8.
[22] Basil Cozens-Hardy, ed., *The Diary of Sylas Neville* (London, 1950), p. 288.
[23] Marsh, *Journals*, p. 417.
[24] Gardiner, *Music and Friends*, vol. 1, p. 46.

annually by Edmund Warren under the auspices of the Catch Club.[25] The Bristol Catch club was additionally the co-dedicatee (with the city's Cecilian Society) of a more general collection including 20 catches and 19 glees compiled by the local composer and publisher Robert Broderip. Canterbury and Bath both produced their own collections, the former being the largest and most important manuscript collection in existence. Up until around 1820 over 1300 entries were made into it by the same hand, 62% of them glees and 32% catches, the remainder consisting of either solo songs or duets. The list of composers most frequently represented is predictable. Like the Warren Collection it is headed by Samuel Webbe the elder and Callcott (see Table 6), although the presence of John Clarke Whitfield (1770–1836) and John Stevenson (1761–1833) among the leaders reflects the later provenance of the collection.[26]

In the case of the Bath Harmonic Society, the proportion of catches and glees is even more heavily weighted in favour of the latter, no less than 77% of the contents of its *Selection* consisting of glees.[27] Such an imbalance runs directly counter to the contents of the Warren Collection, where near-equality of content is granted to the two forms. This is undoubtedly attributable to the later provenance of both the Canterbury and Bath collections; as we have already seen the glee progressively ousted its older companion for both musical and external reasons.

Table 6
Composer Representation in the Books of the Canterbury Catch Club

	No. of works	%
Samuel Webbe the Elder	131	9.8%
John Wall Callcott	80	6%
William Horsley	43	3.2%
John Danby	35	2.6%
John Clarke Whitfield	32	2.5%
William Hayes	27	2%
John Stevenson	26	2%

No uniform picture emerges of the attitude of provincial clubs to the more ribald catches. The Canterbury Collection certainly includes a number of such pieces, while as late as 1789 John Marsh records one Colonel Jones singing for his entry audition to the Chichester club a song 'the words of which were not more chaste than his

---

[25] In Bristol, a copy was owned by a prominent member, the surgeon Richard Smith-Hooper. 'Music in Bristol', p. 201. The Chichester Catch Club owned a copy shared with the subscription concerts, the gift of Thomas Steele, one of the city's MPs and himself a member of the Catch Club. Marsh, *Journals*, p. 526.
[26] It should be noted that the percentage figure in Table 6 includes 151 unattributed works, mostly catches.
[27] *Bath Selection*.

manner of singing them'.[28] Hooper suggests (without providing evidence) that the 'purposeful rearrangement of words to achieve a bawdy result was characteristic of the catches performed by the Bristol club'.[29] In contrast the genteel Bath club seems to have eschewed such rough manners, at least by the end of the century, Rule 1 of its constitution sternly stating that 'This Society is established for the PROMOTION OF HARMONY, in its general signification; in order to preserve which no POLITICAL DISCUSSION shall be suffered to take place, nor shall any INDECENT SONG or SENTIMENT be permitted to be sung or spoken on any account'.[30] As we shall later discover, harmony 'in its general signification' was more easily set in a rulebook than maintained in practice. The refinement of the Bath Harmonic Society may also have been responsible for the comments of the irascible Charles Dibdin, who visited a catch club in Bath (in all likelihood the Harmonic Society) in 1787 and found 'the fashionable gravity' of the proceedings 'beyond credibility'. 'That a meeting' fulminated Dibdin, 'professedly convivial should apparently be held without mirth, is a kind of existence without a soul – a mental death – but it may be reconciled by saying that it is a refinement on politeness.'[31]

Such decorum doubtless accounts at least in part for the unusually low proportion of catches found in the Bath Collection, a mere twenty-nine in a collection consisting of a total of 253 works. We also find Bath to be out on something of a limb when it comes to an analysis of composers represented in the overall repertoire. This is partly due to the number of locals featured in its collection, men like the medical doctor and amateur composer Henry Harington (1727–1816), who was also a glee and catch composer of national significance, and the violinist James Brooks (1760–1809), who between them were responsible for nearly a fifth of the contents.[32] Nonetheless, it is surprising to find Samuel Webbe the elder, the most popular of all glee composers, relegated from his customary first place to third, behind Harington and Callcott, in the Bath Collection. Perhaps the most striking aspect of the repertoire of the provincial clubs is its sheer diversity. Only forty-eight glees are common to the three sources covering the four clubs for which sufficient detail is available (Chichester and Bristol, as we have seen, used Warren). Further indication of the most popular glees sung in the provinces can be garnered from those mentioned by John Marsh, although these include concert in addition to catch club airings. They include works whose popularity endured throughout much of the nineteenth century: R. J. S. Stevens's Shakespearean settings *Sigh no more, ladies* and *Ye spotted snakes*, and Samuel Webbe's *You gave me your heart, Swiftly from the mountain's brow* and *When winds breath soft*. While it is risky to draw categorical assertions from the restricted body of evidence available, the conclusion that the repertoire performed in the provincial clubs was

---

[28] Marsh, *Journals*, p. 462.
[29] Hooper, 'Music in Bristol', p. 204.
[30] *Bath Selection*.
[31] Dibdin, *Musical Tour*, p. 24.
[32] The Harmonic Society of Cambridge went one step further, issuing two collections of *Glees and Rounds for three, four and five voices* (1796 and 1800) entirely composed by such members as Charles Hague, Richard Wheeler and William Dixon. The extensive list of subscribers on the title page of the earlier book includes such names as Samuel Arnold, Thomas Attwood, and R. J. S. Stevens, suggesting that although local the publications achieved widespread circulation.

drawn from a small number of canonic works supplemented by a huge and locally varied stock appears inescapable.

For an understanding of the proceedings and membership of provincial catch clubs, we are yet again much indebted to Marsh. Part of his vivid picture of the Canterbury Catch Club has been quoted above and it can be supplemented by his accounts of the clubs in Salisbury and Chichester. By the time Marsh arrived in Salisbury in October 1776, he found the club well established:

> The winter Catch Club at the Spread Eagle now beginning, I on the 15th. went there & played with Mr Woodyear the leader whose tone was so weak as to require the utmost support I co'd give him. - At this meeting there was always a concert from about ½ past 6 'till after 8. at w'ch time a large table was set out with loaves bricks, cheese & porter, after partaking of w'ch in rather a rough way, the company form'd a circle round the fire & catches & glees were perform'd by Mess'rs Corfe Goss Barrett & Wellman with now & then a song from some other member 'till 11. or 12 o'clock. – The subscription was 7/6s. per qu'tr w'ch paid for the room, fire, candles, bread, cheese & beer at supper pipes & tobacco (w'ch were never used 'till after supper) whatever else was drank being separately paid for by those that called for it. Besides subscribers however there were several professional performers who were admitted gratis & intitled to the same fare as the subscribers.[33]

When Marsh moved from Salisbury to an inherited estate in Kent in 1783 he again found a successful and well-patronised club in Canterbury, at which he made he his first appearance in November of that year:

> The price of admission to this club was only 6d. for w'ch besides the music an unlimited quantity of pipes & tobacco & beer was allow'd, in consequence of which many of the members, amongst the lower kinds of tradesmen etc. used by way of having a full pennyworth for their penny, to go at 6. and smoke away till 11. or 12. On account of this fumigation from 40. or 50. pipes (which was always enough to stifle a person at 1st. entering the room & was very disagreeable to the non smokers) there were 3. ventilators in the ceiling in order, in some degree to get rid of the smoke but the room was so low pitched & bad that notwithstanding this, it appear'd as if we were all in a fog there. – The terms of admission being so low it will naturally be wonder'd how the landlord co'd possibly help losing instead of profiting by it, but the fact was that every member of the Club (of whom there were 50 or 60) paid his 6d. whether he came or not & a great many were always absent (the club being on every Wednesday throughout the winter) besides which many that were present instead of drinking beer had spirits & water & particularly *gin punch* (w'ch Goodban was famous for making particularly palatable) w'ch were paid for extraordinarily.

Not surprisingly, comparison of the formats of the two clubs reveals common features. Both were held at inns, the traditional venue for male clubs during the eighteenth century. This ensured the essential ingredients of drink and social conviviality provided at a modest cost. The choice of inn in Canterbury and Salisbury was in part obviously dictated by the accommodation available, but also in both

[33] Marsh, *Journals*, p. 149.

instances by a landlord who actively participated in club life, both Goodban of the Prince of Orange and Gibbons of the Spread Eagle in Salisbury being violinists. Lichfield, where the society met at the King's Head until 1790, when it moved to the Swan Inn, was almost certainly unusual in expressly forbidding the landlord membership of the society.[34] In Bath and Bristol the clubs also met at an inn, in the instance of the former at the White Hart.[35] The Bristol Catch Club met at the Bush Tavern in Corn Street, where the landlord Jack Weeks was apparently a well-known local character, although it is not clear whether or not he was actively involved. The club founded by John Marsh in Chichester in November 1787 broke with this tradition in meeting at what had become known as the Old Concert Room in East Pallant, a venue that involved food and drink having to be brought in from outside:

> Having now fully establish'd the plan of the Concerts & set them going, the next thing I wish'd to do was to settle a plan for the winter Catch Club at the old Concert Room, in which the vicars & Mess'rs Aylward Webber Humphry etc. all coinciding, we met on Tuesday the 23d. in the even'g at the Room, where we had some oysters etc. & settled the plan as follows – to meet together for 12 nights on every other Friday at the old Concert Room (but so as not to interfere with Subscript'n Concert nights) & amuse ourselves with instrumental music from half past 6. 'till half past 8 at w'ch time we were to sit down to a supper consisting only of oysters & Welch rabbits [sic] (to be provided for us at 10d. per head by Mr Triggs, Serj't at Mace & keeper of the town gaol) & afterwards sing catches, glees etc. around the fire, whetting our whistles with punch, wine etc. as agreed by the members present. These members were however to be confin'd to such gent'n as were capable of either assisting in the instrumental part, or of joining in at least one catch or glee etc. who were to subscribe 7s/6d per quarter to defray the expence of the supper, fire candles & attendance, & forfeit 6d per time for nonattendance or being too late. – To assist in the instrumental part we engaged Mr Payne (at ½ a crown a time) & invited Mr Mitchell the schoolmaster, who played the tenor at the Concerts, Mr Bailey a flute player & his son who played the flute & violin (also amateur players at the Concert) to join us, who except when particularly invited to stay used to go away as soon as the concert before supper was over. – The plan being thus settled, Mr Walker was appointed steward for the 1st. night (Friday Nov'r 2d.) w'ch office was to be taken by each member in rotation for the night, who was to attend a quarter of an hour sooner than the other members to see the fire was lighted the books laid out & everything duly arrang'd.[36]

As is clear from the foregoing, Marsh, as a gentleman, had ideas that differed from the relative informality of the clubs he had known in Salisbury and Canterbury. The strict rules formulated are closer to London models than the more open atmosphere prevailing in Salisbury and, especially, Canterbury. Professional instrumentalists were still hired, but expected to leave after being given supper, itself

---

[34] Lichfield, 'Rules'. The directive was covered by Rule XVIII.
[35] A second catch club may have existed in Bath. In 1804 *A Selection of Catches, Glees etc.*, was published with a dedication to the 'Members of the Bath York-House Catch-Club'. There is of course also the possibility that the Harmonic Society had changed its name. York-House was the principal inn in Bath, rated as 'one of the largest and best inns in the kingdom' by Pierce Egan in his *Walks through Bath* (London, 1819).
[36] Marsh, *Journals*, p. 419.

a more ambitious affair than the bread, cheese and porter served at the Salisbury club. Additionally, Marsh's new club departed from provincial tradition in admitting only those capable of taking part in the singing, thus adding a qualification barrier that provided greater exclusivity than that pertaining in the other clubs under discussion. The use of fines to act as a deterrent against non-attendance or lateness was, as we have seen, a common rule among eighteenth-century clubs, although no such mechanism is recorded as having been in place in Salisbury. In Canterbury the reconstituted club of 1802 levied a small fine of 6d for non-attendance. Surprisingly, the more socially pretentious Bath Harmonic Society seems not to have levied such penalties, although Rule X imposed a heavy punitive fine of half a guinea on a president for not being in his chair at the correct hour. While Bath and Canterbury had a president at their meetings, Salisbury, Chichester, and Lichfield preferred a steward (or stewards), whose function was to manage rather than chair club nights.

Norwich, again following the lead of London, formed its own Anacreontic Society around 1794. It appears to have functioned along lines not dissimilar to those of its London namesake, as is clear from an early nineteenth-century account:

> All the vocal performers were amateurs, but the instrumental players were professors. There was a concert, a collation, and catches, glees, and songs were sung by many of the visitors after supper: no musical party in the place was ever so attractive; the subscription was one guinea and a half per annum, and six concerts were given during the winter months.[37]

Initially membership was restricted to one hundred, but, as in other instances, the popularity of such clubs was such that it became difficult to control numbers, which in Norwich were ultimately swelled by non-resident visitors to a figure of more than double the membership.

The degree of formality adopted by the clubs under discussion therefore varied considerably, and was largely dictated by the social status of the membership. Canterbury unquestionably comes closest to what we might term today a working men's club, with a large membership including 'the lower kind of tradesmen' paying a low nightly admission charge in order to drink cheap beer and smoke their pipes, the resultant fumigation apparently causing one member to own what he called his 'catch club coat', a smoke-stenched garment he reserved especially for his visits to the Prince of Orange.[38] It is not clear from Marsh's account of the club in 1783 whether or not a quarterly fee was levied, but from 1802 the revived club charged a joining fee of half a guinea to go towards the liquidation of debts incurred as a result of the purchase of assets (including an organ and other instruments) of the old club. The wide social mix at Canterbury was obviously maintained following the club's revival, Rule 12 declaring that 'no Articled Clerk or apprentice under the age of Twenty one Years can be admitted as a Member of the Club'.[39] At the opposite end of the scale fashionable Bath attempted to maintain something of the exclusivity of the original Catch Club, considering as candidates for membership only 'Noblemen, Gentlemen,

---

[37] Quoted in Fawcett, *Norwich*, p. 8 from J. Chambers *A General History of the County of Norfolk... (or) Norfolk Tour* (Norwich, 1829).
[38] Marsh, *Journals*, p. 396.
[39] Canterbury 'Minutes'.

and Professional Men, who reside in Bath or its Vicinity, or may occasionally visit it'.[40] As at the Catch Club, those who sought membership were balloted, at least nine members being necessary for an election conducted on the blackballing system. In Bath a ratio of one black ball to four white resulted in rejection.[41] Non-performing applicants in Lichfield also had to face a ballot.[42] Membership numbers and the demand for membership apparently maintained a healthy level. In Bath the list of members in 1799 runs to no fewer than 276 names,[43] while the large attendance noted by Marsh in Canterbury was obviously replicated in Salisbury, as he makes clear in an entry dated only a month later than his first appearance at the established club:

> Mr Corfe having had some disagreement with some of the members of the Catch Club at the opening of that meeting this year, now suggested to me an idea of having (with my assistance as leader & Mr Burgatt's etc.) another club once a fortnight (on the intervening Tuesdays) upon a smaller scale than the other, where there were now so many members that it frequently became disagreeable. This, as may be supposed, I readily acceded to, & on Tuesday Nov'r 5th. we had our first meeting at w'ch Mr Burgat & I played the 1st. fiddle, Mr Gibbons (the landlord) the 2d. Mr Corfe the pianoforte; Mr Still & Mr Beaumont (a musical amateur then at Sarum) the violoncellos Mr Chubb flute with tenors etc. making altogether a very good band. – Having amused ourselves for about 2 hours with instrumental music (in the course of w'ch we played one of Boccherini's quintettos for 2 violins, tenor & 2 obligato violoncellos, of w'ch Mr Beaumont was very fond) we about half past 8. had our bread & cheese etc. after w'ch Mess'rs Corfe Goss Wellman & Barratt sung some glees etc. with now & then a single song till between 11 & 12 o'clock.[44]

The passage is of significance not only for underlining the popularity of the catch clubs – henceforward Salisbury, like Canterbury, would for some years support a weekly meeting throughout the winter – but also for providing further insight into the organisation, activities, and membership of the clubs. Here we find a social mix that encompassed cathedral choristers, the landlord of the Spread Eagle Inn, a dancing master (Burgat), an apothecary, and middle-class professional men such as Chubb, an attorney. In Chichester, as already noted, the membership was much smaller (within a few months of its establishment Marsh records thirty people, including a number of visiting musical amateurs, attending a meeting in January 1788) and in general came from a rather higher social stratum. In addition to Theodore Aylward and the cathedral vicars, the membership named by Marsh at various times includes a clergyman, a surgeon, the boisterous Colonel Jones, and two unidentified gentlemen. The local bookseller Humphry is the only man belonging to a humbler level of society, while Marsh significantly notes that two amateurs

---

[40] *Bath Selection*, Rule II.
[41] *Bath Selection*, Rule IV.
[42] Lichfield, 'Rules', Rule II.
[43] Given Bath's status as a fashionable spa with a fluctuating population, it is unlikely attendance figures for any one meeting approached this figure.
[44] Marsh, *Journals*, p. 151.

admitted as instrumentalists remained members only a short while, 'being not in the habits of intimacy with the other gent'n'.[45]

The Chichester club therefore sought to retain the intimacy of a gathering of friends meeting together to make music and enjoy convivial company, at least after the hired professionals had departed. Such an ethos is obviously quite different from that of the Bath Harmonic Society, where although the membership joined in a cold supper the large potential membership must have precluded any real atmosphere of intimacy. As Marsh's account of a breakaway catch club in Salisbury reveals, size was a common problem and many clubs sought to avoid becoming too large by placing a restriction on the number of members admitted. The Catch Club had passed an early resolution restricting membership to twenty-one,[46] while the Lichfield Cecilian Society restricted its membership to sixty, excluding performers.[47] Most clubs allowed visitors, the cost at Bath being 4s, while Canterbury (post 1802) followed the course taken by many subscription concert series in permitting out-of-town visitors to attend at a cost of 1s when introduced by a member.

The relatively high cost of supper at the Bath Harmonic Society came in addition to an annual subscription of a guinea, for a season that lasted from the last Friday in November until the last Friday in April, a total of some twenty-two meetings. Members who had not settled their dues one month after the commencement of their residency during the season were barred pending a new ballot, although somewhat oddly they do not seem to have been penalised for missing an entire season.[48] The 1799 Bath Harmonic membership list reveals a number of distinguished names: George III's second son, Frederick, Duke of York; the exiled Stadtholder, William V of Orange; and his son Prince Frederick of Orange. They are followed by the Marquises of Bath and Lansdown, and nine peers of the realm. Sir Richard Pepper Arden, Master of the Rolls since 1788 and a friend of Prime Minister William Pitt also graces the list, as do a number of eminent military men and knights. Perhaps surprisingly, from this membership only three out of forty-two were also members of the Catch Club: Lord Hawarden (elected 1806), Sir Charles Talbot (1799), and Sir Walter James (1806). The last named is also one of only two to have been found among subscription lists for catch and glee publications, a striking comparison with members of the Catch Club, many of whom regularly supported such publications. Among the gentlemen and professional men whose occupation can be determined, it is not surprising to find a large body of servicemen (seventy-three, predominantly officers of the Royal Navy) and clerics (forty-nine), while medical men also feature strongly.

We also have some details of the membership of the Bristol Catch Club, thanks to Richard Smith the younger, a member from 1796. In the flyleaf of his copy of the Warren Collection, Smith notes that when his father Richard Smith, a surgeon at the Bristol Infirmary, joined the club in 1785 notable members included: four clerics; two attorneys; a silk mercer; a merchant; a Colonel Andrewes of the Somerset Militia; Robert Broderip, whose publication dedicated to the club has been mentioned; and

---

[45] Marsh, *Journals*, p. 421.
[46] See above p. 39.
[47] Lichfield, 'Rules', Rule I.
[48] *Bath Selection*, Rules V & VII.

the cathedral organist Rice Wasborough. Several were still members when the younger Smith joined, their number supplemented by several members of the Wasborough family; a customs officer; James Hillhouse; a shipbuilder; a doctor; an attorney; Dunbar, 'a private gentleman'; and, interestingly, one Applewaite, described by Smith as 'a West Indian'.[49] Like the clubs in Salisbury and Canterbury, the Bristol club therefore appears to have admitted a diversity of membership that cut across social boundaries.

Although all clubs sought to maintain 'harmony, in its general signification', societies, as Clark notes, 'often experienced internal conflict'.[50] Provincial catch clubs were no exception. We have already seen how a breakaway club was formed in Salisbury because Joseph Corfe disagreed with some of the members, while Marsh also records a new club being set up in opposition to the Canterbury Catch Club, ostensibly on account 'of the badness of the Room at Goodbans', but in reality a reflection of the rivalry between local musicians.[51] In Chichester the gradual erosion of the rules relating to visitors actually led to the demise of the club founded by Marsh. In November 1792 he records that 'by swerving from our original rules in the admission of members [...] we had much injur'd the society'.[52] Marsh's remarks were occasioned by a bad-tempered meeting at which a drunken local visitor (a 'gentleman') insulted one of the founder members, but there is an impression that this upset was only the culmination of a sequence of events. Subsequently, many of the leading members of the club, including Marsh, resigned and the club was disbanded. This rowdiness was by no means exceptional. Years earlier the breakaway Salisbury club was the scene of a bizarre incident that inspired a caricature entitled *Scene at a Catch Club*, now sadly lost. Marsh's account is sufficiently entertaining to be quoted with only minor editing:

> At our last Catch Club for this season (on the 10th.) a most extraordinary thing happen'd [...] It may be recollected that on Capt Mitchell's kicking Burgat down the stairs at the Assembly in Dec'r 1779. the latter sent him a challenge w'ch the other declin'd noticing Burgat determin'd to insult him the 1st. time he met him afterw'ds w'ch [...] did not happen 'till this even'g when during a performance of a violin concerto by Burgat, he came into the room with his friend Mr Richards who was a member of the club [...] As soon as the concerto was finish'd, Burgat looking very significantly tow'ds that quarter of the room, gave a pretty strong *hiss* w'ch after a little pause being repeated, Mr Chafy got up & ask'd Burgat whether it was him & his friend that he did the honor to hiss. "No (replied he) it was *Mitchell*". This imediately brought up him & his introductor Richards who seizing little Burgat by the collar & proceeding to serve him as he had been serv'd at the Assembly, Mr De Hearle the French master [...] imediately came up & threaten'd to be a witness of the assault of his friend, on which Mr Richards [...] threaten'd to throw him behind the fire, & a fine hubbub was created, the whole room being now rous'd, amongst whom Rob't Still mov'd that Burgat for his very extraordinary behaviour in disturbing the amusement of a large company sho'd be turn'd out of the room. This question being therefore put by Boucher the steward to the

---

[49] Hooper, 'Music in Bristol', pp. 202–205.
[50] Clark, *British Clubs*, p. 234.
[51] Marsh, *Journals*, p. 308.
[52] Ibid. p. 526.

company was likely to be unanimously determin'd in the affirmative when Mr Richards perceiving that the little man wo'd hardly retire without force being used, very goodnaturedly, by way of putting an end to the business desired him [...] to resume his fiddle & take his place in the orchestra. But this was too great a condescension for Burgat to submit to who said he sho'd either play or not just as he pleased. Seeing however now a fair opportunity of closing this matter I imediately look'd out a full piece w'ch we all played (except Burgat who kept aloof with his fiddle in his hand) & w'ch concluded the concert after w'ch we according to custom on the last night adjourn'd to a foreroom to supper w'ch afforded Burgat & his friend De Hearle an opportunity of remaining behind & taking themselves off unnotic'd. [53]

In 1790 the Lichfield Cecilian Society was involved in dissension of a more academic nature. A schism had apparently arisen between performing and non-performing members over the question of the powers to enforce the rules, a privilege granted only to performing members in the original statutes. In a magnanimous gesture, the performers agreed to waive this ruling in the interest of 'preserving the Harmony of the Society' while at the same time adding a stern rider that the rules should in future be clearly understood by all new members.[54]

Following the break-up of the Chichester Catch Club attempts to form a new club meeting at the homes of members were short lived. Marsh's account of the first meeting suggests that the new club was in fact little different from the ubiquitous domestic musical evenings that feature throughout his narrative; those attending included such genteel society as Lady Louisa Lennox, the sister-in-law of the Duke of Richmond, and other ladies. While it was the catch clubs in London and the provinces that provided the dynamic for establishing the enormous popularity of catches and glees, they had in fact entered the salon at an early stage, a development that will be examined in the following chapter.

---

[53] Marsh, *Journals*, pp. 233–4.
[54] Lichfield, 'Rules'.

Chapter 6

The Catch and Glee in Other Performance Contexts

This study has so far concentrated on the catch and glee within the context of the clubs and societies that formed the most conducive environment for their performance. The rapid development of the glee to the status of a popular genre with a specific appeal to English audiences ensured that such restricted performance conditions were soon breached. Before the end of the 1760s both the glee and, to a lesser extent, the catch found entry into the wider spheres of domestic music making and the concert platform, while during the following decade the glee would also be taken up by theatre composers. Such incursions would have considerable implications for the later development of the glee. Accompaniment by the increasingly popular piano in the home and by the orchestra on the concert platform and in the theatre would eventually come to undermine the 'purity' of the glee, leading it from a style in which counterpoint and variety of texture played at least some part to one based on predominantly chordal harmony. Widespread amateur demand also led to a simplification of structure to cater for the capabilities of a new market avid to participate in the domestic performance of glees. The result would be a perceptible decline in quality, though by no means of quantity.

The performance of catches and glees in domestic music making was both widespread and an early development. As early as February 1762, just a couple of months after the establishment of the Catch Club, we find Elizabeth Harris, the wife of James Harris (himself soon to become a short-lived member of the club), writing to her son of a domestic concert she had attended. Given by Mrs Foster, the wife of Thomas Foster, MP for Dorchester between 1761 and 1765, it was, she relates, attended by many people of whom 'a select number staid supper[,] among which number was your father and myself. After supper the gentlemen sung catches until two o'clock.'[1] In August of the same year, Elizabeth again recorded catches being sung at Foster's Salisbury home by her husband, Edward Fawkener, already encountered at an Oxford catch club in 1752,[2] and a Mr Ward, possibly the John Ward who was a founder member of the Catch Club. There was 'a little musick after supper', including catches and 'very well they came off'.[3]

We have seen that Lord Sandwich took every opportunity to encourage the singing of catches both at his home at Hinchingbroke and when on visits to others.[4] He was among the guests at another social evening recorded by James Harris in his journal in April 1775 at the Bloomsbury Square home of the Harris's friend Mrs Wilmot. Apparently devoted wholly to the singing of catches and glees the 'large appearance of the best company' included, in addition to Sandwich, Lord Apsley (the Lord Chancellor) and Lady Apsley, Lord and Lady Delawar, Lady Canteloupe, Lord

---

[1] Burrows, *Music and Theatre*, p. 371. Letter of Elizabeth Harris to James Harris jr., 18 February 1762.
[2] See above p. 28.
[3] Burrows, *Music and Theatre*, p. 388. Letter of Elizabeth Harris to James Harris jr., 24 August 1762.
[4] See above p. 34.

and Lady Denbigh, and Baron Smythe.[5] It is worth noting that with the exception of Sandwich, none of these aristocrats were members of the Catch Club, suggesting that the popularity of catch and glee singing had by this time extended beyond the confines of club life. Also significant at this date is not only that a lady should be hosting an event specifically devoted to the singing of catches and glees, but that they were performed in mixed 'polite' company, suggesting that the demand for catches and glees acceptable to female ears existed prior to the publication of Samuel Webbe's *Ladies Catch Book* three years later. Indeed, the Harris papers make clear that by the 1770s amateur ladies were not only listening to catches and glees, but also singing them themselves. In 1770 Harris's daughter Louisa, an accomplished singer who was a pupil of Sacchini, wrote to her brother of 'a superb ball and supper' at which she and her sister Gertrude joined in the singing of two catches.[6] Such interest and participation also accounts for the fair number of women subscribers to catch and glee collections during this period. The third collection of Samuel Webbe, which appeared in 1775, includes six ladies in a total of ninety-nine subscribers, including the actress Martha Ray, the mistress of Lord Sandwich. Two years later Luffman Atterbury's *Collection of Glees and Catches for Three and Four Voices* attracted five ladies in a list of seventy-seven subscribers, Martha Ray, who subscribed for two copies, again appearing on it.

The entrance of the catch and glee into the domestic sphere was not confined to smart London salons and country seats. In October 1772, Elizabeth Harris recorded attending a soiree given in Salisbury at the home in the Close of Dr Gilbert, one of the Prebendaries of the Cathedral. 'A great deal of company' attended to be entertained by catches and glees, a 'kind of music more adapted to the genius of this place than the finest song Millico could sing.'[7] It is not clear from this whether Mrs Harris was passing an ironic comment on the musical taste of Salisbury or providing an early example of national pride in the glee and catch. Three years later she was certainly less ambiguous on the subject after hearing a concert of catches and glees held at the Assembly Rooms as part of the Salisbury Festival. Noting that the concert was greeted with 'a violent burst of applause that surpass'd all I have ever met', she continued in the letter to her son: 'I was much pleased and am thoroughly convinc'd, that this is the only music for our English ears.'[8] Earlier in the same letter Elizabeth noted that her daughter Louisa stayed away from the concert, being now 'too magnificent to contaminate her Italian ears with such stuff', later adding: 'Louisa consol'd herself she had spent the evening like a gentlewomen while we were laughing among the black guards.' Here, then, is the clear suggestion of a body of opinion emerging to claim a distinct preference for the 'Englishness' of the glee and catch over what was perceived as the more refined – and by implication affected – taste for Italian music.

---

[5] Burrows, *Music and Theatre*, p. 819. London journal of James Harris [G838, pp 5–7].
[6] Burrows, *Music and Theatre*, p. 613. Letter of Louisa Harris to James Harris jr., 9 December 1770.
[7] Ibid. p. 688. Letter of Elizabeth Harris to James Harris jr., 10–11 October 1772. The castrato Giuseppe Millico had recently sung at the Salisbury Festival, hence Elizabeth Harris's reference to him. He was, as noted in Chapter 3, a privileged member of the Catch Club.
[8] Ibid. p. 851. Letter of Elizabeth Harris to James Harris jr., 8 October 1775.

The Harris papers note a number of other instances of domestic music making that include the performance of catches and glees, significant among them a concert given by a Mr Ord in London on 23 February 1779.[9] Following songs given by Sarah Harrop, one of the leading sopranos of the day, Harris recorded in his journal that 'with two or three voices more (Webb [sic] in particular) we had many excellent glees, some by Webb himself the best of all – the voices sung in general soft, without the antient English bawl, or French squawl, which rendered the harmony far more exquisite and touching'.[10] Since Harris was a thoroughly experienced observer of the musical scene, his comments on the performances of the glees suggest that such 'exquisite and touching' effects were by no means commonplace. His observation also, of course, provides valuable insight into a performance practice whose ideals seem to have continued to abide by the principles of William Hayes, who, it will be recalled, recommended the singing of anything 'pathetic' or 'delicate' with something less than full tone.[11] That the question of refinement remained an issue is apparent from the words of John Marsh, writing more than thirty years later. Attending a meeting of the Bath Harmonic Society as a guest in January 1800, Marsh observed that the glees 'were very accurately done, tho' not in quite so good a style as I expected, as they sung rather too loud & in too boisterous a manner'.[12]

Marsh records innumerable instances of glees and catches being performed domestically. In July 1776, shortly after his arrival in Salisbury, he records holding a 'grand crash' (Marsh's delightful term for a large concert party) at which he gave a number of the city's leading musicians a cold supper after which they sang catches and glees.[13] December of the same year found Marsh and his wife Elizabeth at a musical party devoted to catches and glees. Hosted by Dr John Stevens, the organist of the Cathedral, the audience included Charles Moss, the Bishop of Bath and Wells and a Prebendary of Salisbury Cathedral, the Dean, and the Harrises. Marsh names the singers as the two principal boy choristers, Steven Sibly and Clark, the alto John Goss and Francis Wellman, later to become organist of Romsey Abbey.[14] That such a party was hosted by the Cathedral organist, performed by some of its prominent choristers and attended by leading ecclesiastics again emphasises the strong and enduring connections between the church and the two musical forms, which in the provinces at least were frequently largely dependent on cathedral singers for performance. Leading visiting singers to the Salisbury Festival frequently became involved in domestic musical parties at which glees were sung, a notable example being Nancy Storace, who appeared at the 1787 Festival some eighteen months after creating the role of Susanna in Mozart's *Le nozze di Figaro*. Marsh's account of the evening at Joseph Corfe's, which was attended by both Storace and her brother

---

[9] James Ord was the son of Anna Ord, a widow and musical enthusiast who was a friend of Charles Burney.
[10] Burrows, *Music and Theatre*, p. 1010. London journal of James Harris [G842, fols. 4ᵛ–6ʳ]. Harris's enthusiasm for the elder Webbe's glees was translated into practical terms; he purchased at least two of Webbe's collections (probably the fourth and fifth, for which subscription lists do not exist), as noted in his London journal in February 1778 (ibid, p. 969) and his account book for 1779 (ibid, p. 1027).
[11] See above p. 29.
[12] Marsh, *Journals*, p. 706.
[13] Marsh, *Journals*, p. 146.
[14] Marsh, *Journals*, p. 155.

Stephen, is of significance for the light it casts on the behaviour of Nancy Storace, whom he found to be 'in such boisterous spirits that she made a noise all the time' and was 'vulgar in her witticisms and manner'.[15] Doubtless Marsh's humour was not improved by Nancy's unflattering and outspoken comparison of his glee *The curfew tolls* with her brother's setting of the same words.[16]

An important development that emerged with the increasing domestication of the glee was its accompaniment by the piano, an instrument that as early as the 1760s had started to replace the harpsichord as the most popular instrument in genteel homes. It has already been noted that the practice of accompanying glees on the keyboard dates at least from the early 1770s, when Arne is recorded as having done so at the Madrigal Society.[17] Nevertheless, no evidence has emerged to support the idea that such accompaniment of glees was widespread at catch clubs, at least during the eighteenth century. But it would appear likely that by the early 1780s at the latest their domestic performance was not infrequently supported by a keyboard instrument, the instance recorded by John Marsh during a visit to Bath in April 1782 doubtless widely emulated elsewhere. Following a social breakfast, he tells us 'we sang some glees, accompan'd on the harpsichord by Miss H'.[18] While there is little doubt that the accompaniment of the glee in domestic performance during the last two decades of the century became increasingly prevalent, the practice evidently remained controversial, as we learn from Marsh himself, who in January 1793 found himself embroiled in just such a controversy during an evening's domestic music making:

> On Monday the 21st. we all went to a musical party at Mr Middletons to whom I lent my piano forte for the occasion on w'ch amongst other things I accomp'd a new glee sung by Mrs S. Heming, Mess'rs Moore & Toghill, the latter of whom imediately [sic] afterw'ds observ'd that it wo'd have a better effect another time *without* accompaniment, on w'ch I co'd not help observing that it was at Mr Middleton's desire that I accomp'd it & not from any officiousness of my own having no notion of any accompaniment on a small piano forte having any ill effect, that was not injudiciously played, w'ch I co'd not help thinking his observation seem'd to imply tho' he tried in not the best humour, to do it away by saying he did not mean to criticise on *my* accompaniment in particular, but on accomp'ts in general.[19]

Clearly Marsh himself, who as we will see maintained an unambiguous attitude to the question of performing catches and glees with single voices to a part, was prepared to adopt a pragmatic approach to the question of accompaniments. On a visit to the Nottingham Catch Club in September 1796 he heard 'some glees &c. very decently done, some of w'ch I accompanied on the piano forte'.[20] Notwithstanding Marsh's ready acceptance of accompanied glees, there can be little doubt that the

---

[15] Marsh, *Journals*, p. 414.
[16] Ibid. Both settings were published in 1782, Marsh's by Bland, Storace's by Dale.
[17] See above p. 25.
[18] Marsh, *Journals*, p. 262. Miss H. refers to the daughter of the prominent amateur glee composer Dr Henry Harington.
[19] Marsh, *Journals*, p. 533.
[20] Marsh, *Journals*, p. 627.

practice, widespread among amateurs in the domestic sphere, played a considerable part in the glee's downward progression from a finely wrought professional vehicle to a genre within reach of the most modest of dilettante singers.

The introduction of the catch and glee into public concerts and the London pleasure gardens was an innovation that followed closely in the wake of the establishment of the Catch Club. The gardens were important venues for promoting the music of native composers and encouraging English musicians. Surviving records of concert programmes from the period show that it was indeed in the pleasure gardens that the glee (and to a lesser extent the catch) made the most significant incursions onto the concert platform, at least initially.[21] The first recorded example of catches and glees being given at a public concert dates from 1765 and took place at Marybone, a pleasure garden situated rather out of town and one of the less fashionable of the garden venues.[22] Toward the end of the 1765 season, Thomas Lowe, who had been manager of Marybone since 1763, promoted a concert of 'Songs, Catches and Glees by Purcell and other eminent Masters'. Lowe, a singer himself, had apparently lost a substantial amount of money during the preceding three seasons and he particularly appealed to the public and his friends to support this concert, in which the catches and glees were to be sung by 'three Gentlemen', who would be 'in proper habits' and 'in Character'.[23] It seems significant that Lowe turned to a concert involving catches and glees in an attempt to recoup his losses, since it clearly indicates not only the rapidly increasing popularity of the two genres, but moreover that they were by this time already considered to be a sound commercial proposition for a public concert.

There is no surviving record to tell us whether or not Lowe's venture was successful, but two years later Thomas Arne started to promote concerts including catches and glees at both Marybone and Ranelagh Gardens, the latter the most fashionable of all the gardens. By the late 1760s Arne's popularity in the theatre had waned significantly, and it seems likely he turned to the promotion of catch and glee concerts in an attempt to regain notice. Such an activity was of course an ancillary to his membership of the Madrigal Society and his privileged membership of the Catch Club, the latter of which was associated at least by name with some of the early pleasure garden concerts, including the first of Arne's catch and glee concerts. This took place at Ranelagh on 12 May 1767 and was announced as a programme of catches and glees 'selected from the collection of the Catch Club'. Although yielding precedence to Thomas Lowe's Marybone concert of two years earlier, the event was still sufficiently novel to be advertised as 'the first of the Kind publicly exhibited in this or any other Kingdom' and to receive considerable press coverage. The report in the *Public Advertiser* noted that 'the Entertainment consisted of the most favourite Catches and Glees, with the elegant and humorous Music, composed of the most

---

[21] I am especially grateful to Simon McVeigh for his generosity in providing information from his invaluable database, 'Calendar of London Concerts 1750–1800', Goldsmith's College, University of London. The Calendar is based on systematic research in London newspapers for details of concert programmes across the whole spectrum of concert giving. Unless otherwise stated, all information regarding London concert details and programmes is taken from this source.

[22] Edward Croft Murray and Simon McVeigh, 'London V. Musical life: 1660–1800; 3. Pleasure Gardens' in revised *New Grove*.

[23] Molly Sands, *The Eighteenth-Century Pleasure Gardens of London* (London, 1987), p. 65.

eminent Masters of the last and present Age'.[24] At least some of the items included instrumental accompaniments and choral arrangements made by Arne 'to give the Catches and Glees their proper Effect in so large an Amphitheatre',[25] the first recorded instance of the repertoire being expanded from one-per-part *a capella* performance.[26] No fewer than thirty choral singers and six boys are advertised as being involved in addition to the named soloists, Samuel Champness (like Arne a founder privileged member of the Catch Club), the tenor and actor Joseph Vernon, Charles Vernon, Charles Dibdin, and one Parsons. The report then goes on to give a somewhat over-refined historical background to the evening's events, noting that 'these Kinds of Entertainment (in the time of Mr Henry Purcell) were so much in Fashion, that in most polite families, after Dinner and Supper, it was a Custom to lay the choicest Collections of Catches and Glees on the Table, and it was thought a Deficiency of Education in those who could not readily perform a part'. Also stressed is the conviviality associated with this type of music making in 'select Clubs and private Companies', they being places where 'the Performers by their expressive Gesticulations have added Life and Spirit to Harmony, and in Hamlet's Words "set the whole Table in a Roar"'.[27] This extract is notable for providing the only known reference to the performance of catches or glees being accompanied by gesture.

Arne's hand can be suspected in at least part of the above review, which was followed up by a critique in the *Monthly Review* in its July edition of the printed texts of the 'Favourite Catches and Glees, performed at Ranelagh House, on the Twelfth of May. The Music by Dr Arne'.[28] The review is of interest for quoting the anonymous (Arne?) preface, which not only still found it necessary to provide definitions of both forms (as did the *Public Advertiser* review), but also made clear that the glee had yet to achieve a fully distinctive character. The writer drew attention to the fact that the Catch Club's medals for glees 'have graciously extended the appellation of Glee to every composition, in three or four parts, which is not contrived in the manner of a Catch', a point taken word for word from the *Public Advertiser*'s review. In fact, and contrary to Rubin's assertion that 'the distinction between the catch and glee was definitely established with [the] formation of the Noblemen and Gentlemen's Catch Club in 1761',[29] ambiguity still existed even in deciding the differences between catches and glees. This is well illustrated by *Which is the properest day to drink*,[30] one of the most popular of Arne's pieces at this time, which although invariably referred to as a glee might more properly be considered a catch. The *Public Advertiser*'s reviewer quotes the words of several of the pieces contained. Noting that the 'greater part are dedicated to Bacchus', the poem of *Which is the properest day* is extolled for its 'easy and agreeable' humour, although the reviewer drew attention to the apologia in the preface, which makes clear that 'the reader is requested to consider, that if the poetry of one or two of the ancient catches will not

---

[24] *Public Advertiser*, 14 May 1767.
[25] Ibid.
[26] Rubin, 'The English Glee', p. 289ff includes a general discussion of instrumentally accompanied glees.
[27] *Public Advertiser*, 14 May 1767.
[28] *Monthly Review*, July 1767, p. 58.
[29] Rubin, 'The English Glee', p. 140.
[30] Included in the fourth of Warren's collections.

bear a critical examination they were so written, with a more particular regard to the Music'. 'The catch and glee poet', claims the reviewer, therefore 'has little more to do than to observe Swift's words: "Suit your words to your music well".' This dictum would well serve much of the catch and glee culture throughout its period of ascendancy.

In the summer of 1767 catches and glees start to appear regularly in Marybone programmes alongside the songs that had always been one of the main attractions at the pleasure gardens. The diarist Sylas Neville records visits to Marybone on 8 and 17 June, noting on the second occasion that he heard *Which is the properest day* and *The Silent Cock and hen that crows*,[31] and that the evening's entertainment also included fireworks.[32] On 9 June a special evening at Marybone was held to celebrate the birthday of George III, although the announcement that it was 'originally' in honour of the occasion suggests that it may have been a repeat of a concert held closer to the king's actual birthday on 4 June. A more elaborate event than customary, it involved choral music in addition to the usual songs, catches, and glees, the usual admission price of 1s being raised to 3s 6d, for which a firework display was also included. The only catch or glee mentioned was a 'prize catch' by Samuel Webbe that can be identified as *The Moon and Woman*, the recipient of a Catch Club prize earlier in the year, and the first of a long list of his catches and glees to be so honoured.[33]

The Marybone Gardens 1767 season was almost certainly the first concert series to programme catches and glees systematically. Regrettably few details of the repertoire performed have come down to us, however. The most frequently performed identifiable work is Arne's *Which is the properest day*, which appeared on no fewer than eight occasions, thus setting a precedent for what is one of the defining characteristics of concert performance of the repertoire: the constant repetition of a relatively small number of works. Of the eight hundred or so catch and glee concert performances McVeigh records, fully a third are distributed between fewer than twenty titles. The lack of a clearly defined glee repertoire at this point in its history is again emphasised by the inclusion as a glee of 'Water parted from the sea', the popular chorus from Arne's English *opera seria Artaxerses*. Only five other composers are named, three of them (Purcell, Aldrich, and John Travers) belonging to earlier generations. Perhaps most significant is the high profile of the young Samuel Webbe the elder, who not only received ten recorded performances of his own catches and glees,[34] but is also listed as a singer for much of the season, an experience the largely autodidactic Webbe almost certainly used to hone his rapidly developing compositional skills. His employment also entitled Webbe to be among five performers granted a benefit evening, which took place on 24 August, an occasion for which the young composer provided three new pieces, a song, a catch and a glee.

---

[31] *The Silent Cock*, probably also by Arne, has not been identified. It may be a song rather than a catch or glee.

[32] *Diary of Sylas Neville*, p. 13.

[33] The catch was published in Book 6 of the Warren Collection and was also written into the third of the Catch Club's books. It obviously retained its appeal, being twice chosen when the Catch Club revisited Book 3 in 1782. 'Records of the Catch Club', BL H.2788.ccc.

[34] The only named work of Webbe's performed during the season was the glee *The Invitation*, which is not listed by Rubin. Along with most of the other catches and glees by Webbe, it was announced as having been newly composed.

The Ranelagh concert that provided the source for the printed texts mentioned above was the inspiration for a repeat performance at Drury Lane Theatre the following year. A bill dated 21 June 1768 informs prospective patrons that the programme to be given includes 'the Favourite Catches and Glees which were exhibited Last Summer at Ranelagh House'. The concert, 'desir'd by many persons of Quality', was again linked to the Catch Club, this time apparently more closely, being announced as given 'by Permission of the Noblemen and Gentlemen of the Catch Club'.[35] Quite why the 'permission' of the Catch Club should be required for a public concert held in a theatre is unclear; possibly it simply means that they loaned their books for the occasion. No director or singers are named, although given the provenance of the concert it seems reasonable to assume that Arne was again closely involved, and that the performers included the majority of those who had performed at Ranelagh. The bill states only that 'a considerable number of the Best Vocal and Instrumental Performers are engag'd', the sole name given being that of the eminent violinist François Hippolyte Barthélemon, who played a violin concerto after the second act, one of two 'desir'd alterations' (the other is not specified) to the Ranelagh concert that had spawned the event.

The juxtaposition of instrumental with vocal music was a standard feature of contemporary concert life, and the appearance of catches and glees in concerts would in future almost invariably fall within a context that encouraged the accompaniment of at least some glees by instruments already *in situ*. To precisely what degree this took place is difficult to determine. Documentary evidence for the practice is sparse, while published glees with orchestral accompaniments are few, their number including two or three by Benjamin Cooke in manuscript,[36] a similar number by Webbe (including *Glorious Apollo* and the 8-part *To love I wake the silver string*, which during the latter half of the 1790s was several times announced as being performed with 'new accompaniments'), and Pieter Hellendaal the elder's *Two glees for four voices with full accompaniments in score, etc.*, published in Cambridge by the composer around 1785 and the only publication during this period of glees in full score. Nevertheless, there can be little doubt that Arne's lead was followed and that the concert devoted solely to catches and glees at Ranelagh on 15 June 1792 was by no means unique in giving some of them with 'treble choir and instruments'.

Over the next two or three years Marybone was seemingly the place to go for those who wanted to hear glees performed in concert, a policy continued even after the now-bankrupt Thomas Lowe ceased management after 1768. Both Lowe's successors, Thomas Pinto and Samuel Arnold, also lost heavily on Marybone, which as previously noted was always a modest undertaking.[37] 1771 seems to be the final season in which a full repertoire of catches and glees was given, the more detailed than usual surviving data clearly illustrating a regular repertoire of five catches and five glees performed throughout the season. Arne was again the most frequently

---

[35] Charles Beecher Hogan (ed.), *The London Stage 1776-1800*. Part 5 of *The London Stage 1660–1800*. (Chicago, 1965–68).

[36] Pink, 'Benjamin Cooke'; Part III 'A Catalogue of Works'. They include *How sleep the brave*, one of Cooke's most popular glees, but interestingly not *Hark, the lark*, which according to McVeigh's data-base was the most frequently performed of all glees on the concert platform.

[37] McVeigh, *Concert Life*, pp. 175–6.

performed composer, accounting for half this repertoire, while the continuing lack of a clear distinction between the genres is borne out by the consistent application of the denomination 'catch' to Giardini's immensely popular glee *Beviamo tutti tre*. Those who made their way across the fields to the gardens during that summer were also entertained with fireworks and a burletta, an Italian comic opera in translation.[38]

The practice of combining a short dramatic work with catches and glees also spread to various London theatres. The original inspiration behind these promotions once again comes from Arne, who may have used such events not only to promote his dramatic works, but also as an attempt to help with the financial difficulties he was experiencing in the early 1770s.[39] The first such mixed concert was advertised for 12 March 1770, when a 'Concert of Catches and Glees' was given at the 'Haymarket Theatre'.[40] The singers advertised included the castrato Tenducci, who had become a privileged member of the Catch Club during the course of the same year,[41] Mrs Barthélemon (the soprano Polly Young), and Mrs Scott. The employment of women to sing the upper parts of catches and glees at such events of course runs counter to the prevailing custom in clubs. It seems reasonable to suggest therefore that such relatively early instances of female participation in the public singing of glees and catches not only played a large part in the shift from the two forms being purely a male preserve, but also acted as direct encouragement for their adoption within a mixed social context. There is a parallel here with the sixteenth-century Italian madrigal, which in its early days, particularly in the case of those with obscene texts, seemed destined for an exclusively male clientele, but was later transformed to accommodate the participation of women both as performers and auditors.[42] The evening in question also included Arne's burlesque *Capochio and Dorinna*, a revival of his earlier *The Temple of Dullness* (Drury Lane, 1745), which had first been given at Marybone Gardens on 28 July 1768. The concert was again given 'by permission of the Noblemen and Gentlemen of the Catch Club',[43] as was another under Arne's direction given at Drury Lane less than three months later on 7 June. On this occasion the catches and glees, which again received top billing, were supplemented by songs and the first performance of the ballad farce *The Country Madcap in London*, a revival of *Miss Lucy in Town* (Drury Lane, 1742), with a text by Henry Fielding and a production that included ten songs by Arne.[44]

The increasing popularity of such events is further confirmed by the choice of such a mixed concert by Barthélemon for his benefit at Marybone Gardens (where he had become leader that year) on 21 August. This was a more miscellaneous affair, with the catches and glees sandwiched between concertos for violin, organ (played by

---

[38] Among a number of such burlettas, Pergolesi's *La serva padrona* (1733), was one of the most frequently peformed.
[39] In 1770 Arne was threatened with legal action for being in arrears with the support payments to his estranged wife, the soprano Cecilia Young. See Peter Holman and Todd Gilman, 'Thomas Arne' in revised *New Grove*.
[40] Beecher Hogan (ed.), *The London Stage*. Possibly the Little Theatre, but not to be confused with the King's Theatre, which was sometimes known as the Haymarket Theatre.
[41] See above p. 46.
[42] Marco Bizzarini, *Luca Marenzio: The Career of a Musician between the Renaissance and the Counter-Reformation*, trans. James Chater (Aldershot, 2003), p. 47.
[43] Beecher Hogan (ed.), *The London Stage*.
[44] Ibid.

Thomas Carter), horn, and trumpet, all composed by Barthélemon, who also produced 'Several New Simphonies' for the occasion. As if all this were not sufficient, the audience were also treated to George Carey's *The Noble Pedlar* and the canon from Barthélemon's burletta *The Magic Girdle*.[45]

Over the course of the next six years, press advertising shows that catches and glees frequently make an appearance in theatre concerts, although none after 1771 are linked with the Catch Club.[46] A letter of Elizabeth Harris dated 5 April 1771 tells her son that his Italian music-loving sister Louisa 'is gone to the catches and glees at the Hay Market',[47] an event not recorded in *The London Stage*, and a concert also held 'by permission of the Catch Club' and directed by Arne.[48] Little more than three weeks later on 27 April, Arne directed a similar event at Drury Lane that also included a performance of *Cymbeline*, an adaptation of Shakespeare's play by Theophilus Cibber, for which Arne had written a dirge when it was first given at the Haymarket in November 1744. The singers on this occasion included Mrs Scott, Frederica Weichsell (a pupil of J. C Bach), the tenor Joseph Vernon, and the bass Samuel Champness, already encountered as a privileged member of the Catch Club. On 6 June Arne revived his third masque *The Judgment of Paris* (Drury Lane, 1742) for a concert at Covent Garden at which 'Catches and Glees' again take top billing. In contrast to reviving older stage works, the following year found Arne introducing a new burletta into a catch and glee concert. This was *Squire Badger*, a short two-act piece with a libretto loosely based on Henry Fielding's *Don Quixote in England*. It received its premiere at the Haymarket on 16 March 1772 and was revived three years later as *The Sot*, when it received three performances, also in harness with catches and glees.[49]

Arne's promotion of catches and glees in the London theatres continued until 1776, the last year of his musical activity, when he mounted an entertainment at the Haymarket.[50] The dramatic work on this occasion was *Whittington's Feast*, a parody of Dryden's *Alexander's Feast* for which Arne felt obliged to apologise in the bill for his act of *lèse-majesté*. The performance, given on 18 April, was announced as 'Dr Arne's last night this season'.[51] In fact it represented his final farewell to the London stage with which he had been involved for more than forty years, and it also appears to mark the end of the tradition of performing catches and glees in tandem with theatrical entertainments. It is also worth noting that in May 1772 the indefatigable composer and entrepreneur Charles Dibdin (1745–1814) had attempted to emulate Arne's initiative by introducing his own catches and glees into three benefit evenings at Drury Lane, the first of which, on 1 May for his own benefit, promised 'Several Catches and Glees, part of which will be entirely New, Composed by Dibdin for that evening, and Part selected from the most admired Composers'. These were performed at the end of an entertainment that also included *Twelfth Night* and

---

[45] Ibid.
[46] Ibid.
[47] Burrows, *Music and Theatre*, p. 631.
[48] It is included in McVeigh's 'Calendar', having been advertised in the *Public Advertiser* during February and March.
[49] Beecher Hogan (ed.), *The London Stage*.
[50] See n. 40.
[51] Beecher Hogan (ed.), *The London Stage*.

Dibdin's own popular afterpiece *The Padlock*. Two further benefit evenings combining drama with catches and glees, 'some composed by Dibdin', were presented on 13 and 19 May, but there is no evidence to suggest that Dibdin, whose extensive surviving output includes relatively few glees,[52] pursued this line further. He did however return to the topic two years later in *The Cobler, or a Wife of Ten Thousand*, an opera with spoken dialogue first given at Drury Lane on 9 December 1774. The action is set mainly in an alehouse and includes a scene set in its clubroom, where eight men, only one of whom takes any further part in the action, 'all talk at once about unrelated matters, until finally they combine in a glee'.[53] Given Dibdin's propensity for satire, it seems more than likely this scene was intended as a barbed comment on the catch club scene.

The linking of catches and glees with theatrical entertainment has a further interesting corollary in an anonymous entertainment entitled *The Sons of Anacreon*, first given at Drury Lane on 18 April 1785. The loss of the text allows only speculation as to its nature, but it appears to have taken the form of some kind of dramatised afterpiece depicting the proceedings of a catch club. Mounted as a benefit performance for the actor and singer John Bannister, it included 'several capital *Catches* and *Glees*, selected from the most Eminent Masters',[54] in addition to which Bannister's father Charles performed 'the *Celebrated Anacreontic Song*'.[55] Other songs were also obviously included, among them 'two *Imitative* songs sung by John Bannister'. The principal singers are listed as Bannister himself, the tenor Charles Dignum,[56] Richard Suett, Matthew Williames, William Barrymore, William Chapman, and a Master Clarke, all of whom were actor/singers closely associated with Drury Lane at the time, lending further weight to the supposition that *The Sons of Anacreon* was a dramatised piece.

The success of *The Sons of Anacreon* can be gauged by the fact that over the next seven years it was revived on twenty-two occasions. Significantly almost all were benefits, when it was performed alongside dramatic works ranging from William Shield's popular opera *Rosina* to *The Beggar's Opera* and Sheridan's *The School for Scandal*. Three years after its first production the piece underwent the first of three changes of name, becoming known as *The Catch Club*,[57] perhaps in homage to the famous institution. The bill for the performance, given as a benefit for John Bannister at the Haymarket on 22 August 1788,[58] gives us a little supplementary information on the manner in which the piece was performed, naming a President (John Palmer, the creator of the role of Joseph Surface in *The School for Scandal*) and the singers of vocal parts, who included the famous actor James Edwin and 'Master Braham', the fourteen-year-old John Braham, later to become the most renowned English tenor of the day. Several songs, catches, and glees are for the first time

---

[52] Rubin lists just seven glees by Dibdin.
[53] Fiske, *Theatre Music*, p. 373.
[54] Beecher Hogan (ed.), *The London Stage*.
[55] See above p. 73.
[56] Dignum became a privileged member of the Catch Club in 1789.
[57] Undated performances at the Royalty Theatre, Goodman's Fields, inspired the publication of *The Catch Club – A Collection of all the Songs, Catches, Glees, Duets &c as sung by Bannister, Arrowsmith, Leoni, Chapman, Master Braham, Gaudry &c.* (London, ?).
[58] Beecher Hogan (ed.), *The London Stage*.

named, among them Aldrich's popular catch *Hark the bonny Christ Church bells*. Further changes of name to the entertainment took place in 1790, when it became *The Court of Apollo* on the occasion of a benefit performance for the actor/singer Thomas Sedgwick,[59] the performance intriguingly including a performance of Thomas Morley's *Now is the month of Maying*. The last recorded presentation was on 19 April 1792, when it was given as *The Festive Board* at the King's Theatre, once more as a benefit for John Bannister.[60]

In 1775 London gained a new purpose-built concert hall, the Hanover Square Rooms, the building of which was undertaken by the Florentine dancer and impresario Sir John (Giovanni) Gallini in association with J. C. Bach and Abel, who had run successful concert series in London since 1765. Although Bach and Abel moved their concert venue to the new hall, the great talking point of London society during the early months of 1775 were the social entertainments devised by Gallini under the name of 'festinos'. Almost certainly inspired by the glittering society assemblies held under the auspices of Teresa Cornelys at Carlisle House in Soho, Gallini's evenings, which soon became one of the hottest social tickets in London, combined elements of male conviviality with mixed social pleasure, as we learn from Elizabeth Harris:

> There was a new thing last night at Bachs room in Hanover Square, call'd the Festino[;] tis under the direction of Gallini, and it is to be weekly like Almack's [...] As I understand[,] the plan is a dinner for gentlemen[;] at eight or nine the ladies are to come, then catches and glees till supper[,] and after supper they dance.[61]

Significantly, the catches and glees were sung *following* the arrival of the ladies, providing further evidence of their increasing acceptability in mixed society. More than fifteen years later, in 1792, we learn from the *Morning Chronicle*'s 'Mirror of Fashion' that Gallini was evidently still running some weekly form of catch and glee entertainment on Tuesdays and Saturdays at Hanover Square under the name 'The Pasticcio', although no further details have come to light.[62]

Glees and catches also featured prominently in benefit concerts, which by definition required good publicity if they were to provide a satisfactory return for the beneficiary, thus providing greater documented detail than is often available for concert seasons. Throughout the 1780s and 1790s surviving announcements show that many artists chose to include glees (and to a lesser extent catches) in their benefit concerts. Benefit concerts were generally held in the spring, and frequently had a crowded musical calendar with which to compete.

In March 1785, Samuel Webbe the elder and Samuel Harrison held benefits within a week of each other, press reports making clear that both faced stiff competition. In the case of Webbe, his night at the Freemasons' Hall on the 10th

---

[59] Ibid. The bass Thomas Sedgwick (d. 1803) was a pupil of R. J. S. Stevens. He was also one of the professional singers engaged by the Anacreontic Society, for some years singing the Anacreontic Song at all its meetings.
[60] Beecher Hogan (ed.), *The London Stage*.
[61] Burrows, *Music and Theatre*, pp. 802–3.
[62] McVeigh, *Concert Life*, p. 2.

clashed with that of Gertrud Mara, one of the most glittering operatic stars of the period; while six days later Harrison had to compete with oratorios at Drury Lane and the Haymarket, and the Professional Concert at Hanover Square, a striking reminder of the richness and diversity of London's concert life. Notwithstanding such rival attractions, according to press reports both men attracted substantial audiences, the *Public Advertiser* claiming an audience of 'three or four hundred people' for Webbe's benefit,[63] while Harrison's Tottenham Street Rooms concert 'was numerously attended'.[64] Both, particularly Harrison, were able to draw on a loyal personal audience accustomed to hearing them perform in London's concert halls, the report of Harrison's benefit drawing attention to the fact it was attended by 'the principal nobility and persons of fashion, most of whom are subscribers to the Ancient Concerts'.[65] Harrison was a principal tenor at the Concert of Antient Music for some years. Unsurprisingly, given the inevitably close connections between the musicians involved in London's catch and glee culture, Webbe and Harrison each sang in the other's concert, while Harrison's included at least one glee by Webbe.[66] The unidentified selection given at Webbe's concert appears to have consisted largely of glees and songs, a format obviously not to the taste of the *Advertiser*'s reviewer, who noted oddly that the audience had greeted the concert 'without any apparent ill-humour, notwithstanding the unattractive nature of the music given them – which, however good, obviously wanted variety – as out of fifteen articles no less than eight of them were glees and sonacis [sic] of the same school'. Harrison's programme was more diversified, including as it did one of Haydn's recent symphonies and the eleventh of Handel's opus 6 Concerti grossi alongside several glees (four were advertised, but the report refers to three being performed), provoking the reviewer to note that not only had 'this species of composition of late years become very fashionable', but also that the encouragement of the Catch Club 'has raised an emulation and called forth merits that, but for such incitements, might well have lain dormant'.

Benefit concerts for both Webbe and Harrison continued to attract sporadic press attention, Harrison's in 1793 (held on 10 May at Willis's Rooms) drawing from the *Public Advertiser* a view diametrically opposed to that of its critic eight years earlier, when it noted that the glees had formed not only 'the greater part of the Selection', but opined that they had also formed 'the most pleasing part of the evening's entertainment'.[67] In keeping with most reviews of the period, detailed comment on performance and compositions was rare, but the first performance of one of Webbe's finest glees, *When winds breathe soft*, at his benefit on 10 April was greeted with enthusiasm by both the *Gazetteer* and the *Morning Chronicle*.[68] The review in the

---

[63] *Public Advertiser*, 14 March 1785.
[64] *Morning Chronicle*, 18 March 1785.
[65] Ibid.
[66] John Marsh provided an anecdote that well illustrates the camaraderie that existed within the catch and glee coterie. Calling at Harrison's in November 1798, he found assembled among others James Bartleman, Thomas Greatorex and Samuel Webbe the elder, 'some of whom were at whist'. Marsh, *Journals*, p. 680.
[67] *Public Advertiser*, 11 May 1793.
[68] *Gazetteer*, 12 April 1788; *Morning Chronicle*, 11 April 1788. The concert took place at the Freemasons' Hall.

former, probably written by the acerbic anti-Italian Joel Collier, is of interest for its praise of the 'elegant and captivating singing' of Harrison in Handel's 'Angels ever bright and fair' (from *Theodora*), which is contrasted with the 'meretricious ornaments of the Italian school'. In the opinion of this reviewer, Webbe's new glee would 'add to his reputation in this species of composition', praise enthusiastically echoed by the *Chronicle*: 'A musical composition more beautifully expressive, we never witnessed, and the rest of the audience seemed to feel the same sensations, for they testified their pleasure by repeating the very warm plaudit it instantaneously drew from them.'

In addition to Webbe the elder and Harrison, glee composers such as John Danby and other singers closely associated with the repertoire also held benefit concerts that included the performance of glees and catches. They include James Bartleman, Charles Knyvett the elder, John Sale, and Charles Dignum. Perhaps surprisingly given their increasing role in the concert performance of glees, the only women singers to have included them in their benefits were the three Abrams sisters, Harriet, Eliza, and Theodosia, who did so on four occasions. Harriet was herself the composer of the glee *Crazy Jane*, and all three sisters appear to have taken a special interest in the repertoire, their names appearing on publication subscription lists on several occasions.[69] In addition to singers, other notable musicians appear to have felt by the 1780s that glees were a sufficiently established part of concert repertoire to include them in their benefit concerts. Among these were the oboist William Parke, whose membership of the 'alternative' Glee Club, and observations on clubs we encountered in Chapter 4,[70] the noted trumpeter James Sarjant (or Serjeant), who may have become acquainted with the repertoire as a result of his association with Vauxhall Gardens, and the violinist John Hindmarsh, for whom Haydn conducted a Hanover Square Rooms benefit concert on 3 June 1795 that included two unidentified 4-part glees.[71]

Full details of the catches and glees performed at Vauxhall, for many years the most popular of all the London pleasure gardens, and Ranelagh appear only sporadically, information being almost totally lacking for the 1770s. But it is likely that by at least the following decade glees and catches were regularly included in the programmes of both gardens, a practice that can be traced until at least 1795. The opening night of the 1785 Vauxhall season took place on 19 May, an event attended by an assembly 'which was genteel and more numerous than might have been expected from the badness of the weather'. A new catch and new glee (both unidentified) 'were much admired'.[72] We have no further records for that season, but an unusually full record exists for the following summer and is worth looking at in greater detail, since it almost certainly conforms to a general pattern.[73] Concerts at Vauxhall were given every night except Sunday throughout a season that ran from

---

[69] Among publications on which the name appears as a subscriber are Benjamin Cooke's *Nine Glees and Two Duetts*, op. 5 (1795), subscribed to by both 'Miss Abrams' and 'Miss T. Abrams of Charlotte Street', Webbe the elder's *A Selection of Glees* (1812), and Joseph Corfe's *Twelve Glees* [...] *Composed from Ancient Scotch Melodies* (1791).
[70] See above p. 72ff.
[71] Robbins Landon, *Haydn Chronicle and Works*, p. 313. The author incorrectly refers to Hindmarsh as an oboist.
[72] *Morning Chronicle*, 21 May 1785.
[73] All Vauxhall details come from McVeigh, 'Calendar'.

late May until the end of August. The format of the concerts was the usual mix of vocal music (including choruses) and instrumental music, a particular feature being the performance of an organ concerto, often of his own composition, by James Hook (1746–1827), since 1774 the composer and organist in residence.[74] Not surprisingly, the programmes reveal the performance of a substantial number of works by Hook, two early concerts in the 1786 season (10 and 13 June) including an unnamed catch and glee by him, the glee given on the 13th advertised as 'new'.

This pattern of including a single example of each, invariably placed together as the final items of the first half of the entertainment, continued throughout the remainder of the season. From 15 to 23 June no details of composer or title were announced, but from 24 June through to the end of August the titles of both catch and glee are given, although their abbreviated form sometimes make positive identification difficult. While the majority of the programme changed each evening, it is striking that the same catch and glee were paired and performed over a period of time, subsequently alternating with a new coupling. The total repertoire was therefore much smaller than might have been expected in a season consisting of some sixty-five concerts, with no more than seven or at most eight different glees and catches being given. Thus had one attended Vauxhall between 24 and 28 June, the first part of the evening would have concluded with Stephen Paxton's popular glee *How sweet how fresh* and Arne's catch *The Street Intrigue* ('Hark you my dear'),[75] a coupling revived on 14 and 15 July. During the following week (29 June to 5 July) and again between 18 and 19 July, 24–27 July and 29 July to 3 August those attending the gardens would have heard two works of Hook's, the glee *Saw you the nymph* and the catch *The scornful*.[76] Other pieces that can be positively identified include Hook's glee *Come let us all a Maying go* (6–8, 12 and 13, 22 July), Benjamin Cooke's highly successful glee *Hark, the lark* (20 and 21, 28, 31 July; 4 August) in tandem with Webbe's catch *To the old long life*, John Danby's glee *When Sappho tun'd* (10 and 11, 15, 17, 23 August), and Aldrich's *Hark the bonny Christ Church bells* (7–9, 12, 14, 16, 18, 24, 26, 28 and 29 August), which by this time had achieved something like canonic status. No performers are listed and there is no indication as to whether any or all of the pieces included in the repertoire were given with instrumental accompaniment.

Fragmentary surviving details suggest that a similar format to that outlined above was adopted for other Vauxhall seasons, with just one of each genre included in the evenings' entertainment. Indeed, the opening programme of the 1787 season even maintained the same pairing of Cooke's *Hark, the lark* and the Webbe catch. Only the single entry for the 1795 season, the closing evening held on 1 September, deviates from this scheme. Here the programme time allotted to catches and glees has been doubled to four items, three of them composed by Hook.

Less documentary evidence of the performance of catches and glees at Ranelagh Gardens, Vauxhall's grander cousin, has come down to us. Once the most fashionable of the summer venues, Ranelagh went into decline during the last two

---

[74] Hook held a similar post at Marybone between 1768 and 1773.
[75] The glee by Stephen Paxton (1735–87) was published in a number of collections; Arne's catch was included in the second volume of the Warren Collection.
[76] *Saw you* was published in *A Collection of the Most Admir'd Glees and Catches for Three, Four and Five Voices* (Dublin, c.1780). The identity of the catch has not been established beyond its short title.

decades of the century before finally closing in 1803. Only three Ranelagh events of interest to the present survey stand out and they are more accurately described as one, since they consist of identical programmes almost wholly devoted to catches and glees presented on 15 June 1793, and revived on 30 May and 25 June 1794. All three concerts were announced both years in the *Oracle*, the advertisement noting that some of the catches and glees would be given with 'treble choir and instruments'. The conformity of programme and advertisement suggest a special event rather than a regular occasion. A particularly striking feature of the programme is the inclusion of an unusually large number of 'old' works, a practice that had by this time been largely abandoned by the Catch Club. Of a total of seventeen items, no fewer than seven fall into this category, including three of Purcell's catches, in addition to which Michael East's madrigal *How merrily we live*,[77] Thomas Morley's ballet *Now is the month of Maying* (one of the emblematic works of the glee movement),[78] and two part-songs by John Eccles were given, the last named as 'glees'. One is tempted to add to this list of 'classics' Arne's *Hush to peace*, already thirty years old. The contemporary glees performed were tried and tested favourites by Webbe (*Come live with me*), R. J. S. Stevens (*O mistress mine* and *Sigh no more ladies*), and the Earl of Mornington (*Here in cool grot*).

One of the notable features of London's concert life during the last three decades of the century was the intense competition between venues and concert promoters. That between the Professional Concerts and Salomon's Haydn series in 1792 is well known, but numerous other instances abound.[79] No building created a greater stir in this respect than the opening of the magnificent and sumptuously appointed Pantheon in Oxford Street in 1772.[80] The first major project of the promising young architect James Wyatt, the huge and splendid building featured an impressive dome bearing a resemblance to the famous rotunda at Ranelagh. During the 1770s the Pantheon became the most fashionable venue in London, but by the end of the decade the novelty had faded. Until 1786 there is no evidence of the catch and glee playing a part in the Pantheon's history, but during the winter of 1786/7 a series of fourteen weekly concerts introduced both into its programmes. Lasting from 21 November until 27 February, the series, under the direction of Barthélemon, was promoted as the 'Winter Ranelagh', the emulation extending to tickets priced at only 3s 6d, considerably less than the Pantheon had charged its society clientele during its heyday. The opening concert programmed only a single 'glee', Wilbye's evergreen madrigal *Flora gave me fairest flowers*,[81] and Thomas Baildon's ubiquitous 'political' catch *Mr Speaker*, the performance of which according to the *Morning Chronicle* 'set the whole room in ecstasy'.[82] The tenor Daniel Arrowsmith, making 'his first appearance since his arrival from the metropolis of Ireland', was particularly singled out for praise in the performance of the catch, which 'he kept up the spirit of with great

---

[77] Originally published in East's *Second Set of Madrigals* (1606).
[78] From Morley's *Balletts for five voices* (1595).
[79] See McVeigh, *Concert Life*, particularly the early chapters.
[80] The profound effect the Pantheon had on such fashionable concert venues as Teresa Cornelys' lavishly equipped Carlisle House in Soho is colourfully documented by Judith Summers in *The Empress of Pleasure: The Life and Adventures of Teresa Cornelys* (London, 2003).
[81] From the *First Set of Madrigals*, of 1598.
[82] *Morning Chronicle*, 24 November 1786.

humour, and we pronounce him to be one of the finest catch singers in the kingdom'.[83]

The remaining concerts included two glees and two catches alongside the customary miscellaneous selection of songs, concertos and 'full' pieces (symphonies and overtures). In contrast to the pattern noted elsewhere, the Pantheon provided its audiences with a rather broader range of catch and glee repertoire, twenty-six different works being introduced over the course of the season. They include a blend of old and contemporary works, Purcell again being surprisingly well represented by six catches. Among other catches we find William Herschel's famous 'Echo' Catch, given on no fewer than six occasions, when the spatial possibilities offered by the Pantheon were doubtless exploited to the full. The repertoire of glees again tends to confirm an established core repertoire of concert pieces concentrated on works of the more refined, 'sentimental' type, recognition that more convivial glees (let alone those of a risqué nature) were unsuited to concert performance to mixed audiences. Among them are four by Webbe, including *Come live with me* (two performances), *You gave me your heart* (2), *A gen'rous friendship* (3) and *To the old long life* (2), all staple concert repertoire. The same applies to Cooke's *Hark, the lark*, which with four performances was the most frequently sung glee during the 1786/7 season, Mornington's *Here in cool grot* (2), and Steven Paxton's *Go, Damon, go* (2) and *How sweet, how fresh* (1). One also notes the inclusion of works such as William Hayes' *Melting airs* (1) and Arne's *Sweet Muse* (3), both by this time more than thirty years old.

During the 1790s the gentrification of the concert glee repertoire became ever more marked, a development coinciding with the summit of the glee's fashionable status. The violinist and impresario Johann Peter Salomon later recalled that 'the taste for glees superseded that for instrumental music'.[84] Few vocal artists failed to include glees in their benefit concerts, some of which lend support to Salomon's view in that they consisted entirely of vocal music, a departure running counter to the paradigmatic formula of mixed vocal and instrumental concerts. One such, given for the bass John Sale at Willis's (formerly Almack's) Rooms on 1 May 1792, even managed the topical novelty of including 'prize catches and glees determined that day'.[85] Whether or not these were the Catch Club's winning entrants is uncertain;[86] Sale was never a privileged member of the Catch Club, but was at this time deputy conductor of the Glee Club. The latter may have made awards of its own, although there is no record of it doing so until considerably later. The ubiquity of glees in benefit concerts drew sharp criticism from the splenetic William Jackson, who complained 'that of all the numerous Dirges and doleful Ditties with which our Benefit-Concerts are so sorely afflicted – for they are too *precious* for common use – scarce one can be found that has half as much tune as one of Claude le Jeune's Psalms'.[87]

---

[83] Notwithstanding such extravagant praise, Arrowsmith's name appears nowhere else in the annals of catch and glee culture. According to Doane, he appeared at the Handel Commemoration(s) and also sang at Vauxhall Gardens.
[84] Quoted in McVeigh, *Concert Life*, p. 110. The source is a 'Memoir of Johann Peter Salomon' that appeared in *The Harmonicon*, 8 (1830).
[85] McVeigh, 'Calendar'. The announcement appeared in the *Oracle*.
[86] Both prize-winning glees that year (*See with ivy chaplet* and *Father of heroes*) were by Callcott.
[87] William Jackson, *Observations on the Present State of Music in London* (London, 1791), p. 14.

The major impetus behind the elevation of the glee to its highest public popularity was unquestionably the establishment in 1792 of the Vocal Concerts by the singers Samuel Harrison (1760–1812) and Charles Knyvett the elder (1752–1822), both privileged members of the Catch Club, and who also had associations with the Glee Club.[88] As the name suggests, the series took the radical step of including only vocal works in its concerts, mostly songs and glees, and immediately achieved a fashionable success that surprised many observers. By the time of the inaugural concert at Willis's Rooms on 11 February, Harrison and Knyvett were in the happy position of being able to close the subscription. The novelty of the series was observed by the press, *Woodfall's Register* referring to it as 'a new species of musical entertainment'. The newspaper continued by commenting on an audience that included a 'very numerous and brilliant circle, consisting of most of the higher patrons of the harmonic art in this country'. On the evidence of the opening concert, the writer, who one suspects might have had connections with the Vocal Concerts, expressed the view that 'there is every evidence to believe that this novel mode of introducing SINGING without any instrumental accompaniment, will prove a favourite with the public'.[89]

The initial season of the Vocal Concerts consisted of twelve concerts. Eight were held on Saturdays commencing 11 February 1792, while four additional concerts took place on Fridays, with separate subscriptions of 3 guineas and 1½ guineas respectively being available. As noted above, the 1792 series included no instrumental works, but in the following years a few orchestral works, mostly Handel overtures, were played by a small band led initially by the violinist John Mountain. In this form the Vocal Concerts, which had now settled to a season of ten Thursday concerts at a subscription of 4 guineas, existed until 1795, when it was abandoned. In 1801 it was revived in expanded guise, with a full orchestra and chorus employed.

The fact that Harrison and Knyvett were at the hub of London's concert life enabled them to draw on many of the leading vocal performers of the day, doubtless a factor that contributed to the immediate success of the Vocal Concerts. Among those appearing alongside the impresarios themselves are found such familiar figures as James Bartleman, John Sale, John Hindle, John Danby, John Page, Thomas Greatorex, Israel Gore, Samuel Webbe and Thomas Bellamy, all at one time or another associated with the Catch or Glee Club, or both. Significantly, in view of their ready assimilation into concert performances of glees, no woman singer was engaged during the four 1790s seasons of the Vocal Concerts,[90] which also appear to have performed the glee repertoire with minimal or no accompaniment.

The glee repertoire of the Vocal Concerts is remarkable for a wide-ranging diversity unmatched by any other concert-giving organisation, a fact representatively illustrated by the programme for the opening concert (Table 7). It has been reconstructed from press announcements cited in McVeigh's 'Calendar'. As the table shows, over half the pieces were designated as glees, two of which, the unidentified piece by Callcott and the R. J. S. Stevens glee, are listed as newly composed. This is

---

[88] Harrison had become a member in 1788, but resigned in 1790, while Knyvett, who had joined the following year remained a member until 1794, when he too resigned.
[89] *The Diary* or *Woodfall's Register*, 13 February 1792.
[90] Boys were employed to sing treble parts, as the inclusion of Charles Knyvett's son William among the vocalists for the inaugural concert testifies.

untrue of the Stevens, which was claimed by its composer to have been composed three years earlier and submitted to the Catch Club as a prize entry for 1790.[91] Seventeenth-century repertoire is represented by the enduring classics of Rogers and Ravenscroft.[92]

Table 7
Programme of the Opening Concert of the Vocal Concerts Given at Willis's Rooms on 11 February 1792

Benjamin Rogers – Glee *Come all noble souls*
William Jackson – Trio *In a vale*
Luffman Atterbury – Glee *Come let us all a-Maying go*
William Boyce – Song 'Softly rise' (from *Solomon*)
John Stafford Smith – Glee *While fools their time*
Thomas Arne/Jackson – Quartet *Where the bee sucks*
Gaetano Andreozzi – Song *Nel verdermi*
Samuel Webbe the elder – Catch *To the old long life*
John Wall Callcott – Glee *Peace to the souls of heroes*
Callcott – New Glee
John Danby – Glee *O let the merry peal*
Majo (Giovanni Maio) – Song *A morir*
Anonymous – Duet *From morn*
R. J. S. Stevens – Glee *To be gazing on these charms*
Thomas Ravenscroft – Glee *We be soldiers three*
Handel – Song 'Angels ever bright and fair' (from *Theodora*)
Webbe – Glee & Chorus *To love I wake*
Webbe – Glee *Away, away* (Hunting Glee)

Over the course of four seasons, 155 glees and catches by 33 different composers were given by the Vocal Concerts. Not unexpectedly, the repertoire is dominated by the familiar names of Webbe the elder (35 performances), Callcott (15), Atterbury, Benjamin Cooke, and John Stafford Smith (each with 10), who between them account for just over half of all performances. Of greater surprise is once again the remarkably strong showing of older repertoire, which in addition to the Ravenscroft just mentioned also included works by Purcell (5 performances), Rogers (2), Thomas Ford (2), Michael East (Este) (2), John Weelkes, John Hilton, Simon Ives, John Wilbye, John Eccles, and William Byrd. Only within the confines of the Madrigal

---

[91] Stevens, *Recollections*, p. 68.
[92] *We be soldiers three* was published by Hawkins in his *A General History* (vol. 2, p. 569) and written into the books of the Catch Club, the Canterbury Catch Club and the Bath Harmonic Society. It also appears in vol. 18 of the *Warren Collection*. Rogers' *Come all noble souls* was one of four 'glees' included in the 1673 edition of Playford's *Musical Companion* and was also written into the books of the Catch Club and included in vol. 3 of the *Warren Collection*.

Society would one otherwise find such a comprehensive listing of sixteenth- and seventeenth-century composers at this date. The Vocal Concerts' juxtaposition of old and new repertoire therefore bears testimony not only to the remarkably eclectic taste of its organisers, but also to the preservation of an indigenous repertoire viewed not as part of a nostalgia for the past, or in a dry academic sense, but as a living heritage.

Two further distinguishing features mark out the Vocal Concerts. The first is the near disappearance from the repertoire of works designated as catches, which after limited appearances during the first two seasons, ostensibly disappear from programmes. The truth is not so simple however, since in fact programmes simply took to advertising catches as glees, a trait illustrated in Table 7 by the 'glee' appellation given to Danby's catch *O let the merry peal*, an indication of the glee's infinitely more fashionable status in the last decade of the century. Among the works so mislabelled are several of Purcell's catches, including *Would you know how we meet*. Of equal significance is the composition of new glees specifically for the Vocal Concerts,[93] a feature hitherto only found in benefit concerts held on behalf of glee composers. While some were the work of such established glee composers as Callcott, Stevens and Webbe, others amounted to little more than the harmonisation of popular songs by Harrison and fellow performers such as Bartleman, or the erstwhile Salisbury Cathedral organist and Gentleman of the Chapel Royal, Joseph Corfe, whose two volumes of glees (1791) made from popular Scottish ballads achieved great popularity. The development was noted disapprovingly by William Gardiner, who observed that 'after Harrison and his fellow performers had sung the classical glees threadbare, they introduced, as a novelty, a mawkish sort of composition – ballads harmonised for four voices – to which they improperly gave the name of glees'.[94] Gardiner, writing with the benefit of hindsight, has here put an astute finger on one of the principal causes of the glee's decline, while his use of the word 'mawkish' taken alongside Jackson's 'doleful' suggests that musical observers recognised that by the 1790s the glee was not only being taken over by sentimentality, but was also losing the freshness and vitality that had for three decades been the hallmark of its finest examples. The Vocal Concerts may thus be viewed as pursuing a paradoxical aesthetic that espoused both the preservation of a valuable existing heritage, while at the same time undermining a vital contemporary form.

The success of the Vocal Concerts may well at least in part have provided the impetus for one of London's most successful and fashionable concert organisations to introduce glees for the first time. The Professional Concert was founded in 1785 by a co-operative under the direction of the violinist Wilhelm Cramer, one of the

---

[93] The 1792 Vocal Concert season inspired the publication of a book of glees by Longman and Broderip in association with Harrison and Knyvett. *The Favourite New Glees Composed by Dr. Cooke, Mr. Callcott, Mr. Danby and Mr. Webbe, expressly for and performed at Harrison and Knyvett's Vocal Concert* (1792) included 11 glees. However, as we have seen, Rubin is incorrect in stating that all were performed at the opening concert on 11 February (*The English Glee*, p. 68). They were in fact spread over the season. As the example of the Stevens glee given in the opening concert shows, caution also has to be exercised as to works claimed as 'new'.

[94] Gardiner, *Music and Friends*, vol. 3, p. 108. Popular operatic airs were also pressed into service as glees.

dominant figures in London's concert life. William Parke considered its concerts to be 'of the most perfect and gratifying kind' and the orchestra to be composed of 'the first talent in the kingdom'.[95] Its series, which lasted from mid-February to mid-May, consisted of twelve concerts given at the Hanover Square Rooms for a subscription of 5 guineas. At one time it appeared likely that it would be the Professional Concert that would lure Haydn to England, but eventually it would be Johann Peter Salomon, who had fallen out with the directors of the Professional Concert early in its existence and subsequently pursued an independent line, who ultimately succeeded in doing so. The intense rivalry between the Professional Concert and Salomon's first season with Haydn in 1792 was doubtless also in the mind of the directors of the Professional Concert as they prepared for the 1793 season in the full expectation of further competition. On Christmas Eve 1792 an announcement in the *Morning Herald* informed prospective subscribers 'that in Addition to the usual Performances, Glees, Madrigals, Anacreontics, Pastorals, &c &c.' would be included in its forthcoming season, adding the further enticement that such pieces would be 'written and composed by the most famous Authors, expressly for the Concert'.[96] This news was amplified by the *Morning Post* on New Year's Day 1793, the newspaper's 'Winter Musicals' listings stating that 'The Professional Concert follows the popular plan this season of introducing Catches, Glees, &c.'[97] In the event, the Professional Concert had no competition from Haydn to fear that year; he did not return to England until 1794.

In keeping with its promise, the opening Professional Concert on 18 February (reportedly attended by an audience of about eight hundred) included a new glee by Webbe the elder, announced in press advertisements as being 'Addressed to the genius of Britain'.[98] According to the report in *Woodfall's Register*, it was set to poetry by 'Peter Pindar',[99] which allows for conjecture that the glee in question was *Come push round with spirit*, the only glee by Webbe known to have words by Pindar. In the opinion of the *Morning Herald* it had 'great merit'. The reviewer also enjoyed the 'charmingly sung' performance of the other glee on the programme, R. J. S. Stevens' popular Shakespeare setting *Ye spotted snakes*,[100] the soprano part of which was sung by Nancy Storace.[101] John Danby composed the new glee for the second concert on 25 February, *Hark! the chase*, a hunting piece also set to words by 'Peter Pindar' and sung by the soprano Sophia Dussek, the tenor Jonathan Nield, John(?) Buckley and Webbe the elder.[102] Significantly, the glee, which was repeated at the sixth concert on 1 April, was announced as being 'with accompaniments', as was an unidentified new glee by the elder Webbe introduced in the seventh concert on 8 April, suggesting that the concert glee with accompaniments was starting to be recognised as a clearly

---

[95] Parke, *Musical Memoirs*, vol. 1, p. 103.
[96] Quoted in Robbins Landon, *Haydn Chronicle and Works*, p. 212.
[97] Robbins Landon, *Haydn Chronicle and Works*, p. 213.
[98] Patriotic glees became fashionable during the French wars of the 1790s, although to a lesser degree than songs.
[99] *The Diary*, or *Woodfall's Register*, 19 February 1793. 'Peter Pindar' was the pseudonym of the poet John Wolcot.
[100] *Morning Herald*, 19 February 1793.
[101] *Woodfall's Register*, 19 February 1793.
[102] *Woodfall's Register*, 27 February 1793. *Hark! the chase* was repeated at the 6th concert on 1 April. It does not appear in Rubin's listing.

defined genre. The association of both Danby and Webbe with the series is confirmed by Webbe's appearance as a singer in at least two of the concerts (the third and fourth, held on 4 and 11 March respectively), at the first of which John Danby, whose *Fair Flora* was performed, was also engaged as a singer. Other 'new' glees were also contributed by R. J. S. Stevens, works that can be identified from his *Recollections*. One, *When the toil of day is o'er*, was a genuinely new work first performed at the 5th concert on 18 March,[103] but *What shall he have*, advertised as composed for the concert on 11 April (the 8th of the series), was certainly not new, having by Stevens' own account been composed as far back as 1783.[104] Curiously, glees seem to play no further part in the Professional Concert season after the concert on 11 April.

The 1793 season in fact turned out to be the organisation's last, and when Haydn returned to London for a further series of concerts in 1794, Salomon had the field to himself. Salomon's observation on the ubiquity of the glee has already been noted, a view that may account for his decision not to programme glees in his Haydn concerts. Nevertheless, the distinguished visitor could hardly escape contact with the glee's overwhelming late-century popularity. Haydn was elected a member of the Graduates Meeting following his receipt of a doctorate at Oxford in 1791 and he attended meetings on 28 October and 14 December, occasions on which he would certainly have been introduced to glee singing.[105] In addition Haydn directed benefit concerts that included glees in the programme. Among them was one at Hanover Square for the Miss Abrams that included an unidentified glee by Webbe the elder (21 March), while his direction of a benefit for the violinist John Hindmarsh was noted earlier. But Haydn's most lasting contribution to the form was to provide piano (or harp) accompaniments for a group of catches and glees by the Earl of Abingdon, a principal supporter of the Professional Concert, but later a patron and friend of the composer.[106]

The near-frenetic fervour for fashionable concert-going that reached a peak with Haydn's two visits shows a marked decline in the final few years of the century, no doubt at least in part due to increasing weariness with and attendant rising costs of the continuing French war. The glee, too, seems to have at least temporarily reached saturation point. While it continued to feature in benefit concerts, no further instances of glees being performed in regular London concert series are known during the remaining years of the eighteenth century.

The incursion of catches and glees into concerts inevitably spread to the provinces. Rather unexpectedly, the first instance that has so far come to light took place in 1772 at the Three Choirs Festival, a venerable charitable institution founded around 1716 or 1717 and based at the cathedrals of Worcester, Hereford and Gloucester, who took turns to host the festival annually. In addition to the cathedral performances (which invariably included one of *Messiah*), the festival generally also included a secular concert, an event frequently succeeded by a ball.[107] The 1772

---

[103] Stevens, *Recollections*, pp. 89–90.
[104] Stevens, *Recollections*, p. 46.
[105] See above pp. 82–3.
[106] *Twelve Sentimental Catches and Glees, For Three Voices Melodized by the Right Honble The Earl of Abingdon, The Accompaniment for the Harp or Pianoforte by the Celebrated Dr Haydn* (London, 1795).
[107] See Weber, *Musical Classics*, for an important discussion on the Three Choirs and other provincial festivals, p. 113ff.

festival was held in Gloucester between 9 and 11 September, the concert at the Booth Hall on the final evening 'consisting of Full Pieces, some of the most admired Catches and Glees, Solos and Concertos by Messrs Giardini, Fischer, and Crosdale [*recte* Crosdill]'.[108] The vocal performers are listed as Miss Linley, Miss M. Linley, Miss Radcliffe, Messrs Norris, Matthews, and Price. Elizabeth and Mary Linley will have been familiar with the catch and glee repertoire through their father Thomas, and brothers Thomas and William, all of whom composed catches and glees.[109] Thomas Norris (1741–90) also had strong connections with the catch and glee circle. He had become a privileged member of the Catch Club two years before the Three Choirs event and was the composer of a number of glees, including the popular *O'er William's Tomb*, composed on the death of the Duke of Cumberland in 1765. John Marsh heard Norris in what must have been one of his last appearances at the Catch Club before his early death in 1790, an occasion on which the singer's nerves 'were in so shatter'd a state that he spoil'd his own fine glee "*O'er William's tomb*" by bellowing out the tenor of it in a very boisterous and unequal manner…'.[110] Norris' poor health was doubtless responsible for such an uncharacteristic performance, but Marsh's observation again clearly implies that a degree of finesse was expected in the performance of glees.

As is apparent from Elizabeth Harris's afore-mentioned attendance at a 1775 Salisbury Festival concert of catches and glees, the lead (if lead it was) taken by the Three Choirs Festival was soon emulated by other provincial concerts and festivals. The Salisbury Festival, which started life as a celebration of St Cecilia's Day (22 November), was probably modelled on the Three Choirs Festival. Records show that the evening concert that so delighted Mrs Harris was the first occasion on which the festival had included an entire concert of catches and glees,[111] but the event became so successful that it was repeated every year throughout the remainder of the 1770s, the event being advertised in 1776 as being held 'by particular desire'. John Marsh (who had moved to Salisbury earlier the same year) was on hand with a description, observing that 'being something new they were very fully attended & were admirably sung by Norris Corfe Goss and Parry who all enter'd with great spirit into the humorous ones & made me laugh very much at the catch of *Mr Speaker, Beviamo tutti* &c'.[112] In the July of the previous year, Marsh had taken a rather different view of catches being performed at public concerts when he attended the Race Meeting concert in Winchester. Noting that catches and glees were 'beginning now to be introduc'd in concerts', he declared himself 'much pleas'd' with Michael East's seventeenth-century glee *How merrily we live*. However, Marsh felt the performance of Lord Mornington's popular catch '*Twas you, Sir* was less satisfactory, since it 'requir'd humour, & was certainly fitter for a convivial party than a public concert'. While it is possible that the performance lacked the necessary spirit, Marsh observed that the

---

[108] Advertisement in *Jackson's Oxford Journal*, 25 July 1772 and subsequent editions.
[109] William was also a founder member of the Glee Club in 1787, and was later also involved with the Catch Club and the Concentores Society – see above pp. 58 and 85.
[110] Marsh, *Journals*, p. 474.
[111] Douglas J. Reid (assisted by Brian Pritchard), 'Some Festival Programmes of the Eighteenth and Nineteenth Centuries. I – Salisbury and Winchester', *Royal Musical Association Research Chronicle*, 5 (1965), pp. 58–9.
[112] Marsh, *Journals*, p. 148. For Corfe, Goss and Parry see above p. 93.

singers, among them Corfe of Salisbury, were 'apprehensive of meeting with a hiss',[113] thereby articulating a fundamental problem attached to performing what was essentially an intimate, convivial form in large public spaces where subtleties of gesture and expression might well be lost.

Audience discrimination is again apparent in Marsh's account of what would be the last of the catch and glee concerts at the Salisbury Festival. By 1779 these events were no longer a novelty and their audience had by now developed very definite views on what they did and did not like:

> In the evening [of 26 August] I went to the performances of glees etc. which I co'd not resist as Miss Harrop was to sing in some of the principal ones, such as "Come live with me" [Webbe the elder], "You gave me your heart" [Webbe the elder] & "Hark the Lark" [Cooke], which went off inimitably well & were much applauded, but with respect to the other glees & particularly those with humour w'ch were to have been done, from Mr. Norris not being engaged this time who used to take the lead in them, they went off so flat that the performers soon became dispirited & not feeling bold enough to attempt some humorous ones that were printed in the bills, chang'd them for others, w'ch the audience not relishing, they began to hiss w'ch by the time of the concluding one "Beviamo tutti tré" [Giardini] increas'd to the greatest hubbub I ever knew in that room.[114]

That such experienced performers as Joseph Corfe and Robert Parry were apparently unable to project humour again highlights one of the main problems of performing humorous catches and glees in concert. While popular 'sentimental' glees such as those mentioned at the start of Marsh's account were 'much applauded', particularly when involving a leading singer such as Sarah Harrop,[115] efforts to communicate humour failed to impress the audience. It is probably not insignificant that identifiable glees programmed in London concerts after around 1780 overwhelmingly fall within the context of 'serious' pieces.

As is clear from the foregoing and the chapter devoted to provincial clubs, John Marsh took a great interest in the repertoire and its performance. He was himself the composer of twenty glees (and a single catch), which along with some of the most popular pieces of the day he introduced frequently into the subscription concerts he directed in Canterbury and Chichester. Marsh's close involvement makes him by far the most important single source of information on the catch and glee in provincial concert life, his observations on performance practice being of particular value. One area on which he held firm views was the intended one-to-a-part performance of catches and glees. Largely an unchallenged norm in London and more sophisticated provincial towns and cities, it was by no means universally adopted. When Marsh first started reorganising the subscription concerts in Canterbury he discovered

> that the boys were so badly taught by Porter, their master [Samuel Porter, the cathedral organist], that out of so many it was always difficult to find one or 2

---

[113] Marsh, *Journals*, p. 132.
[114] Marsh, *Journals*, p. 204.
[115] Sarah Harrop was widely considered to be one of the finest English sopranos of her day, being particularly noted for the purity of her voice.

fit to sing a single song & even the upper part of a glee without another to support him, on w'ch account when we came to try over the glee of Dr Harington's for a treble, tenor & bass ("Gentle Airs") at the rehearsal, Mr Porter brought 3 boys to sing the upper part, saying that if they were not enough I might have more [Marsh's emphasis], to w'ch I replied that as it was for a glee not a chorus that I wanted them, one or at most 2. wo'd be sufficient.[116]

Marsh's sarcastic dismissal of Porter's offer reveals a man accustomed to hearing glees and catches performed in more refined style, as does his observation on hearing the choir of the Dock Chapel in Portsmouth perform 'glees, elegies &c. in a very solemn style'. 'They might indeed', he continues, 'with as much propriety have been termed chorusses [Marsh's emphasis] there being 9 or 10 singers & of course 2 or 3 to a part.'[117]

As was the case at the catch clubs and domestic musical events held in cathedral cities, Marsh was largely dependent on vicars choral and cathedral choristers for his glee singers at the public subscription concerts he directed. In Canterbury he lists five male singers in addition to the choice of boys offered by Samuel Porter, while in Chichester he was reliant on the services of Toghill, Moore, Middleton and Webber, the vicars choral already encountered as leading singers of the Chichester Catch Club. While their amateur status at subscription concerts (where they sang solo songs in addition to glees) provided a free source of vocal music, it also meant that their attendance was far from guaranteed or reliable, a situation that caused Marsh constant frustration. 'It beginn'g now to be very difficult to get a song from the gent'n or to depend on their coming', he observed in November 1789, 'we had this even'g only two songs [...] & no glee.'[118] By February the following year matters had become more acute:

At this concert [12 February] were neither Mess'rs Toghill, Moore, Middleton or Webber [...] Mr Moore now began to make it so much a favor that I became tir'd of asking him, so that it was now very difficult to get the vocal part of the Concert supplied [...] Having now only Mr T & young Prince [a treble] to sing, we could now seldom raise a glee [...] & could sometimes have but one song in an act w'ch was probably the principal cause of the falling off of the subscription.[119]

Marsh's final words are of significance for the clear emphasis they place on the importance of vocal music in eighteenth-century concert life. His view would seem to be vindicated by the revival of fortunes enjoyed by the Chichester Concert in the 1790s, a period when the vocal forces were strengthened.

While Marsh mentions no specific glee performances at the Canterbury subscription concerts, his listing of adult glee singers and the request to Samuel Porter for boys conclusively proves they formed part of his programming. In Chichester the first concert given under Marsh's direction on 5 October 1787

---

[116] Marsh, *Journals*, p. 300.
[117] Marsh, *Journals*, pp. 367–8.
[118] Marsh, *Journals*, p. 462.
[119] Marsh, *Journals*, p. 467.

included John Stafford Smith's popular hunting glee *Hark the hollow woods resounding*, a work he tells us 'was brought by me to Chichester, where it was quite new'.[120] Over the course of the next quarter of a century some seventy-five glees can be identified from Marsh's writings as being given at Chichester concerts.[121] Given that Marsh did not mention every work he performed the true figure is undoubtedly substantially higher. The identifiable repertoire represents a balanced mix of established 'classics' such as Benjamin Cooke's *Hark, the lark*, the elder Webbe's *You gave me your heart* and *When winds breath soft*, with more recent favourites like the Shakespeare settings of R. J. S. Stevens and the extraordinarily popular Callcott glees *The Friar of Orders Grey* and *The Red Cross Knight*, the former the most often programmed of all glees by Marsh in public concerts. Callcott was also the most frequently performed composer in a list dominated by him and Webbe the elder. Not surprisingly, seven of Marsh's own glees were given, several of which received their first performance at a Chichester concert. The increasing popularity of the harmonised song type of glee that met with William Gardiner's disapproval is reflected in the inclusion of a number of such pieces in programmes dating from the late 1790s and early 1800s. Also worth noting in the concert programmes of the war-torn 1790s is the significant number of patriotic glees, among which was one of the most popular, Callcott's *Peace to the Souls of Heroes*, and two composed by Marsh himself.

While a full-scale investigation of advertised provincial concert programmes is a daunting task that remains to be undertaken, it would be unrealistic to suppose that the evidence drawn from John Marsh's experiences in Salisbury, Canterbury and Chichester marks out those cities as unique in their incorporation of the glee into public concerts. Indeed, even limited research clearly indicates that the practice was widespread not only in major centres where regular concerts were given, but also in smaller towns that mounted only the occasional concert, often an annual benefit for a local musician. In Norwich, one of the largest provincial cities in the eighteenth century, catches and glees made their appearance in subscription concerts by the 1780s at the latest, while analysis of five surviving subscription concert programmes from the spring of 1795 shows the performance of no fewer than nine glees.[122] As in London, glees also made their appearance in the pleasure garden concerts that sprang up in emulation of those of the capital. At the height of their popularity, Norwich had four such gardens, the first established as early as 1750. A programme from one such concert, given on 16 April 1791 at Keymer's Pantheon (a garden that incorporated an auditorium capable of holding a thousand people), shows a typically diversified mixture of orchestral, instrumental and vocal music including John Stafford Smith's glee *Hark the hollow woods resounding* and Webbe's *Swiftly o'er the mountain brow*.[123]

Newly fashionable Brighton also had pleasure gardens that played host to musical events. From at least the mid-1790s the Promenade Grove, situated in what is today

---

[120] Marsh, *Journals*, p. 417.
[121] Brian Robins 'John Marsh and provincial music making in eighteenth-century England: Appendix', *The Royal Musical Association Research Chronicle*, 29 (1996), pp. 107–42.
[122] Fawcett, *Norwich*, p. 50.
[123] 'A. H. Mann Notebooks', No. 2., p. 7. Norfolk Record Office, MS 435. The 'Notebooks', 24 in all, consist of a binding of a collection of handwritten notes detailing concert programmes in Norfolk.

the Steyne, held Friday evening subscription concerts under the patronage of the Prince of Wales. A half guinea subscription entitled the subscriber to three tickets. Described as 'a perfect Vauxhall in miniature',[124] the summer residence of the Prince and his entourage created a sufficiently fashionable society to attract leading London performers, the concerts being jointly directed by two such notable figures, François Barthélemon and Thomas Attwood. A number of programmes advertised in the *Sussex Weekly Advertiser* suggest that glees formed a staple of Promenade Grove concerts, one generally being given in each half. Although there is no indication as to whether they were instrumentally accompanied, the naming of performers shows that they were given one voice per part, one 'Master Welsh' gaining particularly high praise for his contribution to the two glees given at a Promenade Grove concert in July 1794.[125]

Although Brighton had to wait until 1799 for regular winter subscription concerts, there was no shortage of musical activity in the town out of the summer season. Then residents could choose from a variety of singly promoted and benefit concerts mounted by local musicians, who frequently chose to include glees in their programmes. Neighbouring Lewes, less fashionable despite it being the county's administrative centre, was unable to present regular concerts, but benefit concerts given there by local musicians sometimes managed to find three or four singers to cater for the popular taste for glees, which also appear in a benefit concert given in Horsham. Analysis of 24 programmes advertised in the *Sussex Weekly Advertiser* between the late 1780s and 1810 (excluding those given by John Marsh in Chichester) reveal a total of 39 glees being performed in seventeen different concerts throughout the county. As might be expected by this period, only a single catch is included. Callcott's dominance of glee composition in the last decade of the century is again reflected by the number of performances received by four of his glees, the combined total of eleven far in excess of anything achieved by any other composer. Significantly, in view of his good showing in Chichester, not one of Samuel Webbe the elder's glees is listed as having been performed in other Sussex concerts. Since available evidence suggests that Webbe continued to maintain his ascendancy in London concerts during the 1790s, it can be conjectured that Callcott's less demanding writing was perhaps more suited to those provincial concerts that lacked the guiding spirit of a John Marsh or experienced cathedral singers to perform glees.

To conclude this brief snapshot of glee performances in smaller provincial concerts, we might note four events advertised by *Jackson's Oxford Journal* during the late winter and spring of 1779/80. Held respectively at the Cross Keys Inn, Buckingham on 23 February under the direction of Mr Dobney,[126] Woodstock Town Hall on 27 March (given by the Bucks Band under their Master, Mr Cline),[127] the Crown Inn, Bicester on 8 April,[128] and the Blankethall Inn, Witney on 3 May,[129] all were advertised as concerts of vocal and instrumental music consisting of overtures,

---

[124] *Sussex Weekly Advertiser*, 20 August 1798.
[125] *Sussex Weekly Advertiser*, 28 July 1794.
[126] *Jackson's Oxford Journal*, 12 February 1780.
[127] *Jackson's Oxford Journal*, 18 March 1780.
[128] *Jackson's Oxford Journal*, 8 April 1780.
[129] *Jackson's Oxford Journal*, 29 April 1780.

concertos, songs, catches, and glees. No programme details are given, but the mounting of four such concerts within a relatively small geographical area and short space of time is persuasive evidence of the degree to which the catch and glee had entered the provincial concert hall by the start of the 1780s.

The introduction of the glee (and more rarely the catch) into stage works represents a third incursion it made into more general musical life. The loss of many scores from the period means that it is difficult to determine the full extent to which this happened, but from the early 1780s it appears that glees played a significant role in stage works. Attention has already been drawn to the linking of theatrical entertainments with the performance of catches and glees instigated in the 1770s by Arne and others, with Dibdin going so far as to introduce an independent catch club scene into one of his operas. In the following decade composers progressed a step further and started to introduce glees into operas, plays, and music drama. These were either borrowed from the popular established repertoire or newly composed for the work in question. The earliest example established so far dates from 1775, with the inclusion of both a glee and a catch in *The Duenna*, a pastiche first given at Covent Garden on November 21 and a piece set to become one of the most popular English operas of the eighteenth century. Set in Spain with a libretto by Richard Brinsley Sheridan, *The Duenna* drew on a wide variety of sources. The most substantial contribution was that of Thomas Linley the younger, although it was his father who was responsible for the glee 'In our daily occupations', sung in the third and final act by a group of friars (it is also known as *The Friar's Glee*).[130] *The Duenna* also included *Soft pity never leaves*, which was published as a glee but was in fact William Hayes' catch *Epitaph on Sophocles*, while the melody for the finale was taken from Thomas Morley's *Now is the month of Maying*, a madrigal that enjoyed canonical status within the catch club milieu.[131]

There is no evidence that the apparent precedent set by *The Duenna* was emulated until 1782, when the floodgates opened with no fewer than four works introducing at least one glee. The impetus was provided by Samuel Arnold, already encountered as a leading light in the Anacreontic Society and the Glee Club, who led the way with his *Harlequin Teague* (Little Theatre, 17 August 1782) a pantomime that included a single unidentified glee.[132] *Harlequin Teague* satirises a well-known quack philosopher of the day, having a plot not dissimilar to that of Arnold's *The Genius of Nonsense* (Little Theatre, 2 November 1780). The latter included two catches, Purcell's *Soldier, soldier* and Henry Harington's *Look, neighbours look*.[133] Two further works described in the vocal score as catches do not conform to the description. Some three months after the appearance of *Harlequin Teague*, what was destined to become one of Arnold's most successful works reached the Covent Garden stage. The opera *The Castle of Andalusia* (2 November 1782), a reworking of *The Banditti* of the previous year, includes two accompanied glees, one of which, 'Social pow'rs' set an emulated

---

[130] The contrivance of introducing friars into his pantomime *Robinson Crusoe* (Drury Lane, 29 January 1781) offered Linley the opportunity of reviving the glee.
[131] Fiske, *English Theatre Music*, Appendix E, pp. 601–2.
[132] Samuel Arnold, *The Overture, Songs [...] and Glee in the Speaking Pantomime of Harlequin Teague, or The Giant's Causeway*. Opera XIX. London (*c.* 1782).
[133] Samuel Arnold, *The Genius of Nonsense, An Original, Whimsical, Operatical, Pantomimical, Farcical, Electrical, Naval and Military Extravaganza* (London, 1784).

precedent by forming the work's finale.[134] By the end of the year the rival pantomimes staged at Covent Garden and Drury Lane had followed suit by including glees. *The Triumph of Mirth* (Covent Garden, 25 November 1782) was the work of Thomas Linley the elder, who included a single glee,[135] but the title page of William Shield's *The Lord Mayor's Day* (Drury Lane, 26 December 1782) suggests that it must have included at least two glees.[136]

Newcastle-born Shield has previously been encountered as a member of the second Glee Club founded in 1793.[137] In 1784 he succeeded Michael Arne as house composer at Covent Garden, becoming the most prolific and successful English theatre composer during the 1780s. The foundations for Shield's dominance of the decade were laid by the extraordinary popularity of his afterpiece *Rosina*, which received its first performance at Covent Garden on 31 December 1782, thereafter establishing Shield's virtual monopoly of productions at the theatre until he quarrelled with the management in 1797.[138] *Rosina* does not include any glees, but there is an adaptation of a catch in the shape of John Worgan's *Care, thou canker*, one of a number of borrowings incorporated into the opera.[139] Shield's interest in preserving his musical heritage led him to incorporate numerous ballad and folk tunes into his music theatre works, in addition to which a significant number of his dramatic works include glees and, in a few instances, catches. Table 8, without claiming to be exhaustive, details the stage works of Shield after *Rosina* that have been identified as including glees and catches.

Shield's employment of glees and catches in his operas, either of his own composition or drawn from the popular repertoire, is generally clearly differentiated from the many ensembles and choruses also included in them. While content to follow Arnold's exemplar in using glees as set-piece act openers or finales, Shield greatly expanded their dramatic usage, often with a specific purpose. The inclusion of glees in earlier operas such as *Robin Hood* or *The Noble Peasant*, the plot of which is set in Saxon times, perpetuated the tacit association between the glee and 'archaism' and it is no surprise to find several glees in both. *Robin Hood* opens with a glee, *In Sherwood's grove*, and concludes the first act with Lord Mornington's vernal *Here in cool grot*,[140] while the second act was brought to a close with a glee by John Stafford Smith.[141] The 'chain finale', a favourite device of Shield's, incorporates James Hook's catch *Fill the foaming bowl*, an idea Shield had already used in *The Noble Peasant*, whose finale introduces an 'Ancient glee' in the shape of Freeman's madrigal *We be soldiers three* (1614), here renamed 'We three archers be'. The same opera opens with another

---

[134] Samuel Arnold, *The Castle of Andalusia: A comic opera as it is performed at the Theatre Royal in Covent Garden* (London, 1782?).
[135] *The Tunes, Songs, Glee &. in the Pantomime of the Triumph of Mirth or Harlequin's Wedding* [...] *Composed and Selected by Mr Linley*.
[136] William Shield, *The Overture, Duett, Glees etc. in* [...] *The Lord Mayor's Day*. London (*c*. 1782).
[137] See above p. 81. There is no evidence to support the suggestion in revised *New Grove* that Shield was a founder member of the club.
[138] Fiske dates Shield's dispute with the theatre to 1791. See *English Theatre Music*, p. 453.
[139] Fiske, *English Theatre Music*, Appendix E, p. 612.
[140] Fiske observes that Shield spoilt the effect of Mornington's silences near the end of the glee by filling them in with piccolo bird song – *English Theatre Music*, p. 415.
[141] *Robin Hood, or Sherwood Forest. A comic opera* [...] *Compos'd & Compiled by William Shield* (London, 1784).

glee of Smith's, *Come my good fellows*.[142] A later instance of Shield's use of glees in historical drama occurs in his highly successful adaptation of Grétry's *Richard Coeur de Lion*, where the king's adventures are embellished with two glees, 'If health's fair rose', another 'old glee' adapted from an unidentified seventeenth-century source, and 'Sweet peace of mind', adapted from William Hayes' *Melting airs*.[143]

Table 8
Dramatic Works by William Shield Incorporating Glees & Catches

Title and Genre	Venue & Premiere date
The Election -- ?Afterpiece	CG, ?
Friar Bacon – Pantomime	CG, 23 December 1783
Robin Hood – Opera	CG, 17 April 1784
The Noble Peasant – Opera	LT, 2 August 1784
Fontainebleau – Opera	CG, 16 November 1784
The Magic Cavern – Pantomime	CG, 27 December 1784
The Nunnery – Afterpiece	CG, 12 April 1785
Omai – Pantomime	CG, 20 December 1785
Richard Coeur de Lion (Grétry) – Opera	CG, 16 October 1786
The Enchanted Castle – Pantomime	CG, 26 December 1786
The Woodman – Opera	CG, 26 February 1791
Hertford Bridge – Afterpiece	CG, 3 November 1792
Sprigs of Laurel – Afterpiece	CG, 11 May 1793
The Travellers in Switzerland – Opera	CG, 22 February 1794
Netley Abbey – Afterpiece	CG, 10 April 1794
The Mysteries of the Castle – Music Drama	CG, 31 January 1795
Two Faces under a Hood – Opera	CG, 17 November 1807

CG – Covent Garden. LT – Little Theatre, Haymarket.

In two pantomimes, a genre that by definition calls for spectacle and magic, Shield calls on the glee for special effects. *The Magic Cavern* includes a trio that moves into 'Hark from spheres above', a glee directed to be sung with echoes *in lontano*, while the pantomime also includes a four-part glee 'Tis virtue', sung 'by spirits from behind the trees'.[144] In *The Enchanted Castle* a group of enchanted animals is called upon to sing a glee, 'Release us if you pray'.[145] *The Mysteries of the Castle* also includes a glee put to a special purpose, although in this instance the idea of a 'Glee sung by the Boatmen rowing to the shore' was borrowed from Stephen Storace's *The Pirates* (King's

---

[142] William Shield, *The Noble Peasant. A comic opera*, (London, 1784).
[143] *Richard Coeur de Lion. An opera [...] Composed by [...] Gretry, Anfossi, Bertoni, Dr Hayes, Dr Wilson, Carolan and W. Shield* (London, 1786). The unidentified 'old glee' may be an adaptation from a piece by John Wilson.
[144] William Shield, The Overture, Incidental Music and Songs in the Entertainment of *The Magic Cavern* (London, 1785).
[145] *The Pantomime of The Enchanted Castle [...] The Poetry by M. P. Andrews. The Music Selected & Composed by W. Shield* (London, 1787).

Theatre, 21 November 1792).[146] In a few cases, such as 'Thus on bended knees' from act 1 of *The Travellers in Switzerland*, Shield introduced semi-dramatised glees that move the action forward.[147]

Shield's predilection for the inclusion of glees in his stage works appears to have reached a peak in *The Woodman*, a three-act comic opera that took for its subject the contemporary craze for women's archery. No fewer than six glees are introduced,[148] one of those in act 1 being an unaccompanied 'Woodmen's Glee' of Shield's own composition, while act 2 includes a 3-part drinking glee, unsurprisingly as popular a sub-genre on the stage as it was in the clubs, and act 3 a glee accompanied by a bugle horn.[149] Finally, we might note the glee 'Ah, how can I leave' that opens Shield's last comic opera, *Two Faces under a Hood*, its unusual SSA scoring accounted for by its setting in a nunnery. Evidence that Shield had remained faithful to the glee to the last is provided by the inclusion of three further glees in the opera.[150]

Two Faces under a Hood represented a belated and unsuccessful late return to the stage by Shield, the homespun popularity of whose music dramas had been largely supplanted during the 1790s by the more ambitious operas of Stephen Storace (1762 –96). Trained in Naples, and along with his sister Nancy a friend of Mozart, Storace was a more sophisticated composer than Shield. He had two *opere buffe* produced in Vienna before he returned to England, where he became *de facto* house composer to Drury Lane, working alongside the official house composer, the elder Thomas Linley. Although Storace to some extent modelled his English stage works on those of Shield, not being averse to the borrowings that played such a large part in those of the older composer, he displayed markedly less inclination to introduce glees into them. According to Jane Girdham,[151] Storace composed only four glees, three of which, including 'Five times by the taper's light' from *The Iron Chest* (Drury Lane, 12 March 1796), function as the introductory number. The 'musical entertainment' *The Three and the Deuce* (Little Theatre, 2 September 1795) also included at least one glee.[152] *The Glorious First of June* (Drury Lane, 2 July 1794), a one-act pastiche hastily assembled by Sheridan and Storace to celebrate Lord Howe's victory over the French off Ushant, included several glees, and opened with Baildon's *Adieu to the village delights*.[153] Storace's death on 16 March 1796 at the early age of 34 inspired *Mahmood* (Drury Lane, 30 April 1796), a pastiche mounted for the benefit of his widow and child that drew on Storace's own music in addition to that of others, among them Joseph Corfe, whose glee arranged from the ballad *From shades of night* was included.[154]

---

[146] *The Mysteries of the Castle, a Dramatic Tale* [...] *The Music Selected & Composed by Mr Shield* (London, 1795).
[147] *The Travellers in Switzerland, a Comic Opera* [...] *Selected & Composed by W. Shield* (London, 1794).
[148] Fiske's claim that there are six glees in the first two acts is not supported by the vocal score.
[149] *The Woodmen, a Comic Opera.*[...] *Composed chiefly by W. Shield* (London, 1791).
[150] William Shield, *Two Faces under a Hood. A comic opera in three acts* [...] *written by T.Dibdin &c.* (London, 1807).
[151] Jane Girdham, *English Opera in Late Eighteenth-Century London: Stephen Storace at Drury Lane* (Oxford, 1997), p. 194. The author's assertion that Storace 'composed only four glees in his entire career' is misleading. He in fact composed a number of independent glees.
[152] Stephen Storace, *The Three and the Deuce. A Musical Entertainment* (London, 1795).
[153] *The favorite Airs, Duett, Glees and Choruses in the New Musical Entertainment called The Glorious First of June* (London, c. 1795).
[154] *Mahmood. Overture &c.* (London, 1797).

Of James Hook's few larger stage works, at least one includes glees. There are three in *Jack of Newbury* (Drury Lane, 6 May 1795), among them a 4-part 'Madrigal for Minstrels' with harp accompaniment, an instrument R. J. S. Stevens had used in his Ossianic glee *O strike the harp* and a further illustration of the clearly defined link between the glee and 'antiquity'.[155] Among the small number of glees otherwise known to come from the stage, we can note William Linley's *Well, brother, our merry old king is dead*, the opening glee and chorus from *The Merchant of Bruges* (an adaptation of *The Beggar's Bush* (1612) by Beaumont and Fletcher),[156] and *The Naval Pillar*, a patriotic pastiche produced at Covent Garden on 7 October 1799.[157] The later use of glees in music drama lies beyond the scope of the present study, but they certainly continued to be widely introduced, as the presence of some 150 glees in the stage works of Henry Bishop convincingly shows.

While detail concerning the incorporation of the glee and catch into the music theatre of the eighteenth century cannot be other than sketchy, certain generalised conclusions can be drawn. The practice peaked in the 1780s, when the predominant themes of conviviality and gentle sentimentality made them an appropriate vehicle for the operas of Shield, who at times clearly used them for special dramatic effect. Within the context of stage performance, the glee invariably appeared in orchestrated form, often being used to open an opera immediately after the overture, or to close an act in place of a chorus. In common with its performance in the home and the concert, the opera house was never a comfortable home for the true glee, which as this study has shown continued to find its natural milieu in the clubs that had first fostered it.

---

[155] James Hook, *Jack of Newbury, an Opera, in Three Acts with a Masque, in honor of the Royal Nuptials* [...] *Op. 80* (London, 1780).

[156] William Linley, *The Opening Glee and Chorus* [...] *in the revived play of the Merchant of Bruges* (London, 1815).

[157] *The Overture, Songs, Glees and Dance in the New Popular Entertainment of The Naval Pillar...* (London, c. 1799). The entertainment was compiled by the Irish violinist John Moorhead, who also contributed some of the music. It included a Finale based on *The Anacreontic Song*, described as an 'Old Air'!

Chapter 7

The Glee: Aesthetics, Form and Poetry

'That which makes its way most directly into the human heart is the human voice [...] The notes of a man's voice, well tuned and well managed have a mellow variety and energy, beyond those of any instruments' – James Beattie [1]

Any discussion of the glee and the musical aesthetics that informed the period must take as its starting point a fundamental question that exercised musicians and writers on music throughout the eighteenth century: to what degree, if any, is music an imitative art? The question is closely bound to the broader considerations that formed Enlightenment thinking: topics such as the nature of beauty and the expression not just of the passions, but specifically of 'agreeable' passions. Such subjects were widely discussed not only in a general context, but also with specific reference to the arts, which were often compared in their varying abilities to evoke such passions.[2] In 1744 James Harris specifically set out in the second of his *Three Treatises* to compare painting, music and poetry.[3] For Harris, music, which by definition lacked the preciseness of visual art and poetry, could not be an art of imitation without the aid of words. Instrumental music, 'which can only raise affections, which soon languish and decay if not maintained and fed by the nutritive images of poetry' was thus clearly an inferior form. Equally, in Harris's view poetry had its own limitations, since without music it 'must be necessarily forced to waste many of its richest ideas in the mere raising of affections'. Thus 'it is evident that these two arts can never be so powerful singly as when they are powerfully united'.[4]

Harris's conclusions were neither original nor accepted by all, but they were widely influential and frequently echoed by other writers, while his connections with catch and glee culture make them of particular interest to the present study. One who was not prepared to accept Harris' verdict that vocal music at least had certain mimetic qualities was the Newcastle-born composer Charles Avison, who in his important and frequently forward-looking *Essay on Musical Expression* (1752–53) argued that music was in essence not a mimetic art since it was capable only of imitating sounds that bore a relationship with itself.[5] Even when discussing the setting of poetry, Avison's view seems very different from that of Harris, for having mocked the idea of musical word-painting, he is at pains to stress that the musician's

---

[1] James Beattie, *On Poetry and Music* (Edinburgh, 1778), p. 152.
[2] Francis Hutcheson, *An Inquiry into the Original of our Ideas of Beauty and Virtue* (London, 1725), is an early eighteenth-century example of a general survey that takes music into account. Relevant extracts are included in Peter le Huray and James Day (eds.), *Music and Aesthetics in the Eighteenth and Early-Nineteenth Centuries* (Cambridge, 1981), pp. 23–6.
[3] James Harris, *Three Treatises. The First Concerning Art, the Second Concerning Music, Poetry and Painting, the Third Concerning Happiness* (London, 1744). Extracts quoted in *Music and Aesthetics*, pp. 36–9.
[4] *Music and Aesthetics*, p. 39.
[5] Pierre Dubois, (ed), *Charles Avison's Essay on Musical Expression With Related writings by Charles Avison and William Hayes* (Aldershot, 2004).

duty is 'to form his Airs and Harmony', having comprehended the poet's 'general Drift or Intention' rather than 'dwell on particular Words in the Way of Imitation'.[6] This is a viewpoint that, as Pierre Dubois notes, represents a 'divorce of music from the semantic' and a 'decisive step in the movement towards the theoretical autonomy of music',[7] and a development that would reach true fruition only in the following century. Yet paradoxically, Avison's words might also be taken as a blueprint for most glee composers, who rather than attempting to express the emotion of individual words, generally sought to capture a wider sense of poetic mood, while at the same time responding to the changing sentiments of the verse by sometimes dividing a work into several contrasted sections. This avoidance of the highlighting of specific key words in the text represents one of the seminal differences between the glee and the madrigal. We might also note that Emanuel Rubin identifies the Romantic concept of Dubois' 'autonomous music', the notion that music could be a substitute for a text rather than just a conveyor of it, as one of several causes of the glee's decline.[8]

While Avison's philosophy found its followers, it was also strongly opposed, not least by William Hayes, whose preface to his 1757 collection of catches and glees has already been quoted.[9] Among a considerable number of issues Hayes took up with Avison in his *Remarks on Mr. Avison's Essay* (1753), was the question of imitation, which as a conservative and enthusiast for the music of the past he considered to be by no means inconsistent with expression. 'For', asks Hayes, 'may not Imitation be consistent with Air and harmony?' He goes on to cite Handel's setting of John Milton's *L'Allegro ed il Penseroso* as a prime example of a work that 'consisteth chiefly of the mimetic or imitative Kind' without being 'defective in Air or Harmony'.[10] Hayes then moves on to Avison's contention 'that the Energy and Grace of musical expression is of too delicate a Nature to be fixed by Words', challenging it with his assertion 'that without *Imitation* there cannot possibly any such Thing as true *musical Expression*'.[11] He therefore anchors himself firmly within a tradition that believes that music is not only a mimetic art, but also one that relies overwhelmingly on a text from which a composer can draw inspiration. This is a viewpoint that would find echoes in the ethos of subsequent catch and glee composers, many of whom took an interest in music of the past and few of whom were concerned with the composition of instrumental music to any significant degree.

Other writers adopted a less adversarial stance, proposing views that can be seen to incorporate elements of the arguments of both Avison and Hayes. To William Jackson, musical imitation could be divided into two distinct kinds, the 'general' and the 'particular', though Jackson would not have found it acceptable to apply either to instrumental music. He defined general imitation as being 'when the whole of an image is exhibited', while 'particular imitation takes a part only, or catches at the sound of a word instead of expressing the image'.[12] 'General imitation', continues

---

[6] *Avison Essay*, p. 28.
[7] *Avison Essay* p. xxv.
[8] Rubin, 'Introduction'.
[9] See above pp. 29–30.
[10] *Avison Essay*, p. 96. Notwithstanding its Italian title, Milton's great poem was written in English.
[11] *Avison Essay*, p. 97.
[12] William Jackson, Preface to *An Ode to Fancy*, op. 8 (London, c. 1773).

Jackson, 'may belong to the highest style of composition, but particular imitation is to be avoided, except in burlesque music, where it is in its proper providence.' Thus while admitting the validity of a generalised imitation conforming with Avison's 'general Drift or Intention', particularised imitation is suitable only for the 'burlesque', or comic, a category that incorporates most catches, a form for which Jackson reserved particular derision.[13] As Rubin noted, the gradual shift from the kind of particular imitation that found favour with the older, conservative generation represented by Hayes, to a more generalised imitation is reflected by the glee composers, later generations of whom found themselves far more inclined to the general than to the particular.[14] For them, to quote Rubin, 'A poem was not dismembered into separate words, each treated by some musical image; instead the flow of the music was intended to reinforce and underline the total thought of each part of the poem. The poem's structure, then, determined that of the glee.'[15]

Avison and Hayes also had opposing views on the merits of foreign music and, in particular, Italian music. This was a topic that had exercised English writers since the oft-quoted satirical attacks on Italian opera made by Joseph Addison in *The Spectator* in 1711. Avison, though dismissive of Vivaldi and Locatelli, was happy to admit to the merits of such Italian composers as Vinci, Bononcini, Domenico Scarlatti and especially Benedetto Marcello, whose psalm settings gained widespread dissemination in England following their publication by John Garth of Durham, for which Avison provided an introduction.[16] Hayes, on the other hand, adopted an unflinching opposition to Italian music, reserving in his reply to Avison's *Essay* particular opprobrium for the Marcello psalm settings and the music of Geminiani, another Avison favourite. Later, discussing the intelligibility of art, Hayes gives the game away, resorting to the strong national sentiments that would again be articulated in his 1757 preface. 'When', he writes, 'it is highly probable, that what is esteemed Taste and Expression at *Paris*, will entirely be lost upon an *English Audience*, (unless upon those, who, right or wrong, affect to be pleased with every Thing that is foreign), insomuch as the ways of expressing the Passions in Music in different Countries, are adequate to the Idioms of the Languages they speak; which are not easily comprehended by any, except the Natives themselves.'[17]

The belief that for music to make sense it must be in the language of the hearer was widespread and had important implications for the glee. It was not by accident that in choosing *L'Allegro ed il Penseroso* as his exemplar, Hayes selected one of Handel's most quintessentially English works, set to the words of an emblematic and widely revered English poet. His words are echoed by Jonas Hanway, a less strident commentator who sought to distinguish between the sound and the sense of music: 'In considering the charms of *sound*, compared with those of *sense*, we must give the preference to the *Italian*, as most properly adapted to the *music of Italy*, in the same way as *our language* is most agreeable to *our own proper taste* [the italics are Hanway's].'[18]

---

[13] See above pp. 67–68.
[14] Rubin, 'The English Glee', p. 182.
[15] Rubin, 'The English Glee', p. 185.
[16] Avison had initially planned to undertake publication of Marcello's Psalms himself – see *Avison Essay*, p. 197, n. 1.
[17] *Avison Essay*, p. 117.
[18] Jonas Hanway, *Thoughts on the Use and Advantages of Music* (London, 1765), pp. 69–70.

Long after *The Beggar's Opera* (1728), what was seen as the florid, at times empty, virtuosity of Italian opera and its practitioners was a constant butt of English musicians. Their complaints were articulated and summarised by the Doncaster organist Edward Miller, himself a glee composer, in the preface to his *Elegies, Songs &c.*, of 1770:

> The author [...] cannot approve a stile which appears to him more calculated to display the Vanity of the *Singers*, Than to do Justice to the Sentiments of the *Poet*. To please those Public Warblers, what a Quantity of trifling Composition has been obtruded on the World [...] Melody, Harmony, and Expression are all forgot, and a forced Execution only considered. It matters not to Performers of this Sort what Nonsense they sing provided the Audience admire the Volubility of their throat; and that Extent of Compass, which displays itself by the facility of executing the most extraneous and violent Transitions.[19]

Criticism of audiences who were prepared to tolerate such foreign aberrations found voice in *Musical Travels Through England*, a satire on Charles Burney's musical travels:[20]

> Mr Quaver then told me that he had formerly introduced some of these performers [a she-ass, a raven, and six greyhound puppies] to sing at a concert, but without success: and he made great complaints of the unpoliteness of the audience, which he said could sit with patience three hours to listen to the unmeaning trills of heroes in hoop-petticoats, and *Italian* vagabonds in a strange language, while they would not bestow one half-hour on the voice of nature and their brethren.[21]

The barbs in this passage are twofold, being directed not only at the perceived artifice and absurdities of Italian opera, but also at the fashionable and at times amorphous concept of 'nature', which the writer satirises by taking the word literally in the constitution of his 'vocal ensemble'.

Opposition to Italian opera was therefore founded on two key issues: its virtuosic extravagance and its employment of a language that was unintelligible to all but a small minority of its audience, in other words 'the senseless voice of a miserable castrate [sic] in an unknown tongue', again to quote Edward Miller, who goes on to compare such aberrations with the sentiments produced by such ideal combinations of poet and composer as Milton and Handel, or Dryden and Purcell. For Miller 'as the composer is subordinate to the poet, so must the performer be subordinate to them both', a verdict that would have met with widespread agreement among many glee composers.[22] Notwithstanding the prevalence of such views among musicians and writers, we have seen that nationalistic objectives played little part in the early days of the Catch Club, at least in part because some of its aristocratic supporters

---

[19] Edward Miller, Preface to *Elegies, Songs, and an Ode of Mr. Pope's with Instrumental Parts* (London, c. 1770).
[20] Burney's account of his travels in France and Italy appeared in 1771. They were followed in 1773 by an account of his visit to Germany.
[21] Joel Collier (pseudonym of George Veal), *Musical Travels Through England* (4th edn., London, 1776), p. 36.
[22] Miller, Preface.

were also supporters of Italian opera. During the first decade of its existence the club actively solicited foreign entries to the prize competition, Italian composers contributed to the burgeoning repertoire, professional Italian singers were admitted as privileged members and – importantly within the present context – prominent glee composers like Arne, Webbe and Callcott were perfectly happy to set Italian texts as glees.[23]

The question that arises from this openness is the degree to which the noble gentlemen of the Catch Club consciously attempted to export an English form that they were in large part responsible for creating. Whether this all-embracing policy had such intentions or was purely a reflection of a broad-minded tolerance, ultimately the Catch Club was overtaken by events. As we have already seen, the contribution by Italian composers to the glee (and catch) repertoire declined dramatically during the 1770s, while, despite the solicitations of the club, there is no record of any submission in the French or Spanish languages. By the second decade of its defined existence, the glee had become irrevocably an English form, increasingly wedded to the very English notion of poetic sentiment and the natural, unforced expression of a controlled range of 'agreeable' passions.

The nature of those 'agreeable' passions, a topic also addressed by Avison, was clearly laid out in *Elements of Criticism* by the Edinburgh lawyer and philosopher Henry Home, Lord Kames, whose widely read and influential book first appeared in 1762, and subsequently ran to numerous reprints and a German translation. In addition to containing definitions of such seminal Enlightenment concerns as beauty, the sublime, and sentiment, *Elements* takes up the theme of the didactic potential of music, which he believed had the humanising power of 'commanding influence over the mind, *especially in conjunction with words*' [my italics]. By implication, this placed an onus on composers to determine the kind of poetry best suited to musical setting, and the poetic considerations that a composer should take into account:[24]

> In general, as music in all its various tones ought to be agreeable, it never can be concordant with any composition in language expressing a disagreeable passion or describing a disagreeable object [...] Music accordingly is a very improper companion for sentiments of malice, cruelty, envy, peevishness or any other dissocial passion.
>
> With regard to vocal music, there is an additional reason against associating it with disagreeable passions. The external signs of such passions are painful; the looks and gestures to the eye, and the tone of pronunciation to the ear; such tones can therefore never be expressed musically, for music must be pleasant, or it is not music.
>
> On the other hand, music associates finely with poems that tend to inspire pleasant emotions: music for example in a cheerful tone is perfectly concordant with every emotion in the same tone; and hence our taste for airs expressive of mirth and jollity. Sympathetic joy associates finely with cheerful music, and sympathetic pain no less finely with music that is tender and melancholy [...] Melancholy music is suited to slight grief, which requires or admits consolation:

---

[23] See above pp. 42 and 71 and below p. 149.
[24] Henry Home, *Elements of Criticism*, 2 vols (Edinburgh, 1762). Quoted from the 6th edn. (1785) in *Music and Aesthetics*, pp. 76–81.

but deep grief, which refuses all consolation, rejects for that reason even melancholy music.

Home then proceeded to take the familiar dig at Italian (and French) opera, claiming that 'not the least regard is paid to these rules', the general taste for opera being no argument since 'in these compositions the passions are so imperfectly expressed [...]; and it cannot be disguised that the pleasure of an opera is derived chiefly from the music and scarce at all from the sentiments'. Opera, then, is clearly incapable of clarity of expression. This ideal is capable of being achieved only by the perfect union of poetry and music espoused by James Harris, of whom Home and such writers as Daniel Webb are clearly followers.[25]

The views of such as Harris, Miller, and Home formed a powerful philosophy that, consciously or unconsciously, was integral to the approach of the glee composers. As Rubin noted, 'In the glee a classical balance was achieved between the demands of poetic expression and musical design' and that 'More than any feature, it is the way in which composers treated their texts that distinguishes the glee [...]. To view the eighteenth-century glee as a purely musical expression is to miss the point of its importance.'[26] To this might be added that it was not only the treatment of texts, but also the choice of text that mark the eighteenth-century glee out as being as much a literary as a musical phenomenon. To a practising musician like Edward Miller, the composer had a clear duty 'to chuse such poems as abound with sentiment and pathos',[27] a dictum that would have met with the approval of Home. It would also have done so to the anonymous writer of *Euterpe*, a polemic on the place of music in education addressed to the subscribers of the Concert of Antient Music. Making clear that he is speaking specifically of vocal music, the author states that it 'is to be understood as a powerful assistant to *sentimental expression*, which by the power of its charms, inforces our attention to some particular *subject*, adapted to some *natural* passion of mankind [...] But to produce the sounds of nature, the means must not be *unnatural*; and to raise the idea of certain passions, the means should be consonant with the passion itself, and confined within the simple bounds of nature.'[28] Within these few lines lie the key words that informed the ideal ethos of native vocal composition: 'sentimental', 'natural', 'passion', words closely tied to the concept of sensibility that took such firm root in the novels of the second half of the century.

Analysis of the subject matter of glees reveals how closely composers in the eighteenth century adhered to the maxims set out by Home. Table 9 is an analysis based on 254 glees published in Warren's annual collections. The division of categories in the table needs to be treated with some degree of caution since many glees cannot be categorised quite so conveniently, and a number of sub-categories could be introduced. Pastoral glees, for example, include those employing Anacreontic poetry and descriptions of nature, but omit May and spring songs

---

[25] Webb's *Observations of the Correspondences between Poetry and Music* (London, 1769) makes similar observations to those of Home on the topic of 'agreeable' and 'disagreeable' passions. See especially pp. 1–35.
[26] Rubin, 'The English Glee', pp. 170 and 168 respectively.
[27] Miller, Preface.
[28] Anonymous, *Euterpe; or Remarks on the Use and Abuse of MUSIC* (London *c.* 1778).

(3.5%) and those I term 'pastoral sentimental', the latter a not insubstantial sub-category (3.5%) that might have been included in either the 'sentimental' or 'pastoral' categories. The relatively large number of epitaphs includes serious pieces in addition to those taking a humorous approach, the latter having been placed in the 'humour' grouping.

Table 9
Principal Topics of the Glees Included in the Warren Collection, Vols 1–32

Sentimental	-	73 (29%)
Convivial	-	48 (19%)
Epitaphs	-	23 (9%)
Pastoral	-	18 (7%)
Musical	-	15 (6%)
Philosophical	-	15 (6%)
Humorous	-	14 (5.5%)

Notwithstanding caveats, the table does allow a number of conclusions to be drawn. Perhaps the most notable is the relatively restricted range of topics, compared with those found employed in catches. The glee is concerned overwhelmingly with subjects that either exploit the increasingly popular vogue for the sentimental – a trend to which the rise of the sentimental novel can be accounted – or with celebrations of the conviviality that forms the core of catch club culture. Those celebrations might range from simple honouring of Bacchus to expressions of male bonding in friendship, the two not infrequently extolled in the same piece. A number of glees juxtaposed these central tenets with romantic sentiments that find in drink a release from the pains of love. *Jolly Bacchus*, a 3-part glee by the Irish amateur Frances Ireland (Francis Hutcheson), provides a typical example:

> Jolly Bacchus hear my pray'r
> Vengeance on the ungrateful fair
> In thy smiling cordial bowl
> Drown all the sorrows of my soul.
>
> Jolly Bacchus save O save
> From the deep devouring grave
> A poor despairing, dying swain.
>
> Haste away lash thy tigers
> Do not stay
> I'm undone if thou delay.
>
> If I view those eyes once more
> I shall still love and still adore

And be more wretched than before.[29]

The poem, by the dilettante gentleman poet William Somerville (1675–1742), is ideal for a glee, allowing its composer to respond to the varying word-setting requirements of a text that incorporates elements of the Anacreontic and the sentimental. Indeed, although the glee was awarded the 1772 Catch Club prize for a 'cheerful' glee, Ireland responds to the mock-pathos of the second verse by turning from his cheerful opening C major Allegro to a 3/4 A-minor passage marked Largo e piano. At 'Haste away' the music returns to a vigorous G-major Allegro in duple time, reverting to triple time and a Largo affettuoso marking for the final verse, the glee being brought to a conclusion with a repeat of the second Allegro. The form here is thus a satisfyingly rounded A (fast) B (slow) C (fast) D (slow) C (fast) structure incorporating contrasts of time and key, with passages in both the relative minor and dominant. Above all, the glee conforms to the ideal of responding to the varying emotions of the text in a generalised fashion, which is set with relatively little departure from a predominantly homophonic texture, although the pleasure of the 'smiling cordial bowl' is treated to effective imitative entries.

Another significant feature of Table 9 are the topics not treated, or only very occasionally visited. It is noteworthy that when the Catch Club came to set up the categories of glee eligible for its prize competitions, it originally chose the designations 'serious' and 'cheerful', the latter in preference to 'humorous'.[30] Outright humour is indeed conspicuous by its neglect, fewer than 6% of glees conforming to such a description, as against the huge number of catches that can be so described. Ribald glees are all but non-existent, only Thomas Arne's *The Unconscionable* ('Is the devil in you?') truly conforming to a genre that belonged specifically to the catch. In contrast to the catch, political topics play no part in the glee repertoire, since politics were supposedly left behind at the doors of the clubs and societies, even (or perhaps particularly) in the instance of a club like the Catch Club, dominated as it was by political membership. It was doubtless this admirable policy that enabled a radically minded musician like Samuel Webbe the elder, a member of the extreme London Corresponding Society, to mix in easy conviviality with men whose political views differed widely from his own. Likewise satire and comment on current events are also virtually exclusive to the catch. In marked contrast to the large number of patriotic songs and ballads dating from the period (particularly in the 1790s after the outbreak of the French wars), the glee generally stood more aloof from overt sentiments of a more jingoistic nature. More popular were elegies for fallen heroes, either particularised or general. A notable example of the former is *On the death of the Duke of Cumberland*, the epitaph composed by Thomas Norris following the death of George III's uncle William Augustus, the so-called 'butcher of Culloden', at the end of October 1765. As an English hero who had put down the Jacobite rebellion of 1745, Cumberland's early death was widely mourned, being also the subject of *How silent lies the chief*, a glee by William Bates. The poem of Norris's glee by H. Read is no

---

[29] *Jolly Bacchus* was included in the eleventh of Warren's collections and Book 5 of the Catch Club's collection.
[30] These designations were dropped later.

literary masterpiece, but it admirably caught the mood of national grief, ensuring its considerable popularity:

> O'er William's tomb with silent grief opprest
> Britannia mourns her hero now laid at rest
> Not tears alone but praises too she gives
> Due to the guardian of our laws and lives
> Nor shall that laurel ever fade with years
> Whose leaves are water'd with a nation's tears.[31]

Norris sets the poem as an E flat Largo in triple time (3/2), both halves of the binary form structure being repeated. The second half modulates to the dominant and briefly touches on C minor. While containing little of a contrapuntal nature, the glee makes its affect by virtue of a directness that underlines the melancholy subject matter. While general elegies for the fallen included no fewer than three settings of William Collins' splendid *How sleep the brave* (Benjamin Cooke, Francis Ireland and the little-known Joseph Holder) and Callcott's immensely popular *Peace to the souls of heroes*, perhaps one of the most touching essays in the form is another glee by Cooke that combines simplicity with an infinitely touching quality. *Epitaph on a dormouse* has a moralising text of almost childlike naivety; indeed the title page credits the poem as being 'Said to have been written by a child', although it was more likely the work of Cooke himself:

> In paper case
> Hard by this place
> Dead a poor dormouse lies
> And soon or late
> Summon'd by fate
> Each prince, each monarch dies
>
> Ye sons of verse
> While we rehearse
> Attend instructive rhyme
> No sins had Dor
> To answer for
> Repent of yours in time.

Like Norris, Cooke sets the poem in repeated section binary form and the key of E flat, with a modulation to the dominant in the second half (from the words 'Ye sons of verse'). Although the prevailing texture is homophonic, the composer introduces both a degree of part writing and numerous melismatic solo flourishes, such as the bass descent on the word 'dead', while the moral of the piece is underlined by arriving at its climactic point (both as to tessitura and dynamics) on 'repent'. The whole of this miniature gem demonstrates admirably how closely the best glee composers worked in close harmony with their texts.

Many of the finest sentimental glees conform to this simplicity of approach, depending for their affect in performance on sensitive observation of frequently

---

[31] Included in the fifth of Warren's collections and several other anthologies.

scrupulous markings of expression and dynamics. One of the elder Samuel Webbe's most enduringly successful glees falls into this category. The five-part (SATTB) *You gave me your heart* is set to a brief sentimental poem by Joseph Craddock, previously encountered as Lord Sandwich's host at his Gumley Hall residence.[32]

> You gave your heart t'other day
> I thought it as safe as my own.
>
> I've not lost it but what can I say
> Not your heart but mine can be known.[33]

Webbe set this innocuous little verse in flowing triple time as an A-major Andante in binary form, with a modulation to the dominant by the double bar. The two lines of the first stanza are each repeated, the dynamic marking throughout being *piano* until the repeat of line two, when Webbe emphasises the growing emotion by marking it *forte*. The opening line of stanza two is also repeated, the first statement *piano*, but the reprise is again intensified by the crescendo marking that guides the glee to a climax released in quiet ambiguity of the final line.

Similar care for affect also informs Webbe's 4-part setting of *Breathe soft ye winds*,[34] a pastoral elegy by the Cambridge poet Ambrose Philips that caught the imagination of at least four glee composers, most famously William Paxton:

> Breathe soft ye winds, ye waters gently flow
> Shield her ye trees, ye flow'rs around her grow;
>
> Ye swains, I beg you pass in silence by
> My love in yonder vale asleep doth lie.

The glee, which dates from around 1777, is again set in binary form and 3/4 metre, this time as an E flat-major Andantino. The tender invocation of the opening line is accentuated by the pianissimo marking and the slight crescendo on its second clause, where Webbe also introduces a suggestion of Jackson's 'particularised imitation' by setting the words 'gently flow' to a placid rocking rhythm, thus deviating from the writer's assertion that such a device was suited only to the 'burlesque'. In the second line a pedal point in the treble and tenor parts is introduced on the word 'grow', bringing the first part (28 bars) to a reposeful cadence in B flat. In the shorter (20 bars) second half the plea of the first line is given greater emphasis by the *poco crescendo* marking, while the poignant denouement of a final line that reveals the point of the poem's supplication is marked by a dramatic move to *forte* and the modulation to the subdominant.

William Paxton's setting of the same text was probably composed at much the same time as Webbe's. Never written into the Catch Club books or published in Warren's collections, it nevertheless became extremely popular, appearing in many

---

[32] See above p. 35.
[33] *You gave me your heart* was widely published, appearing in Warren Collection No. 15, Webbe's *4th Book of Catches and Glees* (c. 1776), and Webbe's *Selection* (1812), in addition to at least seven other anthologies.
[34] Included in Warren Collection No. 17 and Webbe *Selection*.

nineteenth-century anthologies after being published posthumously in his brother Stephen's *A Collection of Glees, Catches etc.* (*c.* 1782). Paxton's version is scored for three voices (ATB), in triple time (3/2) and E major. Like Webbe's, it is cast in binary form, entirely homophonic, and is embellished only by the occasional restrained melisma. Nothing could be simpler, yet so fitting and distinctive is the melodic invention that Paxton's glee leaves a gentle sentimental impression far outlasting that achieved by many more ambitious and sophisticated pieces. In that sense, it fits perfectly the paradigmatic aim of the glee: a perfect synthesis of words and music.

As noted in the opening chapter, by no means all glees conform to such simplicity. Many composers took the multi-movement structure of the Catch Club's first prize-winning glee, George Berg's *On softest beds*, as a blueprint for their own works.[35] *On softest beds* is by no means the finest of glees, but its seminal status makes it worth more detailed comment. It is set to an anonymous poem:

> On softest beds at leisure laid
> Beds of pinks and myrtle made
> While the easy hours I spend
> Love my festal shall attend
> Love, his robe behind him bound
> Love shall serve his goblet round
>
> Swift in this terrestrial strife
> Turns the rapid wheel of life
> Swift as speeding from the bar
> Turns her wheel the rapid car
>
> Soon, my friends, to cruel death
> I alas must yield my breath
> Soon dissolve, too soon I must turn to an undistinguished death
>
> Do not then, when I am dead
> Flow'rs, or wines, or odours shed
> Fruitless love, superfluous care
> Spare me now what you can spare
> Rather in these present hours
> Bring your odours, wines and flow'rs
> O Cupid bind my hair
> Summon now the tender fair
> That before I'm doomed to go to the ghosts who sport below
> I may taste with those that live
> All the sports which life can give.

The poem is mediocre, but it serves admirably the purpose of providing a framework for the composer to embody contrasting sentiments, and its topic, the desire to enjoy transitory life to the full, accords with the general notion of conviviality that plays such a central role in catch and glee culture. The 3-part glee

---

[35] *On softest beds* was included in Warren Collection No. 2, and written into the first of the Catch Club's books. Despite its historic place in the club's annals, the glee does not appear to have achieved enduring popularity, being selected only once by members when the club revisited its early books in 1780. The choice was that of Lord Sandwich on 12 December 1780.

was subjected to an excellent analysis by Emanuel Rubin, to which the following is indebted.[36] Berg's setting divides the long poem into four unequal sections, distinguished in the manner laid out in the above text. Each is clearly demarcated by a change of tempo, key and texture that reflect the changing moods of the poem. The opening section (marked 'Slow & Pia.') in F major is characterised by flowing triplet figures with trills, initially imitated between the two upper parts in unison and the lower, and gentle roulades. The second section (ff. bar 18) brings an increase in tempo to Allegro and a move to C major effected with no modulation. Phrases such as 'the rapid wheel' and 'speeding from the bar' are given additional dynamic impetus by means of brief imitative counterpoint. The third section reverts to a slow tempo, ('Andantino a pia.') but the change of key to A minor is reserved until the word 'death'. The climax of the poem is its hedonistic final passage, marked by a return to F major and set in rather unimaginative homophony as a pastoral allegro in 12/8 time, the cheerful mood disrupted only by a momentary return to A minor at the words 'the ghosts who sport below'.

As we will shortly see, glee composers frequently turned to poetry of a rather more elevated quality than that of *On softest beds*. No author was more frequently called upon to provide inspiration than Shakespeare, although composers proved just as inclined to alter his texts when it suited them as did the eighteenth-century theatre. Probably the earliest Shakespeare glee is *Fear no more the heat of the sun*,[37] the elegy from Act IV, scene 2 of *Cymbeline*, which was set by the Chapel Royal organist and Master of the Children, James Nares (1715–83). It dates from around 1768, two years before Nares was awarded a Catch Club medal for his glee *To all Lovers of Harmony*. Those familiar with the original text will recognise that Nares has omitted the two middle verses and also changed the final lines of both verses, that of the last from Shakespeare's infinitely more powerful 'And renowned be thy grave!'

> Fear no more the heat of the sun
> Nor the furious winter's rages
> Thou thy worldly talk has done
> Home art gone to take thy wages
> Golden lads and lasses must
> All follow thee and turn to dust
>
> No exorciser harm thee
> Nor no witchcraft charm thee
> Ghost unlaid forbear thee
> Nothing ill come near thee
> Quiet consummation have
> Unremoved be thy grave.[38]

Nares' effective 3-part (ATB) setting opens with a *Vivace e allegro* in C minor in common time that after 20 bars modulates to the tonic major at the words 'No

---

[36] Rubin, 'The English Glee', p. 187ff.
[37] Published in Nares, *A Collection of Catches, Canons and Glees* (London, c. 1772), and also included in Warren Collection No. 8, and the third of the Catch Club's books. The glee's subsequent popularity can be gauged by its inclusion in no fewer than eight anthologies.
[38] Alexander, *Shakespeare*.

exorcisor', which open with an alto solo and also bring a change of time to 6/8. The final section (from 'Ghost unlaid') reverts to 4/4 with a change of tempo marking to Largo. There is some pleasing counterpoint reflecting the composer's cathedral training and, as one of the earlier glee composers more prone to 'particularised' imitation, he is fully alive to the possibilities of word painting on 'rages' and 'furious'.

Glee collections are notorious for not attributing the name of the poet, but a survey of the poets whose work can be positively identified reveals an astonishing diversity of authors.[39] Chronologically they range from the unsurprisingly large number of settings of Anacreon, the sixth century BC Greek poet who might with some justification be considered the patron saint of eighteenth-century glee composers, to Sir Walter Scott. His substantial showing can be credited to the interest taken in his poems by the generation of glee composers who came to the fore in the early years of the nineteenth century, in particular Thomas Attwood and Joseph Mazzinghi.

As already noted, the overwhelmingly dominant name is that of Shakespeare, who with 83 glees set to his lyrics accounts for a total just over twice that of his nearest challenger, Anacreon (40). Shakespeare's popularity with glee composers comes as little surprise. The plays enjoyed considerable popularity throughout the eighteenth century, the bard's high profile being yet further enhanced by the extravagant Shakespeare Jubilee mounted by David Garrick in 1769, an event for which Garrick wrote an *Ode to Shakespeare* with music by Thomas Arne. They also, of course, fulfilled the increasingly nationalistic tendencies of glee composers, who consistently revisited the songs in the plays. Most notable among those who did so was R. J. S. Stevens, a fifth (11) of whose glees are Shakespeare settings. Among the more popular texts were *Take, Oh take those lips away*, set by Tommaso Giordano, Sir John Stevenson, and John Stafford Smith, *Tell me where is fancy bred* (Thomas Arne, Stevens, and Matthew King) and *Who is Sylvia?* (Stevens and Samuel Webbe the younger). In addition Arne's immensely popular songs *Blow thou winter wind* and *Where the bee sucks* were both translated into glees, each on two separate occasions.

The eighteenth century's fascination with the literary forms of Primitivism has at least some analogy with the vogue for old music, a vogue that interested so many of the men associated with catch and glee culture. It is ostensibly reflected in glee literature by the high number of glees set to James Macpherson's epic poetry, which purported to be a faithful translation of poems by an ancient bard, Ossian.[40] In a similar category is Thomas Percy's *Reliques of Ancient English Poetry*, which created something of a stir when first published in three volumes in 1765, inspiring the pseudo-archaism of the tragically short-lived Thomas Chatterton, three of whose texts were set as glees. Closer examination, however, reveals caveats as to the true extent of the influence of literary archaism on the glee, the settings of Ossian and Chatterton in particular owing their prominent place substantially to the efforts of one man – the indefatigable autodidact John Wall Callcott. No fewer than thirteen of

---

[39] Rubin, 'The English Glee'; Catalogue V List A is a list of glee poets. Of the 2528 glees for which the author provides incipits, he provides the poet's name for 908. However, considerable caution is required in attempting to analyse the catalogue since it reveals a number of errors and ambiguities.

[40] Macpherson's Ossianic writings include *Fragments of Ancient Poetry* (1760) and *Fingal, an Ancient Epic Poem* (1762).

the Ossian glees were the work of Callcott and they include one of his most successful, *Peace to the souls of heroes*. In addition three of the four Chatterton settings also came from his pen. Three further Ossian glees came from R. J. S. Stevens, whose high literary pretensions are already clear from the large number of Shakespeare texts he set, and they too include one of his most enduringly successful works, *O strike the harp*.

The relatively large number of glees set to poems from Percy's *Reliques* and those based on Robert Burns have also to be treated with caution. In both instances they belong almost entirely to the category of the harmonized ballads that became so fashionable during the 1790s – William Gardiner's 'mawkish sort of composition' – although the *Reliques* also inspired *It was a fryar of orders gray*, one of Callcott's most frequently performed glees.

Rather more interesting are the glees that took their texts from three major eighteenth-century English poets: William Shenstone (19 settings), Thomas Gray (12), and Alexander Pope (10), the last–named himself becoming the subject of a 4-part *Epitaph to Pope* ('Heroes kings at distance keep') set to his own words by the composer and tenor Charles Dignum. Shenstone's predominantly pastoral poetry found favour with a number of glee composers, including (once again) Callcott and Stevens, in addition to James Hook, Jonathan Battishill, Stephen Paxton, and Benjamin Cooke's ill-fated son Robert.[41] Most notable of all the Shenstone settings is Lord Mornington's *Here in cool grot*, a Catch Club prize winner in 1779 and a delightful 'classic' that taps into the theatrical vogue for fairy songs, its widespread popularity clearly evident from the number of mentions in Chapter 6. Gray also attracted the attention of a number of composers, most conspicuously the ubiquitous Callcott, who employed four of his poems. Others included John Danby, who produced another of the classics of the repertoire in the shape of *Awake Aeolian lyre*, which won a Catch Club medal in 1783 and was thereafter included in innumerable collections; the Bath amateur Dr Henry Harington; and Thomas Attwood. Curiously, given the glee composers' fondness for elegies, few composers attempted to set any part of one of the most famous poems in the English language, *Elegy Written in a Country Churchyard* ('The curfew tolls the knell of parting day').[42] Some of Pope's most famous lines, *Vital spark of heav'nly flame* ('The dying Christian to his soul') were also the subject of glee settings by several composers, including Jacob Cubitt Pring, whose 3-part setting was published in 1794, and the Lancashire amateur Edward Harwood, a version that became popular among nineteenth-century parish choirs.[43] Both Samuel Webbes were drawn to Pope, possibly a reflection of empathy for a fellow Roman Catholic, and in the elder Webbe's *A gen'rous friendship* we find an archetypal celebration of convivial friendship and another of the repertoire's staples.

The literary-minded R. J. S. Stevens also turned for inspiration to the poetry of Ben Jonson, the only other author to achieve ten or more listings in Rubin's catalogue, which includes two three-part arrangements of the familiar ballad *Drink to me only* under the heading of the Jacobean playwright. A glance at the list of less

---

[41] Robert Cooke committed suicide by hurling himself into the Thames in 1814.
[42] Two who did were Stephen Storace and John Marsh – see p. 106.
[43] See Peter Holman's note for the CD 'Vital Spark of Heav'nly Flame' (Hyperion CDA67020), which includes Harwood's work.

frequently set authors reads almost as a who's-who of English poets. Taking Chaucer as its chronological starting point it proceeds through Christopher Marlowe to the Cavalier poets James Shirley, Robert Herrick, Abraham Cowley, and Thomas Carew. From the other side of the seventeenth-century political divide, John Milton's beautiful *Song: on May Morning* ('Now the bright morning star') was set by George Berg, Benjamin Cooke, the Rev. Robert Greville, and Maria Hester Parke, the niece of the oboist William Parke and one of the very few women glee composers, making it one of the most frequently set texts. Another Milton text that carried resonance among musicians is *Blest pair of sirens*, which provided the text for an ambitious four-movement glee for 5 voices by John Stafford Smith.[44] John Dryden's *Go tell Aminta*, the basis for glees by Maria Hester Parke and the Earl of Mornington, was one of several of his texts selected by glee composers, while from the following generation of poets come three Congreve settings, all to texts devoted to music. Naturally, the work of many eighteenth-century poets was employed, among the more notable of those not already mentioned being William Cowper, whose sensitive nature poems caught the imagination of several composers, among them Samuel Webbe the elder (*Rose had been washed*).

Classical Greek and Roman literature is also well represented, with translations of poetry by Homer, Virgil, Catullus and Pindar in addition to the already mentioned Anacreon. Despite his seventeenth-century popularity in England having waned, three glees have words adapted from Petrarch, two in translation, the one in the original Italian (*O voi che sospirate*) being the work of Callcott. Modern and more fashionable Italian poetry is represented by Metastasio, who surprisingly failed to attract those of his fellow countrymen who composed glees, leaving it largely to the youthfully prodigious Reginald Spofforth, who employed Metastasian texts on four occasions, in each instance in the original language, as did the linguist Samuel Webbe the elder in his *Non fidi al mar che femo*, a glee whose popularity suggests that even as late as 1790 there was no intrinsic objection to glees employing foreign texts.[45]

Even this cursory summary reveals the scope and depth of the literature trawled by the glee composers in their search for texts that might fulfil the quest for the ideal marriage of poetry and music. A number of them were well-educated and well-read men who sought to unite their music with poetry of an elevated literary standard. Nonetheless, as has frequently been observed, the best poetry does not always lend itself to music and some of the finest glees are those in which the verse does not aspire to the highest level. In a few cases such poetry as can be identified was the work of the composer himself, creating the potential of a fusion developing in a single mind. Inevitably, the names involved include those of Webbe and Callcott, in addition to that of Arne. It is also highly likely that modesty regarding their literary efforts prevented many other glee composers from identifying themselves as the authors of their texts. While further detailed work is needed on the relationship between the glee and its poetry, there seems little doubt that it was closely related, if not always consciously, to the prevailing aesthetic concerns of the period.

---

[44] Awarded a Catch Club prize medal in 1775, Smith's glee appeared in Warren, No. 14, and was included in a number of anthologies.

[45] *Non fidi al mar* was included by Warren in the 29th of his collections and thereafter appeared in several anthologies.

Chapter 8

Epilogue: Later Reception of the Eighteenth-Century Catch and Glee

The death of the elder Samuel Webbe at the age of 75 on 25 May 1816 draws a final line under the catch and glee culture of the eighteenth century. Webbe had ceased to compose some years previously and there is evidence to suggest that he spent his final years in poor health and reduced circumstances.[1] Nevertheless, in the years immediately following his death Webbe's stock stood high, his place as the pivotal figure in eighteenth-century catch and glee culture widely recognised. Webbe's standing during this period is reflected in *The Euterpeiad*, a short-lived publication that probably represents the only attempt ever to run a weekly musical newspaper. Published in Boston, Massachusetts, from the start of April 1820, the first musical biography in the paper was not that of Handel, not that of Haydn, Mozart or Beethoven, as might be expected, but a laudatory two-part survey of the life of Samuel Webbe the elder in which his glees are extolled for their 'precision of harmony, beauty, and expression'.[2]

In the immediate aftermath of Webbe's death we find in the writings of contemporary observers not only stirrings of a sense of nostalgia for past glories, but equally a conscious movement to elevate what was perceived as the innate 'Englishness' of the madrigal and glee repertoire to the status of a national music, a sentiment echoing the prescient words of Elizabeth Harris written nearly fifty years earlier.[3] In his *General History*, the first major English music history of the nineteenth century, Thomas Busby follows Burney's example of using 'modern' music as a stick with which to beat that of earlier times: 'Modern Europe', he claims, 'has evinced its ability to conceive and execute designs more elaborate and sublime, than any within the scope afforded by the ancient *unisons, octaves* and *discrepant* intervals'. While conceding that Italy 'has proved itself the region of fancy, feeling and elegance' and Germany 'demonstrated its theoretical profundity and felicitous contrivance', Busby believed that 'the lustre of this country has not been dimmed by the radiance of *foreign* models'. Indeed, 'England [...] may boast, that from their contrasted garlands she has culled a consistent wealth of her own; that in her Blow and her Purcell, her Greene and her Arne, her Boyce and her Battishill, she has evinced a power of deep research, a clear and prompt conception, and a taste and sensibility not uncongenial with the pathos, dignity, and manly fervour indispensable to the production of fine Music.'[4]

---

[1] R. J. S. Stevens and the Catch Club both organised benefits for Webbe in 1808, further benefits for him being held in April 1809 and April 1814.
[2] *The Euterpeiad*, vol. 1, No. 2.
[3] See above p. 104.
[4] Thomas Busby, *A General History of Music from the Earliest Times to the Present*, 2 vols (London, 1819), vol. 2, pp. 522–3. The italics are his.

Some three years later the anonymous writer of an article in the *New Monthly Magazine* could be found returning to that old English bugbear, Italian opera. Having suggested 'that the genius of the English is averse to opera' and that 'The recitatives [of Italian opera] are heard with absolute disgust by three-fourths, or even a much greater proportion of the audience', the writer goes on to propose his solution to the problem of vocal music in England. 'Some establishments in favor of English music are on foot which have considerable weight. – The public have of late been attracted very much by glees, the works of English composers, and Dr Callcott has been the author of some songs which combine much of the enchantment of Italian music, with the strength and dignity of a genuine English expression.'[5] Here again, then, we find some of the key words that were consistently applied to the glee in its key role of purveyor of 'Englishness' – 'strength', 'manly', 'dignity', 'pathos'.[6]

Pride in national heritage would find a still more strident nationalistic voice in the words of Richard Clark, a Gentleman of the Chapel Royal, writing in 1824. Clark certainly had a vested interest, since he was not only a past secretary of the Glee Club (from 1812 to 1824), but was also promoting a volume of the poetry of the most popular glees, catches and songs.[7] Nonetheless, Clark's observations are of significance not only for their strong patriotic fervour, but also their trenchant criticism of the foreign domination of English music. His polemic, lacking as it does the optimism of the *New Monthly Magazine*'s writer, centres around the exclusion 'of the beautiful compositions of our own countrymen from public concerts and evening parties, to make way for foreign compositions, and singers (for fashion's sake) who [...] flock to this country in swarms, and devour what Englishmen, by their birthright, ought to enjoy'. He continues with a long list of English composers whose neglect 'for the honour of our countrymen' he abhors. Among them are not only the great names of the Tudor and Elizabethan era, but also those of the more recent past and present, which along with the names mentioned by Busby, also includes Webbe, Callcott, Danby, Cooke, R. J. S. Stevens and John Stafford Smith. Clark was in no doubt that were it not for the Catch Club and like societies who value 'the indefatigable study and labour of the above composers, their works would be laid, untouched, neglected, and almost forgotten, on the shelf'.[8]

Clark's desire to preserve a native musical heritage in the shape of the madrigal and glee repertoire would subsequently find more scholarly articulation in the work of three men in particular, two of whom have already made an appearance in these pages. The senior is Edward Francis Rimbault (1816–76), an avid antiquarian and collector who in addition to his groundbreaking work on rounds, catches, and canons,[9] undertook important, if flawed, research on early English church music and the organ. David Baptie (1822–1906) was a Scottish writer whose compilation of glees, madrigals and English part-songs started in 1846, and involving, in the words of the author 'the pursuance of 100s of volumes and thousands of single glees' resulted in both a huge and detailed manuscript catalogue of such works and his

---

[5] 'Elements of Vocal Science', *The New Monthly Magazine*, vol. III, No. 3, 27 April 1822.
[6] See also the quotation from W. A. Barrett's lecture on p. 4.
[7] Clark, *First Volume of Poetry*, Introductory Remarks.
[8] Ibid.
[9] See Chapter 1, n. 19.

valuable little *Sketches of the English Glee Composers*.[10] While less rigorous in his research than Baptie, with whose work he was certainly familiar, William Alexander Barrett (1834–91) was encountered in the first pages of this book as an enthusiastic proponent of the glee, an interest that led from his 1877 lectures to the publication of his own book on the topic.[11]

All three writers took up the now-familiar theme of the strongly nationalistic character of the music with which they were concerned. Having observed that the English had been content to follow Italian and German models in all other kinds of music, Rimbault goes on to assert that 'we cannot, however, produce a foreign glee, round or catch: no such thing exists. This class of composition is of English origin.'[12] Baptie agreed, stressing that 'the peculiar form of the glee is essentially English', going on with unbounded enthusiasm to declare that 'while in the madrigal our composers have never been *surpassed* [author's italics], we can proudly add that in the glee we are – and ever have been – absolutely *unrivalled*'.[13] Unlike Rimbault, both Baptie and Barrett believed that foreigners had attempted to compete with English glee composers. Baptie cited a list of composers, including Gounod, Ambroise Thomas, and Mendelssohn, who had tried to challenge the English composers on their own ground and failed, since 'excellent as the music is – it is in a different *style* from the English glee, and *that* is still the best'.[14] More scientifically, Barrett drew the analogy of learning to speak a foreign tongue, pointing out that however proficient a linguist might become, 'some trick of emphasis or form of phrasing, will sooner or later betray him'. Therefore, Barrett continues, 'Mendelssohn in his imitation of our great English writers, his Glees for men's voices, has produced some admirable works, they are beautiful, they are expressive, but they never approach the excellence of the English glee, which holds its own in individuality and distinctiveness against the genius even of a Mendelssohn.'[15] It is pertinent to add that there is no evidence to suggest that either Mendelssohn, who never used the term 'glee' for his part songs, or the other composers mentioned by Baptie sought to emulate or 'imitate' the English glee.

Both Baptie and Barrett, unlike some later writers, had no doubt that there was a clearly defined 'golden age' of the glee. While Baptie expressed the hope that 'musicians and music lovers may be induced to glance back to the period when our great glee writers Callcott, Webbe, Stevens, Danby, Cooke, and others gave their compositions to the world',[16] Barrett is even more explicit in claiming that by the time of Webbe's death 'the glee had reached its highest point of development'.[17] For Barrett that 'golden age' had indeed been inaugurated by Webbe, who 'was the first that gave the glee its recognised classical form, as it is called, and out of the

---

[10] David Baptie 'Descriptive Catalogue of Glees, Madrigals, Part Song, Etc.' 4 vols (Glasgow, 1895–98), BL Shelfmark M.R.Ref.3.a. *Sketches of the English Glee Composers* (London, 1895).
[11] William Alexander Barrett, *English Glees and Partsongs* (London, 1886).
[12] Rimbault, *Rounds*, p. vii. As we have seen, Rimbault's assertion that there was no such thing as a foreign catch or glee was incorrect.
[13] Baptie, *Sketches*, Prefatory Remarks.
[14] Ibid.
[15] Barrett, Lectures.
[16] Baptie, *Sketches*, Prefatory Remarks.
[17] Barrett, *English Glees*, p. 236.

excellence of his own interpretation of the 'hints' furnished in the writings of his predecessors grew the new pattern which was in turn imitated by his contemporaries, and accepted by his successors as the model of perfection to which the glee had been tending through a long course of years'.[18] Baptie, too, recognised in the industrious, self-made Webbe, a man whose life might in some ways be said to reflect Victorian moral values, 'one of the greatest glee composers in every sense'. He also reserved high praise for Callcott, who was also lauded by Barrett for writing 'true glees that never once suggest any tendency towards part-song writing'. Paradoxically, Barrett also considered Webbe's *Glorious Apollo*, which for all its renown is generally accepted as one of its composer's weaker glees, to be the harbinger of the new, harmonised style that would be fatal to the pure glee. Yet ultimately it was Webbe who was the true hero. 'While he was yet alive,' Barrett wrote, 'he seemed to be able to control and influence the character of the glee, and restrain it from overstepping the borders of that classicality which he himself had helped to formulate. He was the central sun round which the minor planets of the musical world, his contemporaries, revolve in regulated order.'[19]

The high estimation in which Baptie and Barrett held the 'classical' glee did not of course extend to the catch. Baptie simply ignored its existence, while Rimbault's bowdlerisation of many of the texts of the catches he published was noted earlier.[20] Richard Clark, in the Remarks to his collection of poetry, castigated Warren for publishing 'so many compositions which could not, by the nature of the words, be left open to the inspection of our families. Those obscene Catches were meant to be sung only among the wits of that time, but were never intended to appear in print.' Clark goes on to claim that while some of Warren's volumes were destroyed by a fire at their compiler's house, others were bought up and destroyed on purpose, creating a sought-after scarcity and high values for some numbers.[21]

Picking up on Clark's words, Barrett found in Warren 'some of the most exquisite gems of vocal composition ever written, together with productions of so questionable or rather unquestionable a character that it is a pity the fire that consumed the greater portion of the stock, or copies did not consume the whole'.[22] Barrett was in no doubt where the original blame lay. 'Catches', he fulminated, are 'an ever-shameful monument to the licentiousness of the [Restoration] age which gave them birth.' Rimbault was of the same view, though more inclined to point the finger specifically at the demon drink: 'Of the tavern-life of the Restoration, and its feats of conviviality, we know more than enough; and if Purcell's catches serve as a criterion of the extravagance of the merriment prevailing, we may have a glimpse of the musician in such unbending hours as no longer indulged in cultivated society. The drinking habits of the day shortened the career of much genius.'[23] Unsurprisingly, both Barrett and Rimbault found grist for their mill in William Jackson's outburst

---

[18] Barrett, *English Glees*, p. 223.
[19] Barrett, *English Glees*, p. 236.
[20] See Chapter 1, n. 19.
[21] Clark, *First Volume of Poetry*, Introductory Remarks.
[22] Barrett, *English Glees*, p. 209.
[23] Rimbault, *Rounds*, p. xxix.

against the catch.[24] Barrett went so far as to believe that Jackson's polemic had played a role in halting the progress of the catch. 'It could not ensure the destruction of what had been done in the way of catches in the past, but it checked and finally stopped their production, and the composition of the catch became an abandoned art.'[25] Jackson's invective also served as a catalyst to raise the blood pressure of Rimbault, who declared 'it is not the *mirth* [author's italics] of the catch which offends him, but its vulgarity and indecency. And every properly constructed mind must go along with him in censuring in the loudest terms the filthy rubbish which disgraces the books of the Nobleman and Gentleman's Catch Club.'[26] That Barrett and Rimbault were motivated more by bigotry than by fact is confirmed by an examination of the catch texts of the period, which reveals Barrett's claim that 'there are scarcely more than a dozen catches whose humour does not raise the blush of shame' to be by any standard a wild exaggeration.[27]

Today it is all too easy to smile at the patriotic effusions of men like Clark, Rimbault, Baptie, and Barrett, to find something even faintly absurd in their desire to elevate the unpretentious glee to the status of a national music capable of warding off foreign domination. It is even easier to be amused by their outraged condemnation of the humble catch, a not-quite innocent victim of the 'politeness' that from its stirrings in the eighteenth century developed into the full blown prudery of the nineteenth. Yet before allowing ourselves to become too superior, it was worth recalling that the assiduous work of Rimbault, Baptie, and Barrett has found few subsequent echoes, few successors with the interest to build on the foundations they laid. While the earliest editions of *Grove's Dictionary of Music and Musicians* carried an insightful entry on the glee by John Hullah, a pupil of the glee composer William Horsley, later editions have been distinguished only by the inadequacy of their treatment of the topic. The contribution made to the subject by most twentieth-century music historians has been at best perfunctory or condescending. At worst it has been merely dismissive.

The object of the present study has been to show that far from occupying an ephemeral place on the fringes of musical life in later eighteenth-century England, the culture of the catch and glee played a crucial dynamic role that came to extend beyond the limits of club into every sphere of musical activity. The great, if possibly unwitting, achievement of the noblemen and gentlemen who founded the Catch Club late in 1761 was to give to native composers the inspiration to create a large body of lyric compositions that would come to fill the purpose of restoring pride in the concept of Englishness in music. That their initial ambitions for the Catch Club were founded on the more prosaic precepts of conviviality and sociability is not only a mirror of the Georgian era in which they lived, but also in itself somehow very English.

---

[24] See above pp. 67–68.
[25] Barrett, *English Glees*, p. 215.
[26] Rimbault, *Rounds*, p. xxxiii.
[27] Barrett, *English Glees*, p. 216.

Appendix A

Appendix A
Members of the Catch Club

Those marked with an asterisk are identified as Members of Parliament.
Those marked + were listed as subscribers of the King's Theatre in 1783.
Members who for one reason another left and subsequently rejoined account for repeated names.

Subscribing Members 1761–1800

Original Members – November 1761
Earl of Sandwich
Earl of Eglinton
Earl of March +
Maj. Gen. John Barrington
Lt. Gen. Robert Rich
John Ward +
Hugo Menil * +
Richard Phelps

Additional Members – April 1762
Sir George Armytage
Earl of Rochford
Earl of Oxford
Viscount Weymouth +
Col. Parker
Col. Windus
Marquis of Lorn
Earl of Ashburnham
Henry Peynton *recte* Peyton *
John Manners, Marquis of Granby *
Lord George Sutton
Duke of Kingston
William Gordon *
Viscount Bolingbroke
Col. Montgomery
James Harris

Elected Members

1763
Duc de Nivernois
Duke of Queensbury
Henry Seymour *
Lord Carysfort

1764
Earl of Orford
Charles Sloane Cadogan * +
Earl of Farnham

1764 (cont.)
Duke of Manchester
Richard Aldworth Neville
Dr George Hay
Humphry Morice *
Earl of Charlemont
Marquis Caraccioli
Henry Penton *
Sir George Armytage *

1765
Earl of Plymouth
Thomas Dundas * +
Lord Leigh
Maj. Gen. Irwin

1766
Earl of Buckinghamshire
John Dillon
Sir Harry Bridgeman
Lord Masham
Earl Spencer +
Joseph Gulston *
Hans Stanley *
Richard [?] Burton *

1767
Capt. Boyle Walsingham

1768
Hon. George Hobart *
Hon. Gabriel Hanger *
Duke of Bedford
Earl of Huntingdon +
Earl Ferrers
Sir Watkin Williams Wynn *

1769
? Ayscough
Duke of Dorset +
Earl of Carlisle +

1770
Henry Drummond * +
Lord le Despencer
Lord Pigot
Earl of Ancrum
Duke of Buccleigh
Uvedale Price

1771
Forres Dashwood
Viscount Palmerston
Thomas Brand +
John Duntze *
Sir Richard Phillips *
Earl of Cholmondeley
John [?] Lee *

1772
Earl of Seaforth
Peter Beckford *
Sir Thomas Egerton *
Archibald [?] Douglas *
Marquis of Carmarthen
Lord Paget +
Duke of Argyll +

1773
C. Pelham +
Beilby Thompson *
Archibald [?] Macdonald *
George Pitt *

1774
Earl of Essex
Earl of Warwick
Viscount Guernsey

1775
George Finch Hatton
Hon. William Ward *
Earl of Plymouth
Earl of Winchilsea

1776
Lord Bulkely
George Pitt jun.

1777
Duke of Hamilton
Henry [?] Cecil *
Richard Thompson
Earl of Dunmore
Archibald [?] Douglas *
? Prendergast

1777 (cont.)
Earl of Winchilsea
? Adam

1778
Earl of Berkeley
Lord Brownlow
Viscount Binning
Duke of Hamilton

1779
Eliab [?] Harvey *
? Banks
Anthony [?] St. Leger *
John Lemon *
Hon. Thomas Trevor Hampden * +
Viscount George Legge Lewisham *
Viscount George Capel Malden *
Hon. Hugh Fortescue *
James Graham, Marquis of Graham * +
Charles Preston, Viscount *
Francis Basset *
Munby Goulbourn

1780
Lord Vernon
Earl of Chesterfield
Thomas Dundas *
George Osbaldeston *
Earl of Winchilsea
Sir John Ramsden *
John Campbell * +
Henry Hoare
John Royds
Henry Rosewarne *
Thomas Steele *
Lancelot Brown the younger

1781
Richard Gamon *
John Morshead * +
Earl of Hillsborough
Duke of Hamilton
Earl of Salisbury +

1782
Eliab Harvey *
James Adams * +
Desbrow Taylor
Lord Middleton

1783
Viscount Say and Sele
George Hesse

Appendix A

1783 (cont.)
Reginald Pole Carew *
John Symmons
Viscount Deerhurst
Duke of Athol
Viscount Falmouth +
Sir G. Webster +
Wilson Braddyll *
Sir James Long *
Christopher or Richard [?] Atkinson * + [R]
Sir John Whalley Gardiner *

1784
John Thomas Ellis *
Earl of Berkeley
Duc de Bouillon
Sir Henry Gough Calthorpe *
Capt. Payne

1785
Orlando Bridgeman *
John Maddocks *
Sir Henry Englefield
Sir Ralph Payne *
William Aldersley
Capt. Ashe
Alexander Ross Gray

1786
H.R.H. The Prince of Wales +
George Cousmaker
Welbore Ellis Ager *
Maj. John [?] Lemon *
Gerard Noel Edwards *
Duke of Queensbury
Duke of St. Albans
H.R.H. The Duke of Cumberland +

1787
George Tate
Lancelot Brown *
Viscount Compton
Marquis of Carmarthen
Sir Harry Bridgeman *
W. Churchill
H.R.H. The Duke of York

1788
John Calcraft *
Viscount Fitzwilliam +
Robert Burton
James Clitheroe
Sir G. Cornwell
H.R.H. The Duke of Gloucester +

1788 (cont.)
George Tierney *

1789
William Champion de Crespigny *
Baron Perrier Speed
John Montague (Viscount Hinchingbroke) *
George Pocock *
H.R.H. The Duke of Clarence
Duke of Ancaster +

1790
John Dent *
Earl of Darnley
George Hardinge *
Thomas Lewin
Thomas Hibbert
Sir G. Young
Francis Drake
F. Calvert
Joseph Foster Barham *
Edward Cotsford *

1791
David W. Hartley *
Sir. J. Coghill
Lord Eardley
Edward Loveden *
Viscount Molyneaux
John Cawthorne * +
James Bland Burgess
Lord Delavel
Earl of Tyrconnel
Earl of Strathmore
Hon. John Vaughan *
Col. William [?] Popham *
Lewis Montolieu

1792
Thomas Thompson *
Thomas Steele *
? Thoyts, Esq
Hon. Peniston Lamb *
Lord Craven
Joseph Scott *
J. L. Kaye
Lord Macdonald

1794
Sir Watkin Williams Wynn *

1795
George Pocock *

1797
James Meyrick
Earl Temple
Marquis of Carmarthen

1798
Thomas Wilkinson

1799
W. B. Martin
John Lloyd *
Samuel Gambier
Temple West
Charles Shaw Lefevre *
Sir Charles Talbot *
John Griffiths
John Weyland
Bryan Edwards *
Sir William John Heathcote *
William Egerton *
Sir Edmund Cradock Hartopp *
Edward Ravenscroft

1800
Sir William Geary *
William Gosling
William Lowdnes *

Professional Members 1763–1807

1763
John Beard
Jonathan Battishill
Thomas Arne
Gaetano Quilici
Carl Friedrich Abel
? Cowper (or Cooper)
William Savage
Samuel Champness
Felice Giardini

1764
George Berg

1765
William Hayes

1766
Cristiano Tedeschino
Mattia Vento
Ercole Ciprandi
? Grassi
Tommaso Guarducci

1767
François-Hippolyte Barthélemon
Benjamin Cooke
Jonathan Battishill

1769
John Abraham [?] Fisher
Gaetano Guadagni

1770
Thomas Norris
Giusto Tenducci
Frederick Charles Reinhold

1771
Samuel Webbe the elder
Rev. D. Bailey [Bayley]

1772
John Dyne

1773
Michael Leoni

1774
Giuseppe Millico
John Stafford Smith
Jonathan Battishill

1775
Edward [?] Meredith
Martin Renoldson [Rennoldson]

1777
? Wood

1778
Francesco Roncaglia
Gabriele Mario Piozzi

1779
Luffman Atterbury
Gasparo Pacchierotti

1780
Stephen or William Paxton
Venanzio Rauzzini
Felice Giardini

1781
Charles Knyvett snr
Giusto Tenducci
? Nonini

Appendix A

1783
R. J. S. Stevens
Samuel Harrison
John Hindle

1784
Joseph Corfe

1785
William Parsons
John Sale
Israel Gore

1786
Luigi Tasca
Nehemiah [?] Griffiths
? Stephenson or Stevenson

1787
? Salmon
James Billington
John Wall Callcott
John Danby
Robert [?] Parry

1789
Thomas Greatorex
Frederick Charles Reinhold
Charles Dignum
John [?] Pearson

1790
John or Richard Guise
James Bartleman
Richard or Thomas Bellamy
John [?] Saville
Matthew Cooke

1791
Samuel Webbe the younger
Robert Cooke

1792
Charles Knyvett jnr
Jonathan Nield
John Page
Robert Leete

1798
Thomas Greatorex
William Knyvett
James Bartleman

1799
John Bernard Sale

1803
Thomas Welsh

1805
John Goss
Frederick Charles Reinhold
? Vaughan
Thomas or William Elliott

1806
William [?] Hawes
Charles or Thomas [?] Evans

1807
Thomas [?] Taylor
Richard or Thomas Bellamy

Source: Membership details included in the Catch Club Minutes, BL H.2788.rr. - ww. Supplemented by lists included in Gladstone, *Story*.

Appendix B
Prize Medals Awarded by The Catch Club

1763
Canon – William Hayes *Alleluja*
Catch – Joseph Baildon *On a dram*
Glee – George Berg *On softest beds*
Glee – William Hayes *Melting airs*

1764
Canon – William Hayes *Resonate jovern totus*
Catch – Joseph Baildon *My sledge and hammer*
Catch – Thomas Arne *Good neighbours be quiet*
Glee – Samuel Long *Where e'er you tread*
Glee – George Berg *Compagni amor*

1765
Canon – Juan Bautisita Braugera *Beatus vir*
Canon – William Hayes *Come follow me*
Glee – George Berg *Si beviam vezzosa dori*
Glee – Thomas Arne *Which is the properest day*

1766
Canon – Thomas Arne *Ombré a mene*
Glee – Joseph Baildon *When gay Bacchus*
Glee – Thomas Arne *Gia ride primavera*

1767
Catch – Samuel Webbe *The moon and woman*
Glee – Benjamin Cook *The longitude*

1768
Canon – Samuel Webbe *From everlasting*
Catch – Gioacchino Cocchi *Quando, quando*
Glee – John Dyne *Fill the bowl*
Glee – Samuel Webbe *A gen'rous friendship*

1769
Canon – Peter Hellendaal *Glory be to the Father*
Catch – Charles Jenner *Ancient Phillis*
Glee – Thomas Arne *Make haste to meet*
Glee – Theodore Aylward *A cruel fate*

1770
Canon – Samuel Webbe *Alzate o porte*
Catch – William Bates *Sir you are*
Glee – John Alcock *Hail ever pleasing*
Glee – James Nares *To all lovers of harmony*

1771
Canon – Samuel Webbe *Iddio e quell che micinge*
Catch – Francis Ireland *As Colin one evening*
Glee – Jonathan Battishill *Come bind my hair*
Glee – Benjamin Cooke *How sleep the brave*

1772
Canon – John Alcock *Like as the hart*
Catch – James Hook *One morning Dame Turner*
Glee – Francis Ireland *Jolly Bacchus*
Glee – Samuel Webbe *Discord dire sister*

1773
Canon – not known
Catch – J. Stafford Smith *Here flat on her back*
Glee – Benjamin Cooke *In the merry month*
Glee – Francis Ireland *Where weeping yews*

1774
Canon – Samuel Webbe *Who can express?*
Catch – Samuel Webbe *To the old long life*
Glee – John Alcock *We'll drink*
Glee – J. Stafford Smith *Let happy lovers fly*

1775
Canon – Benjamin Cooke *Amen*
Catch – J. Stafford Smith *Since Phillis*
Glee – J. Stafford Smith *Blest pair of sirens*
Glee – Samuel Webbe *Now I'm prepared*

1776
Canon – G. B. Cirri *Nos autum gloriam*
Catch – Lord Mornington *When first I was wed*
Glee – J. Stafford Smith *While fools their time*
Glee – Samuel Webbe *You gave your heart*

1777
Canon – Samuel Webbe *Glory be to the father*
Catch – Lord Mornington *As Dolly and Nan*
Glee – Samuel Webbe *Rise my joy*
Glee – J. Stafford Smith *Return blest days*

1778
Canon – John Alcock *O give thanks*
Catch – Luffman Atterbury *As t'other day*
Glee – Samuel Webbe *Great Bacchus*
Glee – Luffman Atterbury *Adieu ye streams*

Appendix B

1779
Canon – William Paxton *O Lord in thee*
Catch – Luffman Atterbury *Some modern wives*
Glee – Lord Mornington *Here in cool grot*
Glee – Stephen Paxton *How sweet, how fresh*

1780
Canon – William Paxton *O Israel trust*
Catch – Anon (? Wright) *Quoth Hodge*
Glee – Luffman Atterbury *Begone dull care*
Glee – Luffman Atterbury *Oh thou sweet bird*

1781
Canon – S. Webbe *O all ye works of the Lord*
Catch – not known
Glee – John Danby *When Sappho tun'd*
Glee – Stephen Paxton *Round the hapless*

1782
Canon – John Danby *Lift up your heads*
Catch – Samuel Webbe *My lady Bantum*
Glee – R. J. S. Stevens *See what horrid tempests*
Glee – Benjamin Cooke *As now the shades*

1783
Canon – Samuel Webbe *To thee all angels*
Catch – Stephen Paxton *Ye muses inspire me*
Glee – John Danby *Awake Aeolian lyre*
Glee – John Danby *Music has pow'r*

1784
Canon – John Danby *And why my soul*
Catch – Samuel Webbe *When youthful Harriet*
Glee – Samuel Webbe *The fragrant painting*
Glee – Stephen Paxton *Blest pow'r here see*

1785
Canon – John W. Callcott *Blessed is he*
Catch – John W. Callcott *A beauteous fair*
Glee – J. W. Callcott *Dull repining sons of care*
Glee – John Danby *The nightingale who tunes*

1786
Canon – John W. Callcott *Bow down thine ear*
Catch – J. W. Calcott *On a summer's morning*
Glee – R. J. S. Stevens *It was a lover*
Glee – John Danby *The fairest flow'rs*

1787
Canon – John W. Callcott *Thou shalt shew*
Catch – Matthew [?] King *A rough country priest*
Glee – Robert Greville *Now the bright morning*
Glee – J. W. Callcott *Whan battayle smethynge*

1788
Canon – S. Webbe *O Lord shew us thy mercy*
Catch – Matthew King *We'll drink t'other glass*
Glee – S. Webbe *Swiftly from the mountain's*
Glee – Robert Cooke *Concord is conquer'd*

1789
Canon – J. W. Callcott *O thou wouldst' hide me*
Catch – John W. Callcott *Have you?*
Glee – John W. Callcott *Go idle boy*
Glee – John W. Callcott *Oh thou where'er*

1790
Canon – John W. Callcott *Call to remembrance*
Catch – Samuel Webbe *Juliet is pretty*
Glee – Samuel Webbe *Non fidi al mar*
Glee – John W. Callcott *O voi che sospirate*

1791
Canon – John W. Callcott *I am well pleased*
Catch – not known
Glee – John Danby *O salutaris hostis*
Glee – John W. Callcott *Triumphant love*

1792
Canon – John W. Callcott *O Israel return*
Catch – not known
Glee – John W. Callcott *Father of heroes*
Glee – John W. Callcott *See with ivy chaplet*

1793
Canon – John W. Callcott *Christ being raised*
Catch – Benjamin Cooke *Nature for defence*
Glee – Reginald Spofforth *See smiling*
Glee – R. Spofforth *Where are those hours?*

1. The principal source is Catch Club Prize Winners (British Library Add. E.1858.c), a listing that is unfortunately incomplete. It has been supplemented where possible by information from the Warren Collection and Rubin, 'The English Glee', pp. 108–10.
2. Samuel Webbe is every case the elder Webbe

Appendix C
Select List of Eighteenth Century Catch & Glee Publications

I – Individual Composers

Atterbury, Luffman: *A Collection of Catches and Glees for three and four voices* [...] *by Luff[man] Atterbury, musician in ordinary to His Majesty.* G. & S. Thompson; London, *c.* 1777.
_____ *A Collection of 12 Glees, Rounds &c* [...] *op. 2.* G. Goulding; London, *c.* 1788.
_____ *A Collection of Glees, Canzonets, and Rounds* [...] *op. 3.* T. Skellern for Mrs Atterbury; London, *c.* 1790.
Aylward, Theodore: *Elegies & Glees* [...] *op. 2* [...] *Printed for the Author.* London, *c.* 1785.
Baildon, Joseph: *A Collection of Glees & Catches for three and four voices, as they are performed at the Noblemen & Gentlemen's Catch Club. Never before printed.* Randall & Abell; London, 1768.
Battishill, Jonathan: *A Collection of Songs for three & four voices. Never before published.* Welcker; London, *c.* 1775.
Callcott, John Wall: *A First Collection of Catches, Glees, Canons for three, four and five voices* [...] *op. 4.* Longman & Broderip; London *c.* 1790.
_____ *A Select Collection of Catches, Canons & Glees.* London, *c.* 1790.
Cocchi, Gioacchino: *Twelve Italian Glees for two or three voices after the manner of the Catch Club.* Welcker. London, *c.* 1770.
Cooke, Benjamin: *A Collection of Glees, Catches and Canons for three, four, five and six voices. Printed for the Author,* London, *c.* 1775.
_____ *Nine Glees & Two Duets (never before printed) composed by the late Dr Benjamin Cooke. Published from the original manuscripts by his son, Robert Cooke. Op. 5.* Longman & Broderip; London, 1795.
Danby, John: *Danby's First Book of Catches, Canons & Glees for three, four & five voices &c.* J. Bland; London, *c.* 1785.
_____ *Danby's Second of Catches, Canons & Glees* [...] *Op. 3. Printed for the Author.* London *c.* 1789.
_____ *Danby's Third Book of Catches, Canons & Glees for three, four & five voices* [...]. J. Dale; London, *c.* 1791.
Dibdin, Charles: *A Collection of Catches & Glees for two, three or four voices with accompaniments for guittars and flutes.* I. Johnston; London, *c.* 1772.
Harington, Henry: *A Favorite Collection of Songs, Glees, Elegies and Canons* [...] Longman & Broderip. London, *c.* 1780.
Hayes, William: *Catches, Glees & Canons for three, four and five voices. Printed for the Author.* Oxford, 1757.
_____ *Catches, Glees & Canons for three, four, five, six & eight voices, including such as gained prize medals at Almack's AD 1763 & 1764. Book II. Printed for the Author.* Oxford, 1765.
Hellendaal, Pieter the elder: *Two Glees for four voices with full accompaniments in score, &c. The Author;* Cambridge, *c.* 1785.
Nares, James: *A Collection of Catches, Canons and Glees.* Welcker; London, *c.* 1772.
Paxton, Stephen: *A Collection of Glees, Catches &c for three and four voices. Op. 5. Printed for the Author.* London, *c.* 1782.
Smith, John Stafford: *A Collection of Glees for three, four, five & six voices, including some of the more serious cast* [...]. Welcker, London, *c.* 1776.
_____ *A Select Collection of Catches, Canons & Glees* [...] *for three and four voices.* Welcker; London, *c.* 1780.
Stevens, R. J. S: *Eight Glees for four and five voices* [...] *Opera 3.* Broderip & Wilkinson; London, 1792.

_____ *Eight Glees, expressly composed for ladies* [...] *Op. 4.* Printed for the Author; London, 1796.

_____ *Ten Glees for three, four, five and six voices* [...] *Op. 5.* Printed for the Author; London, 1800.

Webbe, Samuel the elder: *The Ladies Catch-Book, being a collection of Catches, Canons & Glees, the words of which will not offend the nicest delicacy.* Welcker; London, *c.* 1775.

_____ *A Second Book of Catches, Canons & Glees, &c* [...]. Longman & Broderip; London, 1771.

_____ *A Third Book of Catches, Canons & Glees for three & four voices.* Welcker; London, 1775.

_____ *A Fourth Book of Catches, Canons & Glees for 3, 4, 5 & 6 voices.* Welcker; London, *c.* 1778.

_____ *A Vth Book of Catches, Canons & Glees for three, four, five & six voices.* J. Bland; London, *c.* 1780

_____ *A Sixth Book of Catches, Canons & Glees for 3, 4, 5 & 6 voices.* A. Hamilton; London, *c.* 1780.

_____ *A Seventh Book of Catches, Canons & Glees for three, four & five voices.* J. Bland; London, *c.* 1784.

_____ *An Eighth Book of Glees, Canons & Catches* [...] *Printed for the Author*; London, *c.* 1795.

_____ & Samuel Webbe the younger: *A Collection of Vocal Music in two, three, four & five parts. Ninth Book.* Longman and Broderip for the Authors; London *c.* 1795.

II – Collections

A Collection of Catches, Glees, Canons, Canzonets, Madrigals &c. Selected from the works of the most Eminent Composers. J. Bland; London, *c.* 1785.

A Collection of Catches, Canons, Glees, Duettos &c. Selected from the works of the most eminent composers ancient and modern. J. Sibbald & Co; Edinburgh, *c.* 1780.

A Collection of Glees & Rounds for three, four and five voices. Composed by Members of the Harmonic Society of Cambridge and Publish'd by W. Dixon. Cambridge, *c.* 1796.

A Collection of Glees from the MSS of the Concentores: being the compositions of Dr Callcott, R. Cooke, W. Horsley, W. Linley, J. C. Pring, Dr Smith, R. Spofforth, S. Webbe & S. Webbe Jr. Broderip & Wilkinson; London, 1801.

A Collection of Vocal Harmony consisting of Catches, Canons & Glees [...] *to which are added several Motetts & Madrigals composed by the best Masters. Selected by Thomas Warren.* Welcker; London, from *c.* 1765.

A First [to 32nd] *Collection of Catches, Canons and Glees* [...] *most humbly inscribed to the Noblemen & Gentlemen of the Catch Club* [...] *Thomas Warren.* Longman & Broderip; London, 1763–1794.

Apollonian harmony: a collection of scarce & celebrated glees, catches, madrigals, canzonetts, rounds, & canons, antient & modern, with some originals. / Composed by Aldrich, Arne, Atterbury, Battishall, Boyce, Brewer, Dibdin, Eccles, Est, Giardini, Green, Handel, Harington, Hayes, Hook, Morley, Nares, Purcell, Ravenscroft, Travers, Webbe, and other eminent masters; most of which are sung at the Noblemens' Catch-Club, theatres, & public-gardens. The words consistent with female delicacy. Vol. 1–[VI]. S. A. & P. Thompson; London, 1781–1790.

Catch Club Harmony: being an entirely new set of near one hundred Catches, Songs & Glees for two, three & four voices. Compiled by John Arnold. Longman, Lukey & Co.; London, *c.* 1769.

Musicae vocalis deliciae, being a collection of [...] *Madrigals, Glees, Canzonets, Rounds & Canons* [...] *composed by* [...] *eminent masters* [...] *the words consistent with female delicacy. Vol I.* Printed for T. Skellern. London, *c.* 1790.

The Essex Harmony: being an entire new collection of the most celebrated Songs & Catches, Canzonets, Canons & Glees, for two, three four, five, & nine voices. From the works of the most Eminent Masters. Vol. II. By John Arnold, Philo-Musicae [...] R. & M. Brown; London, 1769.

_____ *The Essex Harmony* [...] *Vol. II. The Second Edition with large additions* [...]. G. Bigg. London, 1777.

The Favourite new Glees composed by Dr Cooke, Mr Callcott, Mr Danby and Mr Webbe, expressly for and performed at Harrison & Knyvett's Vocal Concert, 1792 [...] *Printed for Harrison and Knyvett.* Longman & Broderip. London, *c.* 1792.

The Professional Collection of Glees for three, four and five voices; composed by [...] *Callcott, Cooke, Danby, Hindle, Stevens & Webbe.* Longman & Broderip for the Authors. London, *c.* 1791.

Bibliography
Primary Sources

A Selection of Favourite Catches, Glees, &c. as Sung at the Bath Harmonic Society with the Rules of the Society, and a List of Members. Second edition with considerable additions. Bath, 1799.
Andrews, John: *An inquiry into the Manners, Taste and Amusements of the Last Two centuries in England.* London, 1787.
Anon: *Letters Concerning the Present State of England Particularly respecting the Politics, Arts, Manners and Literature of the Times.* London, 1772.
Arnold, John (comp.): *The Essex Harmony*, 2 vols. London, 1769.
Arnot, Hugo: *The History of Edinburgh from the Earliest Accounts to the Present Time.* 2nd edn, Edinburgh, 1788.
Burney, Charles: *A General History of Music*, 4 vols. London, 1776–89. Reprint ed. Frank Mercer. 2 vols. New York, 1957.
Busby, Thomas: *A General History of Music from the Earliest Times to the Present.* 2 vols. London, 1819.
By-Laws of the Musical Society at the Castle Tavern, in Pater-Noster-Row. London, 1731.
Callcott, John Wall: 'Essays on Musical Subjects'. British Library, Add. MS 27646.
_____ Notes for 'A Dictionary of Music'. British Library, Add. MS 27699.
_____ 'Plan of a General Dictionary of Music'. ?1798, British Library, Add. MS 27693.
Clark, Richard (comp.): *The First Volume of Poetry: Revised, Improved, and Considerably Enlarged, containing The Most Favourite Pieces, as Performed at The Noblemen and Gentlemen's Catch Club.* London, 1824.
Coke, Lady Mary: *Letters and Journals of Lady Mary Coke.* Edinburgh, 1889.
Collier, Joel (George Veal): *Musical Travels Through England.* 4th edn, London, 1776.
Craddock, Joseph: *Memoirs*, 4 vols. London, 1828.
Dibdin, Charles: *The Musical Tour of Mr Dibdin.* Sheffield, 1787.
Doane, Joseph: *A Musical Directory for the Year 1794.* Reprint, London, 1993.
Euterpeiad, or Musical Intelligencer, 1. Boston (USA), 1821.
Gardiner, William: *Music and Friends; or, Pleasant recollections of a dilettante*, 3 vols. London & Leicester, 1838–53.
Greene, Maurice: *Catches and Canons for Three and Four Voices.* London, 1747.
Grosley, M: *A Tour of London; or New Observations on England and its Inhabitants*, Translated from the French by Thomas Nugent, 2 vols. London, 1772.
Hanway, Jonas: *Thoughts on the Use and Advantages of Music.* London, 1765.
Hawkins, Sir John: *A General History of the Science and Practice of Music.* London, 1776. Reprint, 2 vols. New York, 1963.
_____ 'An account of the Institution and Progress of the Academy of Ancient Music, by A Member'. London, 1770.
Hayes, William: *Catches, Glees and Canons for 3,4, 5 Voices.* ?London, 1757.
_____ *A Supplement to the Catches, Glees and Canons, Lately published by Dr Hayes.* London, 1765.
_____ 'Remarks on Mr. Avisons's Essay on Musical Expression'. London, 1753.
Hoare, Prince: *Memoirs of Granville Sharp.* London, 1820.
Home, Henry: *Elements of Criticism*, 2 vols. Edinburgh, 1762.
Jackson, William: *The Four Ages and Essays.* London, 1798.
_____ *Observations on the Present State of Music in London.* London, 1791.
_____ *Preface to An Ode to Fancy, op. 8.* London, c. 1773.
Letters Concerning the Present State of England Particularly respecting the Politics, Arts, Manners and Literature of the Times. London, 1772.

'List of the Society for the Encouragement of Arts, Manufactures, and Commerce.' London, 1765.
'Madrigal Society', Records of: British Library, Add. MadSoc.F1/2/5.
Mann, A. H.: 'Notebooks', Norfolk Record Office, MS 435.
Miller, Edward: *Elegies, Songs, and an Ode of Mr. Pope's with Instrumental Parts*. London, *c.* 1770.
'Minutes of the Canterbury Catch Club'. Canterbury Cathedral Library, MS CC/W7/1.
'Minutes of the Catch Club'. British Library, Add. H2788.rr-ww. 1761–1796.
Monthly Review, 37, July 1767.
———— 44, January 1771.
New London and Country Songster; or A Banquet of Vocal Music. London, 1781.
New Monthly Magazine, vol. III, No. 3. April 1822.
Oliphant, Thomas: *An Account of the Madrigal Society*. London, 1835.
'Papers of the Concentores Society, Rules and Minutes.' Guildhall Library, London, MS 8593c.
Parke, William T.: *Musical Memoirs*, 2 vols. London, 1830.
Playford, Henry: *The Pleasant Musical Companion*. London, 1701.
Ravenscroft, Thomas: *Pammelia. Mvsicks Miscellanie*. London, 1609. Facsimile: Amsterdam, 1971.
'Rules and Orders of the Society, Established in London for the Encouragement of Arts, Manufactures, and Commerce.' London, 1758.
'Rules of the Lichfield Cecilian Society.' Lichfield Record Office. Add. MS D127.
Simpson, Christopher: *Compendium, or Introduction to Practicall Musick*. ?London, 1656.
'The Academy of Vocal Music 1725–1730.' BL Add. MS 11,732.
Warren, Edmund Thomas: *A Collection of catches, canons and glees*. (ed. Emanuel Rubin). Rep. with Introduction. 4 vols. Wilmington, De (USA), 1970.
Webb, Daniel: *Observations of the Correspondences between Poetry and Music*. London, 1769.
'Words of the Favourite Catches and Glees, Performed at the Ranelagh House, on the Twelfth of May.' London, 1767.

Secondary Works

Argent, Mark (ed.): *Recollections of R. J. S. Stevens: An Organist in Georgian London*. London, 1992.
Baptie, David: 'Descriptive Catalogue of Glees, Madrigals, Part Song, Etc.' 4 vols. Compiled in Glasgow, 1895–98. British Library Add. M.R.Ref.3.a.
———— *Sketches of the English Glee Composers*. London, 1895.
Barrett, William Alexander: 'English Glee and Madrigal Writers.' Two lectures read at the London Institution on 18 January and 15 February 1877. London, ?1877.
———— *English Glees and Partsongs*. London, 1886.
Beecher Hogan, Charles (ed.): *The London Stage 1776–1800*. Part 5 of *The London Stage 1660–1800*. Chicago, 1965–68.
Blom, Eric (ed.): *Grove's Dictionary of Music and Musicians*. 5th edn 9 vols. London, 1954.
Blume, Friedrich (ed.): *Die Musik in Geschichte und Gegenwart*. 17 vols. Kassel, 1949–79.
Borsay, Peter (ed.): *The Eighteenth-Century Town: A Reader in English Urban History 1688–1820*. London, 1990.
Boydell, Brian: *A Dublin Musical Calendar*. Dublin, 1988.
Brewer, John: *Pleasures of the Imagination: English Culture in the Eighteenth Century*. London, 1997.
Burrows, Donald and Rosemary Dunhill (eds): *Music and Theatre in Handel's World: The Family Papers of James Harris 1732–1780*. Oxford, 2002.
Caldwell, John: *The Oxford History of English Music, vol. 2: c. 1715 to the Present Day*. Oxford 1999.
Chappell, William: *Popular Music of the Olden Time*, 2 vols. London, 1859.
Chevill, Elizabeth Jane: 'Music societies in musical life in old foundation cathedral cities, 1700–1760'. Ph.D. Diss. University of London, 1993.
Clark, Andrew (ed.): *The Life and Times of Anthony Wood*. 3 vols. Oxford, 1892 & 1894.

Bibliography

Clark, Peter: *British Clubs and Societies 1580–1800.* Oxford, 2000.
_____ *The English Alehouse 1200–1830.* Harlow, 1983.
Colley, Linda: *Britons: Forging the Nation 1707–1837.* Yale, 1992.
Colman, Lawrence, H. C. G. Matthew, Brian Harrison (eds): *Oxford Dictionary of National Biography.* Oxford, 2004.
Cozens-Hardy, Basil (ed.): *The Diary of Sylas Neville.* London, 1950.
Cudworth, Charles: 'Two Georgian Classics: Arne and Stevens.' *Music and Letters,* 45 (1964).
Dubois, Pierre (ed.): *Charles Avison's Essay on Musical Expression With Related writings by Charles Avison and William Hayes.* Aldershot, 2004.
Elkin, Robert: *The Old Concert Rooms of London.* London, 1955.
Fawcett, Trevor: *Music in Eighteenth-Century Norwich and Norfolk.* Norwich, 1979.
Fiske, Roger: *English Theatre Music in the Eighteenth Century.* Oxford, 1986.
_____ (ed.) *Michael Kelly: Reminiscences.* Oxford, 1975.
_____ and H. Diack Johnstone (eds): *Music in Britain: The Eighteenth Century.* Oxford, 1990.
Ford, Boris (ed.): *The Cambridge Cultural History: Seventeenth-Century Britain.* Cambridge, 1989.
Fraser, Antonia: *Cromwell: Our Chief of Men.* London, 1973.
Fuller-Maitland, John A: *Grove's Dictionary of Music and Musicians.* 2nd edn. 5 vols. London, 1904–10.
Girdham, Jane: *English Opera in Late Eighteenth-Century London: Stephen Storace at Drury Lane.* Oxford, 1997.
Gladstone, Herbert John: *The Story of the Noblemen and Gentlemen's Catch Club.* London, 1930.
Highfill, Philip H., A. Kalman and Edward A. Langans: *A Biographical Dictionary of Actors, Actresses, Musicians, Dancers, Managers and other Stage Personnel in London, 1660–1800.* 16 vols. Carbondale (USA), 1973–93.
Holman, Peter: *Four and Twenty Fiddlers: The Violin at the English Court, 1540–1690.* Oxford, 1993.
Hooper, Graham: 'A Survey of Music in Bristol with Special Reference to the Eighteenth century'. MA Diss. University of Bristol, 1963.
Johnson, David: 'The 18th-century glee.' *Musical Times,* vol. 107 (1979), pp. 200–2.
Klima, S. G. Bowers, and Kerry S. Grant (eds.): *Memoirs of Dr Charles Burney.* Nebraska, 1988.
Latham, Robert (ed.): *The Shorter Pepys.* London, 1985.
Le Huray, Peter and James Day (eds): *Music and Aesthetics in the Eighteenth and Early-Nineteenth Centuries.* Cambridge, 1981.
Lovell, Percy: '"Ancient Music" in Eighteenth-Century England.' *Music and Letters.* 60 (1979), pp. 101–15.
McVeigh, Simon: *The Violinist in London's Concert Life, 1750–1784: Felice Giardini and his Contemporaries.* New York, 1989.
_____ *Concert Life in London from Mozart to Haydn.* Cambridge, 1993.
_____ 'Calendar of London Concerts 1750–1800.' Database, Goldsmith's College. University of London.
Namier, Sir L. and J. Brooke (eds): *The History of Parliament: The House of Commons 1754–1790.* 3 vols. London, 1985.
Pink, Andrew: 'Benjamin Cooke (1734–93).' MA Diss. Anglia Polytechnic University, 2000.
Price, Curtis, Millhous, Judith and Hume, Robert D: *Italian Opera in Late Eighteenth-Century London: The King's Theatre, Haymarket 1778–91.* Oxford, 1995.
_____ *The Impressario's Ten Commandments: Continental Recruitment for Italian Opera in London, 1763–64,* RMA Monographs, 6. London, 1992.
Raynor, Henry: *A Social History of Music: From the Middle Ages to Beethoven.* London, 1972.
Reid, Douglas J (assisted by Brian Pritchard): 'Some Festival Programmes of the Eighteenth and Nineteenth Centuries. I–Salisbury and Winchester.' *Royal Musical Association Research Chronicle,* 5 (1965), pp. 51–63.
Rimbault, Edward Francis: *The Rounds, Catches and Canons of England.* London, c. 1860.
Robbins Landon, H. C. : *Haydn Chronicle and Works: Haydn in England, 1792–1795.* London, 1976.

Bibliography

Robins, Brian: 'John Marsh and Provincial Music Making in Eighteenth-Century England.' *Royal Musical Association Research Chronicle*, 29 (1996), pp. 96–142.

_____ 'The Catch Club in 18th-Century England.' *Early Music*, 28 (2000), pp. 517–29.

_____ (ed.): *The John Marsh Journals: The Life and Times of a Gentleman Composer (1752–1828)*. Stuyvesant, NY, 1998.

Robinson, B. W. and R. F. Hall (eds): *The Aldrich Book of Catches*. London and Sevenoaks, 1989.

Rubin, Emanuel Leo: 'The English Glee from William Hayes to William Horsley.' Ph.D. Diss. U. of Pittsburgh, 1968.

Sadie, Stanley and John Tyrrell (eds): *New Grove Dictionary of Music and Musicians*. Revised; 29 vols. London, 2001.

Sands, Molly: *The Eighteenth-Century Pleasure Gardens of London*. London, 1987.

Scholes, Percy A: *Music and Puritanism*. Vevey (Switzerland), 1934.

Spink, Ian 'The Old Jewry Musick-Society: A 17th-Century Catch-Club.' Musicology II: Journal of The Musicological Society of Australia, 1965–67, pp. 35–41.

_____ (ed.): *The Blackwell History of Music in Britain: The Seventeenth Century*. Oxford, 1992.

_____ (ed.): *The Works of Henry Purcell*, vol. 22a. London, 2000.

Summers, Judith: *The Empress of Pleasure: The Life and Adventures of Teresa Cornelys – Queen of Masquerades and Casanova's Lover*. London, 2003.

Timms, J: *Club Life of London: With anecdotes of Clubs, Coffee-Houses and Taverns of the Metropolis during the 17th, 18th and 19th Centuries*. 2 vols. London, 1866.

Walker, Ernest: *A History of Music in England*. 3rd edn, revised by J. A. Westrup. London, 1952.

Weber, William: *The Rise of Musical Classics in Eighteenth-Century England*. Oxford, 1992.

Weinreb, Ben and Christopher Hibbert (eds): *The London Encyclopaedia*. Revised edn. London, 1993.

Wilson, John (ed.): *Roger North on Music*. London, 1959.

Wollenberg, Susan: *Music at Oxford in the Eighteenth and Nineteenth Centuries*. Oxford, 2002.

_____ and Simon McVeigh (eds): *Concert Life in Eighteenth-Century Britain*. Oxford, 2004.

Wright, B. F. : 'The Glee.' *Monthly Musical Record*, 89 (1959).

Young, Percy M. : *A History of British Music*. London, 1967.

Index

Abel, Carl Friedrich, vii, 40–42, 45, 90, 114
Abingdon, Earl of, 124
Abrams, Eliza, 116, 124
Abrams, Harriet, 116, 124
   Crazy Jane, 116
Abrams, Theodosia, 116, 124
Academy of Vocal (Ancient) Music, 19, 20–25, 27, 37, 40, 46, 70, 73, 77, 79, 82, 84, 93
Actor's Remonstrance or Complaint, 8
Adams, James, 76
Addison, Joseph, 137
Ah! Robin, gentil Robin, 4
Albion Tavern, 84
Aldrich, Henry, 14, 48, 109, 114, 117
   On Tobacco, 14
   Christ Church Bells, 14, 114, 117
Almack, William, 32, 36, 38, 55–56, 114
Almack's Assembly Rooms (Willis' Rooms) 32, 55, 115, 119–21
Almack's Club (Pall Mall), 32, 48, 55
Anacreon, 72, 147, 149
Anacreontic Society, 57, 72, 74–78, 92, 114, 130
Anacreontic Song, 73–74, 113–14, 134
Anderson and Colvil, 60
Anderton's Coffee House, 76
Andion, Dr, 82
Andreozzi, Gaetano, 121
   Nel verdermi, 121
Andrewes, Colonel, 100
Applewaite, Mr, 101
Apsley, Lady, 103
Apsley, Lord, 103
Arden, Sir Richard Pepper, 100
Argent, Mark, 84
Argyle, Duke of, 58
Arne, Michael, 41, 45, 131
   Almena, 41, 45
Arne, Thomas, vii, 25–26, 34, 40, 42, 48, 66, 69–70, 106–12, 117–19, 121, 130, 139, 142, 147, 149–50
   Artaxerxes, 109
   Blow thou winter wind, 147
   Capochio and Dorinna, 111
   Country Madcap in London, The, 111
   Fair the op'ning lily blows, 66
   Già riede prima vera, 42
   Hush to peace, 118
   Judgement of Paris, The, 112
   Love in a village, 34
   Miss Lucy in Town, 111
   Ode to Shakespeare, 147
   Ombré a mene, 42
   Silent cock and hen that crows, The, 109
   Squire Badger (The Sot), 112
   Street Intrigue, The, 117
   Sweet Muse, 119
   Tell me where is fancy bred, 147
   Temple of Dullness, The, 111
   Unconscionable, The, 142
   'Water parted from the sea' (*Artaxerses*) 109
   Where the bee sucks, 121, 147
   Which is the properest day to drink, 108–9
   Whittington's Feast, 112
Arnold, John, 51, 72, 89
   The Essex Harmony, 72, 89
Arnold, Samuel, 74, 77, 80–82, 95, 110, 130–31
   Banditti, The, 130
   Genius of Nonsence, The, 130
   Harlequin Teague, 130
   'Social pow'rs' (*The Castle of Andalusia*), 130–31
Arnull, George, 83
Arrowsmith, Daniel, 118
Ashley, Charles or Charles Jane, 81
Astarto, Re di Tiro, 42
Atterbury, Luffman, 25–26, 69–70, 78, 104, 121
   Collection of Glees and Catches, 104
   Come let us all a-Maying go, 121
Attwood, Thomas, 83, 95, 129, 147–48
Avison, Charles, 30, 135–37, 139
   Essay on Musical Expression, 30, 135
Ayrton, Edmund, 79, 81–82
Aylward, Theodore, 76, 78, 93, 97, 99

Bach, Johann Christian, vii, 42, 46–47, 90, 112, 114
   Carattico, 46
   Catone in Utica, 46
   Orione, 47
   Zanaida, 47
Bach, Johann Sebastian, 42, 81
Baildon, Joseph, 32, 48, 50, 133
   Adieu to the village delights, 133
   Collection of Glees and Catches, 50
   When gay Bacchus, 50
   When is it best?, 48
Baildon, Thomas, 118
   Mr Speaker, 118, 125
Bailey, Mr & son, 97
Bamfield, Sir George, 58
Banister, John, 12–13
Bannister, Charles, 81, 113

169

Index

Bannister, John, 113–14
Baptie, David, 151–54
Barrett, Mr, 93, 96, 99
Barrett, William Alexander, 3, 4, 12, 151–54
Barrington, Major-General John, 33, 36
Barrington, William Wildman, 36
Barrymore, William, 113
Barthélemon, François Hippolyte, 110–12, 118, 129
   The Magic Girdle, 112
Barthélemon, Polly, (née Young), 111
Bartleman, James, 59, 79, 86, 115–16, 120, 122
Bates, Joah, 34, 59
Bates, William, 142
   How silent lies the chief, 142
Bath Harmonic Society, 89–100, 105
Bath, Marquis of, 100
Battishill, Jonathan, 25, 40–41, 45, 73, 148, 150
   Almena, 41, 45
   I lov'd thee beautiful and kind, 45
Beard, John, 40–41, 82
Beattie, James, 135
Beaumont, Mr, 99
Beaumont and Fletcher, 134
   The Beggar's Bush, 134
Bedford, Duke of, 26
Beethoven, Ludwig van, 150
Beggars Opera, The, 113, 138
Bellamy, Thomas, 80, 82, 120
Bellas, George, 74
Berg, George, 19, 25–26, 48, 145–46, 149
   Now the bright morning star, 149
   On softest beds, 48, 145–46
Bernardi, Francesco, (Senesino), 21
Bever, Thomas, 25, 77
Bishop, Henry, 134
Black Horse, Aldersgate Street, 8
Blake, James, 76
Blankethall Inn, Witney, 129
Blessington, Lord, 58, 68
Blow, John, 14, 15, 150
Boccherini, Luigi, 99
Bononcini, Giovanni, 21–22, 137
Booth Hall, Gloucester, 125
Boswell, James, 72
Boucher, Mr, 101
Bouillon, Duc de, 52
Bowen, Mr, 72
Boyce, William, vii, 36, 69, 121, 150
   An Elegy on the late Earl of Eglinton, 36
   'Softly rise' (*Solomon*), 121
Braham, John, 113
Brewer, John, 65
Brewer, Thomas, 30
Bristol Catch Club, 65, 89–97, 100–101
Bristol Cecilian Society, 92, 94
Britton, Thomas, 13
Broderip, Francis, 79, 85

Broderip, Robert, 92, 94, 100
Brooks, James, 95
Brownlow, Lord, 76
Bruguera, Juan Bautista, y Morreras, 54
   Beatus vir, 54
Brydges, James (Duke of Chandos), 88
Buckingham, Lord, 60
Buckley, John?, 123
Buffalo Tavern, 85–86
Bull, John, 19, 71
Bunbury, Lady Sarah, 39
Burgat, Mr, 99, 101–102
Burney, Charles, 9, 42–43, 46, 81–82, 105, 138, 150
Burns, Robert, 148
Busby, Thomas, 150–51
Bush Tavern, Bristol, 97
Butler, Charles, 34
Byrd, William, 6, 121

Caldara, Antonio, 2
Callcott, John Wall, 3, 32, 36–37, 50, 54, 68–71, 75–77, 81–86, 94–95, 119–22, 128–29, 139, 143, 147–49, 151–53
   'Essay on the Catch Club', 32, 54
   Father of heroes, 119
   Friar of Orders Gray, The, 128, 148
   Go gentle gales, 86
   Hark how the nightingale, 86
   Not, unto us, O Lord, 86
   O voi che sospirate, 149
   Padre del ciel, 71
   Peace to the souls of heroes, 121, 128, 143, 148
   Red Cross Knight, The, 128
   See with ivy chaplet, 119
Calthorp, Lord, 75
Cambridge Harmonic Society, 95
Canteloupe, Lady, 103
Canterbury Catch Club, 89–101
Canterbury Subscription Concerts, 126–28
Carew, Thomas, 149
Carey, George, 112
   The Noble Pedlar, 112
Carlisle House, 114, 118
Carraccioli, Marquis, 52
Carter, J?, 80–81
Carter, Thomas, 81, 112
Caslon, William, 23
Castle Concerts, 18–19, 23, 27
Castle Tavern, Paternoster Row, 18
Catch Club, The (Noblemen and Gentlemen's), viii, 20–21, 24–28, 32–81, 86, 88–94, 98–100, 103–104, 107–12, 115, 118–21, 125, 138–39, 142, 144–46, 148–51, 154
Catullus, Gaius Valerius, 149
Cervetto, James, 74
Chafy, Mr, 101
Champness, Samuel, 40, 45, 48, 108, 112
Chapman, William, 113

Index

Chappell, William, 9
Chatterton, Thomas, 147–48
Chaucer, Geoffrey, 149
Chesterfield, Lord, 56
Chevill, Elizabeth, 88, 91
Chichester Catch Club, 65, 89–102, 127
Chichester Concert, 126–29
Child, William, 7, 71
Chilmead, Edmund, 8–9
Chubb, Mr, 99
Cibber, Theophilus, 112
Ciprandi, Ercole, 46
City of London Tavern, 84
Clark ?, 105
Clark, Peter, 5, 16, 57, 101
Clark, Richard, 151, 153–54
Clarke, Jeremiah, 20
Clarke, Master, 113
Clemens non Papa, 71
Cline, Mr, 129
Clinton, Lord, 58–59
Cocchi, Gioacchino, 54
   Quando, quando, 54
Coke, Lady Mary, 57
Coleman, Robert, 7
Collier, Joel (George Veal), 116, 138
   Musical Travels through England, 138
Collins, William, 143
Concentores Society, 79, 84–87, 125
Concert of Antient Music, 34, 57, 59, 115, 140
Congreve, William, 149
Cooke, Benjamin, 19, 25–26, 37, 49, 50, 54, 57, 63, 65–66, 69–71, 74, 76, 79, 81–83, 110, 117, 119, 121, 126, 128, 143, 148–49, 151–52
   Epitaph on a dormouse, 143
   Hark, the lark, 110, 117, 119, 126, 128
   How sleep the brave, 49, 110, 143
   Interr'd here doth lie, 71
   Now the bright morning star, 149
   'Tis beauty calls, 57
   Welcome friends of harmony, 76
Cooke, Robert, 50, 63, 71, 79, 85–86, 148
   Concord is conquered, 71
Corfe, Joseph, 93, 96, 99, 101, 105, 122, 125–26, 133
   From shades of night, 133
Cornelys, Teresa, 114, 118
Covent Garden, 41–42, 81, 112, 130–32, 134
Cowley, Abraham, 149
Cowper, (Cooper) Mr, 40–41, 44, 48
Cowper, William, 149
Craddock, Joseph, 34–35, 144
Cramer, Wilhelm (William), 74, 122
Croft, William, 21
Crosdill, John, 125
Cross Keys Inn, Buckingham, 129
Crown and Anchor Tavern, 20–21, 73, 78, 80
Crown Inn, Bicester, 129

Crown Inn, Thame, 89
Cumberland, Duke of, 125, 142
Curteys, Mr, 10
Curtis, James, 75

Danby, John, 50, 69–70, 74, 79 94, 116–17, 120–24, 148, 151–52
   Awake Aeolian lyre, 148
   Fair Flora, 124
   Hark! the chase, 123
   O let the merry peel, 121–22
   When Sappho tun'd, 117
D'Angeul, Monsieur, 52
Davies, Cecilia, 41
De Hearle, Mr, 101–102
De la Rue, Pierre, 34
Delawar, Lady, 103
Delawar, Lord, 103
Denbigh, Lady, 104
Denbigh, Lord, 104
Dering, Richard, 7
Devonshire, Duchess of, 75
Dibdin, Charles, 25, 66, 95, 108, 112–13, 130
   The Cobler, 113
   The Padlock, 113
Digest, The, 56
Dignum, Charles, 80, 113, 116, 148
   Epitaph to Pope, 148
Dilettanti Society, 61
Dinwoody, Mr, 76–77
Dixon, William, 95
Doane, Joseph, *Directory*, 45
Dobney, Mr, 129
Dock Chapel Choir, Portsmouth, 127
Dolben, Sir John, 21, 29
Dolben, Sir William, 29
Douglas, Archibald, 56
Dowding, Mr, 76
Drummore, Lord (Hew Dalrymple), 27
Drury Lane Theatre, 81, 110–15, 131, 133–34
Dryden, John, 4, 83, 112, 138, 149
   Alexander's Feast, 112
Dubois, Pierre, 136
Dunbar, Mr, 101
Dunstanville, Lord, 58
Dupuis, Thomas, 77, 81–83
Dussek, Sophia, 123
Dyne, John, 45, 79

East, Michael, 118, 121, 125
   How merrily we live, 118, 125
Eccles, John, 118, 121
Edinburgh Catch Club, 27, 39
Edinburgh Music Society, 27
Edwards, Gerard Noel, 79
Edwin, James, 113
Eglinton, Earl of (Archibald Montgomery), 33, 36, 48

Ellis, William, 9–10, 14, 40
Estwick, Sampson, 20
Euterpe, 140
Euterpeiad, The, 44, 150
Evans, Charles, 70
Exeter, Earl of, 26

Fawkener, Edward, 28–29, 103
Fayrfax Manuscript, 71
Festinos, 114
Fielding, Henry, 111-12
    Don Quixote in England, 112
Fischer, Johann Christian, 125
Fiske, Roger, 81
Fitzwilliam Virginal Book, 19
Flexney, William, 10
Ford, Thomas, 30, 121
Fortescue, Earl of, 58
Foster, Mrs, 103
Foster, Thomas, 103
Fox, Charles James, 79
Frederick, Duke of York, 100
Frederick, Prince of Orange, 100
Freeman, John, 20, 131
    We be soldiers three, 131
Freemasons' Hall, 114
Freemasons' Tavern, 80
Friendly Harmonists, 76–77, 83
From morn, (anon.) 121

Gainsborough, Thomas, 43, 67
Galliard, John Ernest, 20–21
    Calypso and Telemachus, 20
Gallini, Sir John (Giovanni), 114
Galuppi, Baldassare, 42
    L'Arcadia in Brenta, 42
Gardiner, William, 35, 45, 58–61, 63, 68, 93, 122, 128, 148
Gariboldi, Stefano, 74
Garrick, David, 35, 147
Garrick's Head Coffee House, 81
Garth, John, (Durham), 137
Gates, Bernard, 20, 22
Gaudrey, ? 113
Gazetteer, The, 115
Geminiani, Francesco, 21, 137
George III, 54, 67, 70, 100, 109
George, Prince of Wales, 52, 129
Giardini, Felice, 34, 40, 42–44, 53–54, 60, 111, 125–26
    Beviamo tutti tre, 44, 111, 125–26
Gibbon, Edward, 75–76
Gibbons, Mr, 97, 99
Gibbons, Orlando, 43
Gilbert, Dr, 104
Giordano, Tommaso, 147
    Take, Oh take those lips away, 147
Girdham, Jane, 133

Gladstone, Herbert John, viii, 37, 59
Glee Club, The (founded 1787), 25, 73–74, 76–83, 86–87, 93, 119–20, 125, 130, 151
Glee Club, The (founded 1793), 81–82, 116, 131
Gluck, Christoph Willibald, 46
    Orfeo ed Eurydice, 46
Goodban, Mr, 91, 96–97, 101
Goodban, Mrs, 91, 93
Goose and Gridiron, 12
Gordon, William, 39
Gore, Israel, 79, 93, 120
Goss, John, 93, 96, 99, 105, 125
Gounod, Charles, 152
Gough, Sir Henry, 57, 75
Graduates Meeting, 81–83, 124
Granby, Marquis of (John Manners), 39
Grassi, ?, 46
Gray, Thomas, 148
    Elegy Written in a Country Churchyard, 148
Greatorex, Thomas, 59, 87, 115, 120
Greene, Maurice, 18–19, 22, 27–31, 150
    Catches and Canons for Three and Four Voices, 27
Grétry, André Ernest, 132
    Richard Coeur de Lion, 132
Greville, Rev. Robert, 149
    Now the bright morning star, 149
Grey de Wilton, Lord, 65
Guadagni, Gaetano, 46
Guarducci, Tommaso, 46
Guise, Richard, 82

Hague, Charles, 95
Hale, Thomas, 89
    Social Harmony, 89
Hamilton, Duke of, 32, 45–46
Hamilton, William, 53
Handel, George Frederick, vii, 1, 13, 20, 39–41, 45, 90, 115–16, 119, 120, 136–38, 150
    Alexander's Feast, 41
    'Angels ever bright' (*Theodora*), 116, 121
    Concerto grosso op. 6/11, 115
    Esther, 40
    Il Pastor Fido, 40
    L'Allegro ed il Penseroso, 136–37
    Messiah, 124
Handelian Society, 76
Hankey, Sir Richard, 75
Hanover Square Rooms, 114–116, 123–24
Hanway, Jonas, 137
Hardinge, George, 79
Harington, Dr Henry, 95, 106, 127, 130, 148
    Gentle Airs, 127
    Look, neighbours look, 130
Harington, Miss, 106
Harmonic Society, Cambridge, 95
Harmonists Society, 76, 83–84
Harris, Elizabeth, 103–5, 112, 114, 125, 150
Harris, Gertrude, 104

Index

Harris, James, jnr., 103–4, 112
Harris, James, snr., 28, 39, 47, 93, 103–5, 135, 140
   Three Treatises, 135
Harris, Louisa, 104, 112
Harrison, Christopher, 10
Harrison, Samuel, 74, 79, 87, 114–16, 120, 122
Harrop, Sarah, 105, 126
Harwood, Edward, 148
   Vital spark of heav'nly flame, 148
Hawarden, Lord, 100
Hawkins, Sir John, 9, 12–13, 18, 22–23
Haydn, Joseph, 75, 82–83, 90, 115–16, 118, 123–24, 150
Hayes, Thomas, 28
Hayes, William, 25, 28–31, 48, 66, 89, 93–94, 105, 119, 130, 132, 136–37
   Allelujah, 48
   Catches, Glees and Canons, 25, 29
   Epitaph on Sophocles, 130
   Melting Airs, 48, 119, 132
   Remarks on Mr. Avison's Essay, 136
   Soft pity never leaves, 130
Haym, Nicola, 21
Haymarket Theatre, 111–12, 115
Hellendaal, Pieter, snr., 54, 110
   Glory be to God, 54
   Two glees for four voices, 110
Heming, Mrs S, 106
Herbert, Lady Henrietta, 41
Herrick, Robert, 149
Herschel, Alexander, 92
Herschel, William, 92, 119
   Echo Catch, 92, 119
Heseltine, James, 77
Hesse, Prince of, 27
Hibernian Catch Club, Dublin, 14
Hillhouse, James, 101
Hilton, John, 7–8, 11, 30, 121
   Catch that Catch Can, 7–8, 10–12
Hindle, John, 50, 74, 79 120
Hindmarsh, John, 116, 124
Hogarth, William, 21, 65
Hold thy peace, 5
Holder, Joseph, 143
   How sleep the brave, 143
Holywell Music Room, 28–29
Home, Henry, Lord Kames, 139–40
   Elements of Criticism, 139
Homer, 149
Hook, James, 117, 131, 134, 148
   Come let us all a Maying go, 117
   Fill the foaming bowl, 131
   Jack of Newbury, 134
   'Madrigal for Minstrels', 134
   Saw you the nymph, 117
   The Scornful, 117
Hooper, Graham, 95
Horsfall, James, 80, 85–86

Horsham, Sussex, 129
Horsley, William, 85–87, 94, 154
   Softly drops the pensive tear, 86
Howarth, Mr, 76
Howe, Lord, 133
Hudson, Mary, 49, 71
   Applaud so great a guest, 49, 71
Hudson, Robert, 49, 71, 82
   On the Grave Stone of Dr William Child, 71
Hughes, Francis, 20, 21
Hullah, John, 154
Humphry, Mr, 97, 99
Hutcheson, Francis (Ireland), 69–70, 141–43
   How sleep the brave, 143
   Jolly Bacchus, 141

Immyns, John, 23
Incledon, Charles, 81
Ireland, Francis (see Hutcheson)
Isaac, Henricus, 34
Ives, Simon, 121

Jackson's Oxford Journal, 89, 129
Jackson, William, 67–68, 119, 121–22, 136–37, 144, 153–54
   Four Ages and Essays, 67
   In a vale, 121
James, Sir Walter, 100
Janes, Thomas, 10
Jannequin, Clément, 34
Jeacock, Samuel, 23
Jenkins, John, 7
Johnstone, Mr, 81
Jones, Colonel, 94, 99
Jonson, Ben, 4, 5, 148
   The Silent Woman, 5
Josquin des Prés, 34

Kelly, Michael, 36, 72, 74
Keymer's Pantheon, Norwich, 128
King, Charles, 20
   O Absalom, my son, 20
King, Matthew, 147
   Tell me where is fancy bred, 147
King's Head, Lichfield, 97
King's Head Tavern, Oxford, 29
King's Theatre, 35, 42–44, 46, 55, 132
Knyvett, Charles, jnr, 59, 122
Knyvett, Charles, snr, 74, 78–80, 116, 120
Knyvett, William, 59, 87, 120

Lansdown, Marquis of, 100
Lant, Thomas, 4
   Lant Roll, 4, 6
La Rue, Pierre de, 34
Lawes, Henry, 1, 7
Lawes, Henry or William, 30
Lawes, William, 7–8, 71

Index

Le Clerc de la Bruère, Charles Antoine, 52
Lefevre, Charles Shaw, 79
Le Jeune, Claude, 119
Lennox, Lady Louisa, 102
Leoni, ? 113
Lewes, Sussex, 129
Lewis, Mr, 84
Lichfield Cecilian Society, 89–92, 97–100, 102
Lidarti, Cristiano, 48, 53
   Che viva San Martino, 48
   Treman gli spirti, 48
Lincoln Catch Club, 89
Linley, Elizabeth, (Mrs R. B. Sheridan), 58, 125
Linley, Mary, 125
Linley, Thomas, snr, 58, 74, 78, 125, 130–31, 133
   'The Friar's Glee' (*The Duenna*) 130
   The Triumph of Mirth, 131
Linley, Thomas, jnr, 125, 130
   The Duenna, 130
Linley, William, 58, 68–69, 79, 85–87, 125, 134
   'Well, brother, our merry old king is dead' (*The Merchant of Bruges*), 134
Little Theatre, Haymarket, 132–33
Liverpool Catch Club, 90
Locatelli, Pietro, 137
Locke, Matthew, 9, 71
   Domine, salvum fac Regem, 9
London Coffee House, 72–73
London Corresponding Society, 142
London Stage, The, 112
Lonsdale, Lord, 58
Lotti, Antonio, 22
Low, Edward, 10
Lowe, Thomas, 107, 110
Lully, Jean-Baptiste, 1

Macpherson, James, 147
Madrigal Society, The, viii, 23–25, 37, 41–42, 46, 70, 77, 106–7, 122
Mahmood, 133
Mahon, John, 92
Majo, Giovanni Maio, 121
   A morir, 121
Manchester Catch Club, 90
Mara, Gertrud, 115
Marcello, Benedetto, 137
March, Earl of (William Douglas), (see Duke of Queensbury)
March, Lord, 57
Marenzio, Luca, 20, 34, 53
Marlowe, Christopher, 59, 149
Marsh, Elizabeth, 105
Marsh, John, vii, 35, 42, 65, 72–74, 76, 78, 90–91, 93–102, 105–6, 115, 125–29, 148
   The Curfew tolls, 106, 148
Marsh, Dr Narcissus, 10
Marybone (Marylebone) Pleasure Garden, 42, 107, 109–111

Matthews, Mr (Catch Club), 68
Matthews, Mr (Gloucester), 125
Mazarin, Cardinal, 52
Mazzinghi, Joseph, 147
McVeigh, Simon, 1, 109, 120
Melville, David, 6
   Melville Manuscript, 6
Mendelssohn, Felix, 152
Mermaid, Carfax, 88
Metastasio, Pietro Trapassi, 149
Meynell (Menil), Hugo, 33, 35
Middleton, Bartholomew, 93, 106, 127
Miller, Edward, 138, 140
   Elegies, Songs..., 138
Millico, Giuseppe, 46, 104
Milton, John, 136–38, 149
Mitchell, Captain, 101
Mitchell, Mr, 97
Mitre, The, 12
Mollard, Mr, 80
Monck, General George, 9
Monthly Review, The, 66, 108
Moore, John, 93, 106, 127
Moorhead, John, 134
Morales, Cristóbal de, 71
Morley, Thomas, 20, 114, 118, 130
   Now is the month of Maying, 114, 118, 130
Morning Chronicle, The, 114–16, 118
Morning Herald, The, 123
Morning Post, The, 123
Mornington, Earl of (Garret Wesley), 69–71, 118–19, 125, 131, 148–49
   As it fell upon the day, 71
   Come shepherds come, 71
   Go tell Aminta, 149
   Here in cool grot, 118–19, 131, 148
   Twas you Sir, 125
Morris, Mr, 57
Moss, Charles, 105
Mountain, John, 120
Mozart, Wolfgang Amadeus, 14, 46, 83, 105, 133, 150
   Exultate, jubilate, 46
   Le nozze di Figaro, 105
Mug-house Club, 17
Mulso, Edward, 74–76
Musical Travels Through England, (Collier), 138

Nares, James, 146
   Fear no more the heat of the sun, 146
   To all lovers of harmony, 146
Naval Pillar, The, 134
Neville, Sylas, 93, 109
Newcastle Coffee House, 77, 80
New Catch Club, 75–76
New Customs, 5
New London Tavern, 83–84
New Monthly Magazine, The, 151

Index

New Musick Club, York, 91
Nield, Jonathan, 123
Nivernais, Duc de, 51–52
Non nobis Domine, 6, 58, 73, 78, 86, 92
Norris, Thomas, 125–26, 142–43
   O'er William's Tomb, 125, 142–43
North, Roger, 8, 12
Norwich Anacreontic Society, 98
Norwich Harmonic Society, 89, 92
Norwich Subscription Concerts, 128
Nottingham Catch Club, 90, 106

Obrecht, Jacob, 71
Ockeghem, Joannes, 70
Old Concert Room, Chichester, 97
Old Hall Manuscript, 70
Old Jewry Musick-Society, 12
Old-Jury, London, 11
Oracle, The, 118
Ord, Anna, 105
Ord, James, 105
Orford, Earl of, 56
Ossian, 147
Ouseley, Sir Frederick Arthur Gore, 58
Ouseley, Sir Gore, 58
Oxford Catch Club, 28–29, 40, 72, 88–89, 103
Oxford, Earl of, 58

Pacchierotti, Gasparo, 46–47
Page, John, 78–79, 120
Palmer, John, 113
Pantheon, Oxford Street, 118–19
Parke, Maria Hester, 149
   Go tell Aminta, 149
   Now the bright morning star, 149
Parke, William, 72–75, 81, 116, 123, 149
Parry, Robert, 93, 125–26
Parsloe's Coffee House, 83
Parsons, Mr, 108
Parsons, William, 81–82
Parsons, Sir William, 82
'Pasticcio, The', 114
Paxton, Stephen, 93, 117, 119, 145, 148
   A Collection of Glees, Catches etc, 145
   Go, Damon, go, 119
   How sweet, how fresh, 93, 117, 119
Paxton, William, 144–45
   Breathe soft ye winds, 144–45
Paxton, William or Stephen, 74
Payne, Mr, 97
Pearce, George, 76, 83
Pelham, Herbert, 11
Pelling, John, 11
Pepusch, John Christopher, 13, 19–20, 22–23, 69
Pepusch, Margherita (née de l'Epine), 19
Pepys, Samuel, 9, 11
Percival, Lord, 21
Percy, John, 74

Percy, Thomas, 147–48
   Reliques of Ancient English Poetry, 147–48
Pergolesi, Giovanni Battista, 111
   La Serva Padrona, 111
Perot, Charles, 10
Petrarch, 149
Phelps, Richard, 33, 36, 61
Philips, Ambrose, 144
Phillips, Mr, 12
Pidgeon, Charles, 11
Piggot, George, 11
Pindar, 149
Pindar, Peter (John Wolcot), 123
Pinto, Thomas, 110
Pitt, William, 79, 100
Playford, Henry, 15–16
   The Pleasant Musical Companion, 15
Playford, John, 6–8, 10–12, 14, 121
   Ayres and Dialogues, 10
   Catch that Catch Can, 7–8, 10–12, 14
   The English Dancing Master, 6
   A Musicall Banquet, 6
   Musical Companion, 11, 121
Plymouth, Lord, 21
Pope, Alexander, 148
   Vital spark of heav'nly flame, 148
Porter, Roy, 88
Porter, Samuel, 126–27
Price, Mr, 125
Prince of Orange, Canterbury, 91, 97–98
Prince, William, 127
Pring, Jacob Cubitt, 80, 85–86, 148
   Vital spark of heav'nly flame, 148
Professional Collection of Glees, The, 50
Professional Concert, 115, 118, 122–24
Promenade Grove, Brighton, 128–29
Public Advertiser, The, 107–8, 115
Purcell, Henry, 9, 11, 13–15, 23, 27, 30, 38, 49, 71, 107–9, 118–19, 121–22, 130, 138, 150, 153
   Soldier, Soldier, 130
   Sweet Tyraness, 11
   Would you know how we meet, 122

Queensbury, Duchess of, 13
Queensbury, Duke of (William Douglas, formerly Earl of March), 26, 33, 36, 39, 56–57
Queen's Head Tavern, 18, 86
Queen's Theatre (later King's), 20
Quilici, Gaetano, 40, 42, 48

Radcliffe, Miss, 125
Raine, Reverend Matthew, 80
Raleigh, Sir Walter, 59
Rameau, Jean-Philippe, 52
   Dardanus, 52
   'Methode pour faire les canons', 52
   Traité de l'harmonie, 52
Ranelagh Gardens, 107–10, 116–18

Rauzzini, Venanzio, 46
Ravenscroft, Edward, 13
　The Citizen turned Gentleman, 13
Ravenscroft, Thomas, 5–7, 15, 121–22
　Deuteromelia, 6
　Melismata, 6
　Pammelia, 5–6, 15
　We be soldiers three, 121
Ray, Martha, 34, 104
Read, H., 142
Rees' Cyclopaedia, 43
Reinhold, Charles, 74
Rich, Charlotte, 41
Rich, John, 41
Rich, Lieutenant-General Robert, 33, 36, 43–44, 48
Richards, Mr, 101–102
Richmond, Duke of, 39, 102
Richold, Mr, 80
Rimbault, Edward Francis, 151–54
Roberts, John, 77
Robespierre, Maximilien, 52
Rochford, Earl of, 39, 53
Rock, Michael, 87
Rogers, Benjamin, 121–22
　Come all noble souls, 121
Rogers, John, 11
Roncaglia, Francesco, 46
Rore, Cyprien de, 34
Rubin, Emanuel, vii, 4, 33, 36, 45, 49, 66, 68, 86, 108–9, 122–23, 136–37, 140, 146–47
Rutland, Duchess of, 59

Sabbattier, Mr, 73
Sacchini, Antonio, 104
Sale, John, 80, 116, 119–20
Salisbury Catch Club, 89–92, 96–101
Salisbury Festival, 104–5, 125–26
Salisbury Subscription Concerts, 93
Salmon, Mrs, 59
Salomon, Johann Peter, 83, 118–19, 123–24
Salopian Coffee House, 35
Sandwich, Earl of (John Montagu), 26, 33–36, 38, 40, 43–45, 57, 61, 103–4, 144–45
Sarjant (Serjeant), James, 116
Savage, William, 40–41, 45
　Poor Ralpho lies, 41
Scarlatti, Domenico, 137
Scholes, Percy A., 7–9
Scott, Mrs, 111–12
Scott, Sir Walter, 147
Sedgwick, Thomas, 114
Senesino, (Francesco Bernardi), 21
Shakespeare Jubilee, 147
Shakespeare, William, 4, 5, 10, 108, 112, 128, 146–48
　Cymbeline, 112, 146
　Hamlet, 108
　Twelfth Night, 5, 112

Sharp, Granville, 25
Sheepshead, Leicestershire, 93
Shenstone, William, 148
Sheridan, Richard Brinsley, 58, 113, 130, 133
　The School for Scandal, 113
Shield, William, 81, 113, 131–34
　'Ah, how can I leave' (*Two Faces under a Hood*), 133
　Election, The, 132
　Enchanted Castle, The, 132
　Fontainebleau, 132
　Friar Bacon, 132
　'Hark from spheres above' (*The Magic Cavern*), 132
　Hertford Bridge, 132
　'If health's fair rose' (*Richard Coeur de Lion*), 132
　'In Sherwood's Grove' (*Robin Hood*), 131
　Lord Mayor's Day, The, 131
　Magic Cavern, The, 132
　Mysteries of the Castle, The, 132
　Netley Abbey, 132
　Noble Peasant, The, 131–32
　Nunnery, The, 132
　Omai, 132
　'Release us if you pray' (*The Enchanted Castle*), 132
　Richard Coeur de Lion, (Grétry), 132
　Robin Hood, 131–32
　Rosina, 113, 131
　Sprigs of Laurel, 132
　'Sweet peace of mind' (*Richard Coeur de Lion*), 132
　'Thus on bended knees' (*Travellers in Switzerland*), 133
　'Tis virtue' (*The Magic Cavern*), 132
　Travellers in Switzerland, The, 132–33
　Two Faces under a Hood, 132–33
　Woodman, The, 132–33
　'Woodmen's Glee' (*The Woodman*), 133
Shirley, James, 149
Sibly, Steven, 105
Simpson, Christopher, 2
Smith, Clement, 85
Smith, Jack, 74–75
Smith, John Stafford, 47, 50, 54, 69, 70–71, 73–74, 121, 128, 131–32, 147, 149, 151
　Blest pair of sirens, 149
　Come my good fellows, 132
　Flora now calleth forth, 47, 71
　Hark the hollow woods resounding, 128
　Let happy lovers fly, 50
　Musica Antiqua, 70
　Take, Oh take those lips away, 147
　While fools their time, 121
Smith, Richard, jnr, 100–101
Smith, Richard, snr, 100
Smith, Robert, 77, 80
Smith-Hooper, Richard, 94–95

Index

Smythe, Baron, 104
Society for the Encouragement of Arts, Manufactures, and Commerce, 25–26, 29, 37, 47, 70
Sodales Caenantes, 92
Somerville, William, 142
Songsters Companion, The, 66
Sons of Anacreon (The Catch Club; The Court of Apollo; The Festive Board), 113–14
Spectator, The, 137
Spencer, John, 87
Spink, Ian, 12, 14
Spofforth, Reginald, 80, 85–87, 149
Spong, John, 11
Spread Eagle Inn, Salisbury, 96–97, 99
St Alban's Tavern, 55, 75
Stanley, Hans, 61
Star and Garter, Pall Mall, 75
Star-spangled Banner, The, 73
Steele, Thomas, 35, 65, 94
Steffani, Agostino, 20, 21
Stevens, George, 89
Stevens, Dr John, 105
Stevens, R. J. S., 25, 40–41, 45–47, 50–51, 59, 72–74–77, 80–81, 83–85, 95, 114, 118, 120–24, 128, 134, 147–48, 150–52
  Drink to me only, 148
  O mistress mine, 118
  O strike the harp, 84, 134, 148
  See what horrid tempests rise, 45
  Sigh no more, ladies, 50, 95, 118
  Sober lay and mirthful glee, 84
  Tell me where is fancy bred, 147
  To be gazing on these charms, 121
  What shall he have, 124
  When the toil of day is o'er, 124
  Who is Sylvia?, 147
  Ye spotted snakes, 95, 123
Stevenson, Sir John, 94, 147
  Take, Oh take those lips away, 147
Still, Robert, 99, 101
Storace, Nancy, 105–6, 123, 133
Storace, Stephen, 105–6, 132–33, 148
  Curfew tolls, The, 106, 148
  'Five times by the taper's light' (*The Iron Chest*), 133
  Glorious First of June, The, 133
  Iron Chest, The, 133
  Pirates, The, 132
  Three and the Deuce, The, 133
Stradella, Alessandro, 20
Suett, Richard, 113
Sumer is icumen in, 4
Sussex Weekly Advertiser, 129
Swan Inn, Lichfield, 97
Sweet Tyraness, 11
Swift, Jonathan, 109

Talbot, Sir Charles, 100
Tallis, Thomas, 71
Tasca, Luigi, 46
Tasso, Torquato, 4
Taylor, Sir Bernard, 75
Taylor, James, 75
Tedeschino, Cristiano, 46
Tempest, Thomas, 11
Tenducci, Giusto, 46, 111
Thatched House Tavern, The, 32, 35, 55, 57–58, 60, 63
Thomas, Ambroise, 152
Thoresby, Ralph, 13
Three Choirs Festival, 124–25
Toghill, Moses, 35, 93, 106, 127
Tomkins, Robert, 83
Tomlinson, Ralph, 73–74
Tottenham Street Rooms, 115
Travers, John, 19, 109
Triggs, Mr, 97
Twelve Bells (Alehouse), 23

Ulm Gesangbuch, 70

Vaughan, Thomas, 59
Vauxhall Gardens, 116–17, 119
Veal, George, 138
Vento, Mattia, 46
Vernon, Charles, 108
Vernon, Joseph, 66, 74, 108, 112
Vinci, Leonardo, 137
Virgil, 149
Vivaldi, Antonio, 137
Vocal Concerts, 59, 120–22

Waldegrave, Earl of, 41
Walker, Mr, 97
Wallington, Benjamin, 11–12
Ward, Mr, 103
Ward, The Honourable John, 33, 36–37
Ward, William, 60
Warren, Edmund Thomas, 20, 25, 33–35, 38, 45, 47–52, 62–65, 69–70, 75, 94, 153
  The Warren Collections, 20, 25, 33, 37, 38, 41–42, 44–45, 49–51, 53, 64–65, 68–70, 90, 94–95, 100, 108–9, 117, 121, 140–46, 149, 153
Warrender, Sir George, 58
Wasborough, Rice, 101
Webb, Daniel, 140
Webbe, Samuel snr, 25, 35, 37, 45, 50–51, 54, 59, 62–66, 69–70, 74, 76–80, 84–86, 94–95, 104–5, 109–110, 114–124, 126, 128–29, 139, 142, 144–45, 148–49, 150–53
  A gen'rous friendship, 119, 148
  Away, away, 121
  Breathe soft ye winds, 144
  Come live with me, 118–19, 126
  Come push round with spirit, 123

Glorious Apollo, 78, 110, 153
If love and all the world were young, 59
Invitation, The, 109
Ladies Catch-Book, The, 66, 104
Moon and Woman, The, 109
Non fidi al mar che femo, 149
Rose had been washed, 149
Swiftly from the mountain's brow, 95, 128
To love I wake the silver string, 110, 121
To the old long life, 117, 119, 121
When Phoebus was amorous, 86
When winds breath soft, 95, 115, 128
You gave me your heart, 35, 95, 119, 126, 128, 144
Webbe, Samuel, jnr, 25, 70, 85–87, 147–48
   Who is Sylvia?, 147
Webber, Mr, 93, 97, 127
Weber, William, 1, 3, 19, 34
Webster, Anthony, 73
Weeks, Jack, 97
Weelkes, John, 121
Weichsell, Frederica, 112
Wellman, Francis, 93, 96, 99, 105
Welsh, Master, 129
Wert, Giaches de, 71
Wesley, Charles or Samuel, 74
Wesley, Samuel, 81, 84, 87
West, Temple, 58
Weymouth, Viscount, 39
Wheeler, Richard, 95
White Hart, Bath, 97
Whitfield, John Clarke, 94

Wilbye, John, 34, 118, 121
   Flora gave me fairest flowers, 118
Williames, Matthew, 113
William V of Orange, 100
Willis' Rooms (see Almack's)
Will's Coffee House, Cornhill, 83
Wilmot, Mrs, 103
Wilson, John, 10
   Cheerfull Ayres, 10
Windham, Mr, 45
Wise, Michael, 14
Wood, Anthony, 9, 10
Wood, David, 45
Woodfall's Register, 120, 123
Woodstock Town Hall, 129
Woodyear, Mr, 96
Worgan, John, 131
   Care thou canker, 131
Wright, Charles, 77
Wyatt, James, 118
Wynn, Sir Watkin Williams, 61

York-House Catch-Club, Bath, 97
York-House Inn, Bath, 97
York, New Musick Club, 89, 91
Young, Cecilia, 111
Young, John, 18
Young, Talbot, 18

Zingoni (Zirgoni), Giovanni Battista, 48